Studies in Russian
Historical Geography

Studies in Russian Historical Geography

Volume 1

Edited by

James H. Bater

James H. Bater
*University of Waterloo
Ontario, Canada*

R. A. French
*University College London and
School of Slavonic and East
European Studies, London,
England*

1983

Academic Press
A Subsidiary of Harcourt Brace Jovanovich, Publishers
London   New York
Paris   San Diego   San Francisco
São Paulo   Sydney   Tokyo   Toronto

ACADEMIC PRESS INC. (LONDON) LTD
24/28 Oval Road, London NW1 7DX

United States Edition published by
ACADEMIC PRESS INC.
111 Fifth Avenue, New York, New York, 10003

British Library Cataloguing in Publication Data

Studies in Russian historical geography.
Vol. 1
1. Soviet Union—Historical geography.
I. Bater, J. H.   II. French, R. A.
911'.47   DK17

ISBN 0–12–081201–0

Typeset by Oxford Publishing Services, Oxford
and printed in Great Britain by
Whitstable Litho Ltd, Whitstable, Kent

131079

Contributors

T. E. Armstrong
Scott Polar Research Institute
Cambridge
England

J. H. Bater
Department of Geography
University of Waterloo
Ontario N2J 3PQ
Canada

W. L. Blackwell
Department of History
New York University
Washington Sq
New York, NY 10003
USA

R. A. French
Department of Geography
University College London
Gower Street
London WC1.
England

J. R. Gibson
Department of Geography
York University
Toronto
Canada

R. Gohstand
Department of Geography
California State University
Northridge, California
USA

J. Pallot
Christ Church College
University of Oxford
Oxford
England

R. A. Pierce
Department of History
Queen's University
Kingston, Ontario
Canada

D. J. B. Shaw
Department of Geography
University of Birmingham
Birmingham B15 2TT
England

I. Stebelsky
Department of Geography
University of Windsor
Ontario
Canada

To Linda and Anne

Preface

The historical geography of a territory as vast as that of the USSR, over a period of at least seven millenia, is scarcely to be comprehended within the scope of any one book. Certainly the stage has not yet been reached when sufficient work has been done for anyone to take a fully satisfactory overview of so broad a topic. So much basic work remains to be done, before such an all-embracing work can safely be attempted. Yet there are a number of geographers of the English-speaking world, who have been working within the field of Russian historical geography, in some cases for two decades or more, and there are a number of aspects of the subject on which their labours have shed light.

The concept of the editors was that as many as possible of such scholars should be approached to contribute a chapter, or chapters, setting their specific research topics in wider frames and thus to produce a set of studies in the historical geography of Russia. Obviously it was not possible to be comprehensive of all aspects, nor have they sought to be. The hydraulic cultures of Central Asia, the role of the Russian railways are but two of many important, indeed fundamental, themes, which to their regret they have not been able to follow up. Nevertheless, they have been fortunate indeed to have received a positive response from almost all those scholars who were approached. All their contributors have a good command of the Russian tongue, all have spent prolonged periods in the USSR engaged in research, all have a deep acquaintance with libraries, archives and sources of all kinds. To them the editors express a profound sense of gratitude for their participation, for their contributions and, above all, for their patience through the lengthy gestation of this book and for their willing cooperation in every respect.

The editors have not attempted to impose any kind of standardized viewpoint, interpretation or method of approach on the contributors. They have sought merely to create a coherent framework for the individual chapters by arranging them in sections, each introduced by a general essay and by writing introductory and concluding chapters. They are particularly grateful for the generous assistance of two historians in writing two of these scene-setting essays, Richard A. Pierce and William L. Blackwell. If in the eyes of many in the present-day Soviet Union, historical geography is primarily and largely a province of history, clearly demarcated off from geography, the editors hope and believe that such interdisciplinary cooperation has a special role to play in advancing knowledge in this field.

In preparing any book, editors always rely greatly on the help of very many people, and the present ones are no exception. In particular they owe thanks to Mrs C. Daniels and Mr R. Davidson for their skilled care in drawing the maps for Chapters 3, 4, 5, 6, 7, 9, 10, 15 and 16. Dr French has a debt of gratitude to the British Academy for sponsoring research visits to the USSR in 1978 and 1982, and to many colleagues in Great Britain and the Soviet Union for advice and helpful comments on his chapters; notably he would like to thank Hugh Prince and Frank Carter of University College London and Pavel Il'in, lately of the Institute of Geography in Moscow. Dr Bater wishes to acknowledge the continuing support of the Canadian Social Sciences and Humanities Research Council, through grants in 1979 and 1981, which provided the opportunity to undertake research on Russia in European and Soviet libraries. Assistance of a cartographic and secretarial kind by members of the Department of Geography, University of Waterloo is also gratefully acknowledged.

Professor Stebelsky wishes to acknowledge funding provided by the Russian and Far Eastern Institute of the University of Washington for his three-month research trip to the Soviet Union in 1968; the Canada Council Research Grant (1969) for collecting additional information at Stanford University's Hoover Institution of War and Revolution, the New York Public Library and the Library of Congress, and the University of Illinois Russian and East European Center for its Summer Research Fellowship.

London   James H. Bater
June 1983   R. A. French

Contents of Volume 1

Contents of Volume 2

Part III — Rus in urbe

10

11

List of Figures

Figure

List of Tables

Table

Glossary

barshchina: the holding of land in return for labour: corvée.

Cherkas: a Ukrainian Cossack.

chet; chetvert: (1) dry measure; a "quarter"; 2.1 hl; (2) areal measure; half *desyatina*; 0.5463 ha.

desyatina: areal measure; 1.0926 ha.

dikoye pole: lit. "the wild field", the unsettled area of forest-steppe and steppe between Muscovy and the Crimean Tatars.

dvor: (1) a royal court; (2) a town house or building and the land on which it stood; *gostinnyy dvor* building to house visiting merchants or traders; (3) a peasant household and farmstead; tenement; (4) (in Lith.) a manor.

gorod: (1) a town; (2) the citadel of a town; (3) the fortification of a town; (4) a fort.

gorodishche: an earthwork, fortified site, now abandoned.

guberniya: province; the principal administrative division of Tsarist Russia.

khutor: a consolidated plot of land with its farmstead standing on it (cf. *otrub*).

kopek: coin, one hundredth part of a rouble.

kustar': handcraft worker.

lavka: shop, stall.

lyada: slash and burn cultivation.

meshchanin: town dweller, bourgeois.

mir: the village community.

morg: (in Lith.) areal measure, approx. 0.73 ha.

oblast': the principal administrative division of the Soviet Union.

obrok: land holding for money rent.

obshchina: the village commune.

ostrog: (1) a wooden fort; (2) the walls, or fortifications, of a town.

otrub: a consolidated land holding separate from its farmstead.

perelog: long-fallow; land cultivated for several years and then abandoned for long periods.

podseka: slash and burn cultivation.

pomest'ye: an estate held for service to the crown.

pood, pud: measure of weight; 16.38 kg.

posad: part of a town, where artisans and traders resided.

posadskiye lyudi: townspeople, residents of a *posad*.

rayon: Soviet administrative division of an *oblast'*.

rouble, ruble: the basic monetary unit of Russia.

rynok: a market.

sazhen': measure of length; 2.1336 m.

sloboda: suburb; a quarter within a town or an outlying urban settlement.

sosloviye: rank, class.

trekhpol'ye: the three-field system.

tyaglo, tiaglo: (1) a tax; (2) (in Lith.) land holding for labour (cf. *barshchina*).

usad'ba: the settlement of a farm. The farmstead and plot on which it stands.

uyezd: Tsarist administrative division of a *guberniya*; district.

versta: verst, measure of length; 1.0668 km.

voloka: (1) (in Lith.) areal measure, approx. 22 ha; (2) (in Lith.) a holding of land
    after the 1557 reform.

volost': Tsarist administrative division of an *uyezd*.

votchina: hereditary, patrimonial estate.

voyevoda: governor, official in charge of a *guberniya*.

zalezh: long-fallow in steppe, as opposed to forest (cf. *perelog*).

zaseka: a defensive line, consisting principally of abattis of fallen trees.

zemstvo: district council.

1 Approaches to the Historical Geography of Russia

R. A. French and James H. Bater

There is a long tradition of fruitful interaction between geography and history. The patterns of evolution of societies and cultures, the dynamics of economic and political organizations, the human modification of landscapes, the geography of places in past periods, have captured the attention of historically-minded geographers. While historical geography has rarely commanded more than a small share of the collective research effort of the geographical profession, within specific national contexts there have emerged some important and enduring approaches to the subject. One need only mention three rich and imaginative "schools" in historical geographical scholarship: those associated with Vidal de la Blache in France, H. C. Darby in Britain, and Carl Sauer in the United States. What has emanated from the pens of these scholars, and of those who have followed in their footsteps, has weathered well both contemporary critics' judgements and the test of time. In most countries where geography is a well-established and vigorous academic discipline, historical geography is similarly well-established and vigorous.

Such indeed was the case in Russia before the Revolution. Not only was geography a thriving subject under the leadership of such figures as the Semenovs-Tyan-Shanskiy, L. S Berg, and V. A. Obruchev, but historical geography also had a sizeable number of practitioners, whose record of achievement was possibly unmatched in other countries. From the beginning of the nineteenth century, historians had shown interest in such geographical issues as the movement and location of ethnic groups, notably the east Slav tribes, the charting of trade routes, and the location of past boundaries and settlements. The challenging task of building up an accurate picture of the geography of a particular past period, a geographical "cross-section", found occasional, but most noteworthy, exemplification in the writings of historians like Got'ye and Zamyslovskiy. For some historians,

RUSSIAN HISTORICAL GEOGRAPHY VOL. 1
ISBN 0 12 081201 0

historical geography meant simply the influence of geography upon man
and his activities, a viewpoint in keeping with the spirit and purposes of
post-Darwinian determinism. More balanced accounts of the man–land
interaction appeared as well, notably the studies of man's influence in
shaping the landscape, published by the renowned climatologist, A. I.
Voyeykov. In short, the Tsarist legacy of historical geography, bequeathed
to the new Soviet state, was quite rich in content and certainly varied in
approach (French, 1968).

Yet the Soviet Union, where geography is a most active and important
discipline at all levels, is an exception to the general rule. There, geographical enquiry has been, and still is, directed primarily to the task of facilitating the development of the state; applied, pragmatic, policy-oriented
research predominates. Only here and there are signs of an awareness that
better understanding of past places and periods enhances an appreciation of
the present and thus strengthens planning for the future. Two earlier surveys
of historical geography in the USSR noted the paucity of work in the field
(French, 1968; French, 1972). To judge the state of the art during the 1970s
by the volume of published work from geographers could not but result in
the same general observation. The ranks of the devotees are still sadly thin,
their output is limited in quantity and the scope of their enquiry is narrowly
defined.

Given the prominence of historians in writing historical geography in the
pre-Revolutionary era, and given the conditioned concern with the contemporary on the part of Soviet geographers, it is hardly surprising that the bulk
of work produced in the Soviet period has likewise come from historians.
One of them, V. K. Yatsunskiy, was until his death in 1966, largely synonymous with Soviet historical geography. Formally trained in the skills of both
historian and economist and much influenced by traditions of historical
geographical scholarship established before the Revolution, Yatsunskiy
almost single-handed resuscitated the discipline. By many scholarly publications spanning half a century (Spisok . . . , 1970) and by unabashed
proselytization, he kept the subject alive and brought a few new enthusiasts
into the fold. Yatsunskiy contended that historical geographical research
within the Marxist framework was not simply useful for both history and
geography, it was necessary to the full comprehension of the evolution of
society. It demanded adequate training in both history and geography, the
latter in both its physical and economic branches. While training in two
disciplines is difficult enough, the Soviet view that different laws govern the
physical and societal worlds has resulted in the rigid division of geography
into physical and economic compartments, thereby further complicating the
education of the "compleat" historical geographer. In the Soviet academic
scene, there is little to encourage the would-be acolyte.

Writing at the beginning of the 1970s, one of the present editors expressed a rather pessimistic view of future developments in Soviet historical geography and saw a petering out of the mild revival inspired by Yatsunskiy (French, 1972). Ironically, at that very moment, a flurry of interest in the subject was occurring in the USSR, when in 1972 the first Soviet conference on historical geography was convened (Belov and Sokolov, 1973). Sponsored by the Research Council on Historical Geography of the Academy of Sciences and by the Moscow branch of the All-Union Geographical Society, the conference brought together some 200 persons, although what proportion of these were geographers is not known. The gathering was intended to serve as a forum for discussions to bridge the gap between the differing approaches evinced by the various sorts of geographers and the historians. The central question was whether or not a single, "unified" historical geography could co-exist with the philosophically different and bureaucratically separate bases in physical geography, economic geography, and history.

The resolution of this question was not achieved. In 1973, Mil'kov was carefully distinguishing between historical geography, which "faces history", and historical anthropogenic landscape study, which "faces geography", the two "being far from the same thing" (Mil'kov, 1973:166). In 1976 Isachenko was attacking Zubakov's effort (1976) at historical geographical periodization on the grounds that a single historical geography was "impossible" (Isachenko, 1976:525). Nevertheless, the conference did at least try and the military historian L. G. Beskrovnyy, in summing up the sessions, said that the task of the conference was to coordinate forces on the study of the interrelationships of nature and society (Sokolov, 1973:155). Beskrovnyy (1971) himself has written on historical geography and in 1975 a *festschrift* in his honour proved to be one of the highlights of the discipline in the 1970s (Narochnitskiy *et al.*, 1975). Seventeen articles were grouped in three sections—"Territory and Population", "Economic Historical Geography", and "Historical Geography Source Study". It is notable that all the authors are historians, although one, L. A. Gol'denberg, has published a number of papers in geographical journals, relating to cartographic sources for the study of the past. Beskrovnyy himself was the principal editor of one of the few attempts at a cross-sectional reconstruction of past geography, that of the Kievan princedoms in the tenth to thirteenth centuries (Beskrovnyy *et al.*, 1975).

These works apart, the 1972 conference seems to have had little practical effect. Its optimistic resolutions to ask the Academy of Sciences to establish an Institute of Historical Geography, with corresponding developments in republican academies, seem by the early 1980s to have been fruitless. In terms of publishing, one may well imagine that the conference had some influence on the historians at least. In 1973, a university-level textbook on the historical geography of the USSR appeared (Drobizhev et al., 1973). A useful enough overview, it is firmly in the traditional style of Soviet historical writing and offers little new in content or method and little awareness of spatial concepts. Much the same comment might be made about another textbook on the historical geography of the feudal period in western Europe and Russia, with one of the same authors (Murav'yev and Samarkin, 1973). The Kievan cross-section of Beskrovnyy et al. (1975) is almost exclusively concerned with locations. Indeed the concepts of some historians as to the nature of historical geography still appear remarkably naïve and descriptive rather than analytical (see, for example, Shakol'skiy, 1978) and remarkably unaware of earlier, or foreign, work. However, to set against this, there is one of the rare regional studies, the excellent historical geography of Moldavia by L. D. Polevoy (1979), who combines scholarship with an ability to use toponymic, demographic, cartographic, and statistical evidence.

The 1970s have thus seen a number of books within the field and, also on the credit side, the subject is being discussed and fostered by a group of academics. Many of them however take a rather narrow view of it and few support the concept of an holistic, inter-disciplinary historical geography. By far the greater part of achievements to date lies to the credit of historians and few of these appear to have even a passing acquaintance with developments in geographical methodology and theory over the last two or three decades. The geographers meanwhile have continued to set their faces steadily in other directions. At the International Geographical Congress in Moscow in 1976, only five Soviet papers were submitted to the section on historical geography (Annenkov, 1976), principally by historians. The conspectus *Soviet Geographical Studies*, published in 1976 in connection with the Congress, made no reference at all to historical geography. Of approximately 3000 persons listed in the most recent *Directory of Soviet Geographers* (Directory . . . , 1977), only thirteen are designated as having a research interest in historical geography, of whom eleven are still alive (Hausladen, 1979:4–5). Of the eleven, four were historians by training. Soviet geographical periodicals during the 1970s have contained a mere handful of contributions in the field (e.g. Babanin, 1974; Dergachev, 1976).

There have been fine Soviet scholars in the field, whose work can match the best anywhere, scholars for example of the calibre of Vavilov, Gedymin, Fat'yanov, Kirikov, Polevoy and, indeed, Yatsunskiy himself (for a sketch of their contributions, see French, 1972). But so often what is done plods along the traditional lines of approach found before 1970 and in some cases stretching back before the Revolution. For example, Karayev (1975 follows up the pioneering work on river trade routes, begun in the early nineteenth century by Khodakovskiy. Gumilev, whose work provided much of the innovation and interest from the 1960s (French, 1972:120–3), had completed his long series of articles on "Landscape and Ethnos" by 1973 and the individuality of his ideas appears to have made it difficult for him to publish further. Once more the geographers seem to have lapsed into apathy, with only the Moscow branch of the Geographical Society offering any kind of forum to the subject. Some geographers, who are interested, are content to follow Annenkov (1974) in urging an historical approach, a time-dimension, to be adopted by practitioners of other systematic branches of geography, which in fact many do. Such a view surely is but another form of that attacked long ago by Yatsunskiy (1941), which sees the role of historical geography, not as an independent field of study, but as an ancillary aid to other scholars.

Meanwhile in other countries, historical geography is the subject of considerable discussion, debate and continuing scholarship. The relative merits of narrative and cross-sectional methodologies have since passed from the centre stage of debate. Work has long been exploring a wide range of techniques and methods (Prince, 1971). The relative merits of positivist and idealist approaches generate vigorous and articulate argument. Interest in the role of ideology in framing research questions, in the interpretation of evidence, is high (Baker, 1972, 1977. 1978, 1979) and in the associated impassioned ethical and aesthetical controversies. National geographical organizations have specialist working groups or subcommittees in historical geography; annual international conferences (CUKANZUS) span the English-speaking world. There are specialist journals, notably the transatlantic *Journal of Historical Geography*, devoted wholly to this sphere. Its articles and reviews display the range of methods and concepts and the depth of enthusiasm currently being brought to the field in Britain and North America; no less involvement is shown by the geographers of France, Germany, Japan, and many other countries.

This liveliness of the discipline in the West contrasts with the near stagnation in the Soviet Union. It also raises the question, is there not a contribution that Western historical geographers can make towards elucidating problems in the Russian context? Briefly, there is indeed. The absence of a large body of current Soviet work leaves many gaps to be filled, while different approaches have new light to shed. Although access to archival sources is frequently difficult and bureaucratic time-wasting can be frustrating, work is possible on a host of potential and proven research topics, using a wealth of primary sources. Over the last two decades, a group of American, British, and Canadian academics have undertaken investigation of a number of problems in Soviet historical geography. All have a good command of the language, all have spent lengthy periods in the

USSR, working in libraries and archives. It is from this small group that the editors have been fortunate in securing the contributors to this volume, together with the much appreciated reinforcement given by several followers of our sister discipline of economic history.

Naturally, when the workers in so large a vineyard are so few, the topics, which represent the special interests of the contributors, are rather widely diffused. Given the presence of so many lacunae in historical geographical research on Russia, it would scarcely be possible to write an all-embracing book which gave adequate, scholarly cover to all the multifarious geographical aspects of one seventh of the world over more than a millenium. Inevitably, then, this book was conceived as an interdisciplinary, collaborative work, presenting the results of contemporary Western research as a collection of separate studies. It reflects the interests and approaches of geographers and historians. The editors have not attempted to impose any particular research design, methodology, or ideology. Each specialist has been asked to write on topics, within which their research has been located.

The editors have merely attempted to create a general framework, in which each chapter can find a place and a relationship to the others. The traditional "cross-section" approach to the subject, so strongly advocated by Yatsunskiy, which attempts to paint a full picture of the geography of a territory at a given period, was not possible, even if desirable. Nevertheless, the majority of chapters develop themes, which are framed within fairly restricted time parameters and thus at least contribute towards the overall geography of the periods concerned. Rather the structure adopted has been to group the chapters into four sections, or parts, each of which represents what the editors see as a major theme in the relationships between man (in his social, political, and economic organizations) and his geographical environment, through the long centuries of Russian history. Each section has a brief, introductory essay, which is intended to outline the broad setting and to demonstrate the relevance of the chapters comprising the section to the overall theme.

The theme of Part I is one that has long absorbed geographers and others—the relationship between man and his agricultural activities and the land. Since the heyday of environmental determinism, when emphasis was laid on man's subservience to controls of climate and terrain, the tendency has been to stress the role of man and his works in the relationship. In this tendency one can distinguish at least two principal aspects. First there are the various ways in which man, through his activity, has modified the natural conditions. Forest has been burnt and axed, virgin steppe has been ploughed, swamp has been drained, desert has been irrigated, hillsides have been terraced, the sea has been driven back and its bed reclaimed, to provide land for farming. Most of these forms of human adaptation of nature occurred in Russia and one, the clearing of the forest, is the subject of Chapter 2. In such transmogrifications, human wisdom has not always equalled human greed and man has often inflicted fearful, at times incurable, wounds on nature; one of the gravest manifestations of this in Russia has been soil erosion, the topic of Chapter 3. The second aspect of Part I comprises the historical geography of agriculture itself, its systems, its production, its landscapes and its patterns. Two chapters look at the changes, which resulted from two of the most influential developments in Russian agricultural history; Chapter 4 surveys the introduction of the three-field system and its consequences, while Chapter 5 examines peasant land holding in the period of emancipation and the Stolypin reforms.

The theme of spreading agriculture, at the expense of natural landscapes, leads very directly into Part II, which looks at the outward spread of the Russian people and their sedentary, agrarian way of life. Sumner's statement (1944:1) that "throughout Russian history one dominating theme has been the frontier" may be a commonplace of Russian history, but it is none the less true or significant for that. Only of North America can it be said that the expanding, changing frontier of settlement and economic advance against the wilderness of nomadism and hunting had an equal importance. If Russia itself has never produced a Frederick Jackson Turner to interpret its history in terms of the frontier, Western writers have more than once attempted to do so, if with varying degrees of success (Treadgold, 1952; Lobanov-Rostovsky, 1965; Wieczynski, 1976). The southward expansion of Muscovy into the "Wild Field", with its highly significant consequences for agriculture, for the development of towns and for the growth of Russian wealth and power is the burden of Chapter 6; Chapter 7 studies the long, uneasy border of Russia with Central Asia and the defensive measures, which ultimately brought about its settlement; Chapters 8 and 9 follow Russian expansion to the furthest extremity of the Asian continent and across to North America, that ultimate overstretching of the frontier that ended with the sale of Alaska to the United States.

Agriculture by its very nature is the most widespread of man's economic activities and until very modern times it was the most important economically in Russia. Landed nobility and peasantry were the principal elements of social structure. It is appropriate therefore that the first parts should be concerned principally with farming and with its expansion. Nevertheless, in Russia as in any society other than the most primitive, towns had a key importance, wholly disproportionate to their share of the population. Part III looks at aspects of urban historical geography, beginning in Chapter 10 with the early appearance of towns and the subsequent development of the urban network, down to the reign of Peter the Great. Peter's founding of St. Petersburg in 1703, the first planned capital since antiquity, ushered in the beginnings of modern urban development, with its growing industrial production and its creation of an urban proletariat, which in Russia was to be the maker of Revolution. The impact of this modern era and the coming of factory industry on the two greatest cities of Moscow and St. Petersburg form the subject of Chapters 11 and 12. In medieval and modern times alike, town and country were closely linked by the bonds of trade and commerce, activities which were manifested in the fair and market—the content of Chapter 13.

Commerce, the bedrock of capitalism and one of the gateways to the era of modern economic growth, leads directly to the final part of the book, which has as its theme the geographical consequences of economic modernization in the century between Napoleon's invasion and the Bolshevik revolution. In Russia, as elsewhere, the period from the later eighteenth century to the present-day has seen an ever-quickening tempo of economic change (even if rather later than in Western Europe and North America) and therefore ever more considerable and widespread impact on the man-modified environment. The driving force of change was, of course, the industrial revolution, the geographical expression of which is portrayed in Chapter 14. If, as has been remarked, in Russia the agrarian revolution did not antedate the industrial one, at all events agriculture underwent important, modernizing change, as a result first of the belated emancipation of serfs in 1861 and later of the Stolypin reforms. Chapter 15 examines this period of development in the countryside, in the context of peasant farms. A fundamental element in economic development was the improvement in transport, which facilitated, and was itself stimulated by, industrial growth and increase in agricultural production. Railways spread in a relatively dense network over European Russia and a few key lines pushed far out across the Asiatic lands of Tsardom. In their expansion, the railways very largely appropriated the role of the earlier canal system, surveyed in Chapter 16. The canals of Russia may have had but limited economic and geographical significance, but it is perhaps not entirely unapt to end on a theme which reminds us of the Russian rivers, those awesomely great geographical features which have given more than a millenium of service to the Russian people.

In a somewhat arbitrary fashion, 1917 has been set as a terminal date for this collection of studies, principally because the new socio-economic structure of the Soviet era introduces many new and different factors, along with the many continuities. But all geography is historical geography and the process of change in the environment never ceases. Indeed the years since 1917 have seen the fastest, most dramatic changes of all. Towns and cities have grown in size and number at unprecedented rates, the plough has been driven through vast areas of virgin land, the courses of mighty rivers have been turned into chains of inland seas, together sadly with still greater and more horrific levels of environmental destruction. Nevertheless, all the achievements, disruptions, and transformations, however much larger in scale and speedier in execution, are in continuity with the processes of the pre-Revolutionary periods. The geography of today cannot be fully comprehended without knowledge of the past historical geography—a truism which is commonly given as a justification for their studies by Soviet historical geographers. If such an excuse for the search for knowledge is really needed, as in this present time of "applied" and "relevant" geography some would maintain, let it stand also for the editors of this volume.

REFERENCES

Annenkov, V. V., (1974). Istoricheskiye metody na prognozno-konstruktivnom etape geograficheskikh issledovaniy (na primere stranovedeniya). *Izvestiya Ak. Nauk SSSR: Seriya Geogr*, 5, 48–54.

Annenkov, V. V., (ed.), (1976). "International Geography '76: Section 9 Historical Geography", Moscow.

Babanin, G. V., (1976). Tendentsii izmeneniya geografii urozhaynosti zernovykh kultur na territorii Yevropeyskoy Rossii 1883–1915 godu. *Vestnik Mosk. Univ: Geografiya*. 6, 99–103.

Baker, A. R. H., (1972). Rethinking historical geography. *In* "Progress in Historical Geography" (A. R. H. Baker, ed.), pp. 11–28, New York and London.

Baker, A. R. H., (1977). Historical Geography. *Progress in Human Geography* 1, no. 4, 465–74.

Baker, A. R. H., (1978). Historical geography: understanding and experiencing the past. *Progress in Human Geography* 2, no. 4, 495–504.

Baker, A. R. H., (1979). Historical geography: a new beginning. *Progress in Human Geography* 3, no. 4, 560–70.

Belov, M. I. and Sokolov, A. V., (1973). Pervaya vsesoyuznaya nauchnaya sessiya po istoricheskoy geografii, *Izvestiya Vses. Geogr. Obshch.* 105, no. 4, 380–382.

Belov, M. I. and Sokolov, A. V., (1978). The nature of historical geography in the Soviet Union (a debate). *Soviet Geography: Rev. and Trans.* 19, no. 3, 160–4.

Beskrovnyy, L. G., (1971). Spetsifika metodov issledovaniya po istoricheskoy geografii. *In* "Istoriya Geograficheskikh Znaniy i Istoricheskaya Geografiya. Etnografiya" (V. V. Pokshishevskiy and A. V. Sokolov, eds), pp. 48–51, Moscow.

Beskrovnyy, L. G., Kuchkin, V. A., and Pashuto, V. T. (eds), (1975). "Drevnerusskiye Knyazhestva X-XIII vv.", Moscow.

Dergachev, V. A., (1976). Istoricheskiye tsikly khozyaystvennogo osvoyeniya territorii, *Vestnik Mosk. Univ.* 2, 82–6.

Directory of Soviet Geographers, (1978). *Soviet Geography: Rev. and Trans.* 18, no. 7, 433–538.

Drobizhev, V. Z., Koval'chenko, I. D. and Murav'yev, A. V., (1973). "Istoricheskaya Geografiya SSR", Moscow.

10   R.A. French and J.H. Bater

Ford, L. R., (1975). Historic preservation and the stream of time; the role of the geographer. *Historical Geography Newsletter* 5, 1–15.

French, R. A., (1968). Historical geography in the USSR. *Soviet Geography: Rev. and Trans.* 9, no. 7, 551–561.

French, R. A., (1972). Historical geography in the USSR. In "Progress in Historical Geography" (A. R. H. Baker, ed.), pp. 111–128, New York and London.

Hausladen, G., (1979). Soviet historical geography in the 1970s: a preliminary assessment. *Discussion Paper Series, Dept. of Geogr., Syracuse University*, 60.

Isachenko, A. G., (1976). Geografiya i istoricheskaya geografiya (po povodu stat' i V. A. Zubakova). *Izvestiya Vses. Geogr. Obshch.* 108, no. 6, 525–529, (translated in *Soviet Geography: Rev. and Trans.* 19, no. 3, 180–185, 1978).

Karayev, G. N., (1975). O marshrute vodnogo puti 'iz varyag v greki' na uchastke oz. Il'men–r. Zap. Dvina. *Izvestiya Vses. Geogr. Obschch.* 107, no. 2, 154–159.

Lobanov-Rostovsky, A., (1965). Russian expansion in the Far East in the light of the Turnerian hypothesis. In "The Frontier in Perspective", (W. D. Wyman and C. B. Kroecher, eds), pp. 79–94, Madison.

Mil'kov, F. N., (1973). "Chelovek i Landshafty", Moscow.

Murav'yev, A. V. and Samarkin, V. V., (1973). "Istoricheskaya Geografiya Epokhi Feodalizma (Zapadnaya Yevropa i Rossiya v V–XVIII v.)", Moscow.

Narochnitskiy, A. L. et al., (eds), (1975). "Istoricheskaya Geografiya Rossii XII— nachalo XX v.", Moscow.

Polevoy, L. L., (1979). "Ocherki Istoricheskoy Geografii Moldavii XIII—XV vv.", Kishinev.

Prince, H. C., (1971). Real, imagined and abstract worlds of the past. *Progress in Geography* 3, 1–86.

Shaskol'skiy, I. P., (1978). Istoriko-geograficheskiye predposylki osnovaniya Peterburga. In "Iz Istorii Feodal'noy Rossii" (A. Ya. Degtyarev et al., eds), pp. 149–153, Leningrad.

Sokolov, A. V., (1973). Nauchnaya sessiya po istoricheskoy geografii. *Izvestiya Ak. Nauk SSR: Seriya Geogr.* 1, 154–156.

Soviet Geographical Studies, (1976). National Committee of Soviet Geographers, Moscow.

Spisok nauchnykh trudov V. K. Yatsunskogo, (1970). *Voprosy Geografii 83, Istoricheskaya Geografiya Rossii*, 20–30.

Sumner, B. H., (1944). "Survey of Russian History", London.

Treadgold, D. W., (1952). Russian expansion in the light of Turner's study of the American frontier, *Agricultural History* 26, 147–152.

Wieczynski, J. L. (1976). "The Russian Frontier: the Impact of Borderlands upon the Course of Early Russian History", Charlottesville.

Yatsunskiy, V. K., (1941). Predmet i zadachi istoricheskoy geografii, *Istorik-Marksist*, 5/93, 3–29.

Zubakov, V. A., (1978). O soderzhanii i zadachakh istoricheskoy geografii (istorii prirodopol'zovaniya), *Izvestiya Vses. Geogr. Obshch.* 108, no. 6, 516–24 (translated in *Soviet Geography: Rev. and Trans.* 19, no. 3, 170–80).

Part I

Man and the Land

Introduction

R. A. French

To historical geography, the study of the relationships between man and his environment through time is so fundamental as to be almost synonymous with the discipline itself. These relationships have been regarded in various ways. For many historians, the physical environment of the Russians has provided explanations, sometimes unqualified explanations, for the course of their history. To Klyuchevskiy, even the character of the Russians themselves was moulded by physical geographical features such as the great rivers.

More recently, Wieczynski (1976) has attributed that character to the existence of an open frontier of colonization. Even now, long after the ebb of the high tide of determinism, echoes of the search for geographical causation are still not infrequently encountered. For example, there is a fairly common assumption that Moscow's rise to power was an *inevitable* consequence of its location, as shown in the comment of Lobanov-Rostovsky (1965:82) that, "the domination of the whole plain from one center, i.e. Moscow, was to become unavoidable through the very nature of the plain", or again of Kochan (1963:25) that, "certain objective factors would eventually make it (Moscow) the nucleus of a national Russian state. There was the geographical factor, for example." In fact it would be hard indeed to find a single geographical feature favouring the growth of Moscow, which was not equally conducive to the development of Vladimir (Moscow's predecessor as Grand Princely capital), which today is the eighty-ninth Soviet city by size.

Kerner (1942) saw the rivers and portages of Russia as basic determinants of the course of Russian expansion which was itself, as was the whole of Russian history, a conditioned response to the need to find an open sea and to break out of Muscovy's land-locked geographical situation. Gumilev (1964a; 1964b) has attributed both the rise and the fall of the Khazar dominion to the changes in vegetation and agricultural conditions, resulting

RUSSIAN HISTORICAL GEOGRAPHY VOL. 1
ISBN 0 12 081201 0

from cyclical climatic changes. Both Kerner and Gumilev have come under heavy fire for their views, although few would dispute the thought-provoking qualities of their works. Nevertheless, the closer one looks, the less easy it becomes to be convinced of what Vernadsky (1951:6) called "the inevitable logic of geography" as the final determinant of the march of historical events in Russia.

This is not to pretend, of course, that the environment is without an influence on human affairs and therefore on historical happenings. Can anyone doubt that the Russian winter played its part in the eventual demoralization and defeat of La Grande Armée in 1812 and the Wehrmacht in 1941–45, or that the use of the vast spaces of Russia to extend the lines of communication of European invaders, as Russian lines contract, was a factor in overcoming Charles XII of Sweden, Napoleon, and Hitler? Certainly it would seem that the Russians do not, as the award of the Order of Kutuzov to the commander of a successful strategic retreat must surely testify. Nevertheless, whether or not the environment gave more aid and comfort to one side than to the other, can one doubt the even greater significance of human choice—Charles' to turn south to the Ukraine, Napoleon's to retreat, Hitler's to stay and fight at Stalingrad? Some constraints the environment may ultimately impose, if only through economics, but the history of man is the history of his defiance of such limitations.

Rather then in the search for relationships between people and their environment, one needs to look at the basic level of contact between man and land, the level of the plough and the axe, the level where man, far from being subservient to the environment, alters it to suit his economic needs. Ever since George Perkins Marsh's seminal treatise "Man and Nature" in 1864, this theme has always been an element of growing significance in historical geography, although for a long time it had to struggle hard against the post-Darwinian climate of determinism. It is of no little interest that one of the very first to be strongly influenced by Marsh was a Russian, the great climatologist A. I. Voyeykov (Woiekoff): his first article, "The Kinds of Influence of Man upon Nature" in 1892, was followed by two further articles entitled "The Influence of Man upon Nature" in 1894 (Voyeykov, 1957). In them he examined many of the ways in which humans transform the surrounding physical conditions, by destroying vegetation in forest clearance and ploughing grasslands, leading to a range of secondary consequences: lowering of water tables, soil erosion, silting of rivers; Voyeykov also looked at the positive side of the process: counter-erosion methods, plantations, swamp drainage.

The acts of transmogrification are carried out, above all, for the purposes of agriculture, the most extensive spatially of all human activities. There are thus two sides of the same coin in the studies of man and the land in this opening section of the present work—the changes wrought in the natural environment and the changing practices of farming, which bring about differing agricultural landscapes. It is particularly appropriate to begin with a theme so closely bound up with farming. It is no longer questioned that the east Slavs from their first appearance in history were settled folk, engaged in agricultural practices, including the growing of crops. Indeed many of the preceding cultures of the European Russian plain, back to Tripol'ye times, were also agrarian. And if the Russians were agriculturalists in the sixth century AD., agriculturalists the vast majority of them still were when the Winter Palace was stormed. In 1917, 82 per cent of the population lived in rural areas and almost all of these derived their livelihood directly or indirectly from the land; many of the remaining 18 per cent living in urban areas maintained relationships, seasonal or otherwise, with the villages from which they, or their immediate forebears, had come. Man the farmer and his relationship with the physical geographical surroundings must surely be the prime theme in the historical geography of Russia.

As the East Slav tribes spread into the plains of European Russia, from the sixth century onwards, the open steppe-lands were denied them by the succession of nomadic, pastoralist peoples from the Scythians through to the Tatars. Instead, the Slavs moved from their first homeland in the Vistula basin into the zones of forest-steppe and mixed forest. By the ninth century the tribes had settled as far north as Lake Ladoga and eastwards to the Volga-Oka confluence. From then on, until the seventeenth century when colonization began to push out southwards into the steppe, the home environment of the Russians was the forest. Its importance to the Russian is reflected to this day in his language, which distinguishes forest ecosystems with a subtlety that perhaps only the Finnish tongue can match. If the forest was a bountiful provider for the early Russian, he and his successors rewarded it with a ruthless and unceasing attack by fire, axe, and saw in their quest for more and more arable. At first, scattered clearings were made in the mixed forest, especially on those higher, better drained areas with the best soils. As the original colonizing settlements grew in size and daughter settlements sprang up around them, axe met axe and clearings began to coalesce. Each succeeding century saw the rate of clearing increase, as population grew and as the Russians moved slowly southwards into areas of richer, more rewarding soils. By the seventeenth century, as Professor Vikhrov, the Professor of Forestry in Leonid Leonov's novel *The Russian Forest*, says, "There was still plenty of forest wealth in Russia, but it was being ladled out fast with a ladle that kept growing in size" (Leonov, 1966:288). Indeed, if one had to select a single topic in historical geography as the most fundamental in the context of Russia, the longest in operation and most extensive in effect, it might well be the destruction of the forest, the subject of the first chapter in this section. In the last two hundred years before the Revolution, felling removed a third of the forests of European Russia (Tsvetkov, 1957:201) and it has continued with only partially effective abatement since 1917 (Komarov, undated:99–100).

From its forest hearth around Moscow, Russia spread outwards. At first the powers of Tatary to the south and Lithuania to the west confined its expansion to the north into the basins draining to the White and Kara Seas. The mid-sixteenth-century victories of Ivan the Terrible over the Tatars of Kazan' and Astrakhan forced open the barriers to the expansion eastwards into Siberia and southwards towards the Black Sea. The ensuing great saga of the outward spreading frontier is vast enough to form the theme of the separate second part of the book. What concerns us here is the impact of the advancing Russians on the forest-steppe and then steppe environments, when at last they reached them. In these zones the poor, leached podzols of old Muscovy, which needed huge effort for mean returns, gave way first to far more fertile Grey Forest Earths and finally to the humus-rich chernozems, with the stored fertility derived from millenia of dense grass cover. The richness of the soil led to the most intensive ploughing up and ever greater density of settlement. By the later nineteenth century, these zones were no longer frontier regions receiving an influx of settlers, but overcrowded lands exporting surplus population eastwards beyond the Urals.

The decrease in average size of peasant holdings, as families and overall population grew, led to overcropping on peasant lands and the ploughing of dangerously steep slopes. Eventually up to four-fifths of the total surface was under the plough, leaving only the lightest, sandiest soils and the steepest of slopes to be heavily overgrazed, with consequent destruction of the grass cover. At the same time, the growth of the export market in grain to western Europe during the nineteenth century, fostered by the spreading rail network that linked steppes to ports, caused the great estates to indulge in a robber economy of planting wheat year after year, squandering the reserves of soil fertility. The soil erosion which resulted from these short-sighted practices, is examined in Chapter 3. The loss of such a priceless asset as the chernozem soil arouses sympathies with the English long-term resident of the steppes, George Hume (1914:96), when he wrote:

> When passing through the water-worn ravines (often rich in vegetation), my indignation has been aroused that the negligence of man should allow the winter snows and spring rains to run to waste, carrying with them in each succeeding year large deposits of the rich black earth. This can never be replaced.

Alas, that which was true of 1914 is as true of the 1980s.

The pressure of an increasing population on the land during the nineteenth century, and in particular the growing inadequacy of available pasture and hayland to feed sufficient numbers of livestock, led to another aspect of the human modification of the natural landscape—the reclamation of swampland. Although approximately a tenth of present-day Soviet territory is classified as waterlogged, attempts to drain the widespread peat-bogs and grass marshes were few and desultory. Honourable pioneer efforts, all in the vicinity of St. Petersburg, by the German engineers Eberhardt Schroeder in 1775 at Ryabovo and G. Engelmann in 1802 on the Strelka, or by the Frenchman Laubrie along the Moscow highway, or by the English Quakers, Wheeler and Edmondson, in the Okhta and Volkova swamps in 1817–40, failed to find more than a very occasional Russian imitator.

Only in the 1870s were serious efforts made, with the way being shown by the state itself. Drainage "expeditions", led by army engineers, were set up by the Ministry of State Property. After overcoming considerable opposition and technical problems, the Northern and Western Expeditions laboured for the remainder of the century in scores of swamp areas throughout the central and northern mixed forests of European Russia, most notably in the huge swamps of Poles'ye along the river Pripyat' (French, 1959), in the Meshchera swamps south-east of Moscow and in numerous swamps within a 200-kilometre radius of St. Petersburg. By 1900, thousands of kilometres of canals had been built, tens of thousands of square kilometres of land had been reclaimed: to give new pasture, hayland and arable, to improve forest growth and to eradicate the endemic diseases of the wet lands, malarial fever and anthrax. By the outbreak of the First World War, the impact of drainage operations was being felt in the wide marshes of western Siberia, along the Trans-Siberian railway, and colonists were moving in to settle the newly-won lands (French, 1964).

The second half of the nineteenth century, when the first significant transformations of swamp environment took place, also saw the Tsarist Empire expand into the desert lands of Central Asia in a series of brief military campaigns. If most Russian expansion was into empty "Wild Field" or to thinly populated lands of nomads, in Central Asia their conquests brought within their dominion many settled Turkic peoples, who were no strangers to the process of deliberate landscape change. Indeed the irrigation necessitated by the arid climate of the region has a history extending back more than 7000 years. The people of the Jeitun culture, who lived along the foot of the Kopet-Dag mountains from the sixth millenium B.C., constructed simple gravity canals to water their fields, but long before the dawn of the Christian era, highly sophisticated irrigation agriculture and no less sophisticated societies dependent upon it had evolved along the main rivers of Central Asia, the Amu-Dar'ya, Syr-Dar'ya, Zeravshan, Murgab, and Tedzhen.

By the mid-sixteenth century, when Anthony Jenkinson made his pioneering journey to Bukhara and, en route, visited "Sellizure" south of the Aral Sea, withdrawals of water for irrigation were so heavy as to threaten a negative, rather than positive, landscape change;

> The water that serueth all that Countrey is drawen by diches out of the riuer *Oxus*, vnto the great destruction of the said riuer, of which cause it falleth not into the Caspian sea as it hath done in times past, and in short time all that lande is like to be destroyed, and to become a wildernes for want of water, when the riuer *Oxus* shall faile, (Morgan and Coote, 1886:70).

Jenkinson's prophecy was only too accurate. "Sellizure" is today the ruined site of Dev-Kesken-Kala on the Uzboy, the dried-up ancient course of the Amu-Dar'ya, or Oxus.

After the coming of the Russians in the nineteenth century, the suitability of the area for cotton-growing led to new, large-scale projects for irrigation in the Hungry Steppe and on the river Murgab, where the Grand Duke Nikolay Konstantinovich supervised the bringing into cultivation of over 27 000 hectares (Semenov-Tyan-Shanskiy, 1913:430); it was the continuation of an age-old process, but the beginning of a larger scale of operation that was to develop still more after 1917.

All these various modifications of the land from its natural state in the process of extending the farming base of human economy were large-scale, affecting anything from thousands to millions of hectares at different periods. At a far more local level, there has been, as there still is, a myriad of landscape changes resulting from agriculture, each tiny in itself, but the totality adding up to a largely, or even wholly, humanized environment—a fence erected or removed here, a row of threshing barns built there, a dam for a mill-pond on this river, a terrace for vines on that hillside. The nature and intensity of such changes in the detail of geography depend very greatly on the type of agriculture practiced. Every system of farming creates its own landscape.

In the dawn of East Slav colonization of the forest, and perhaps even earlier among the pre-Slav cultivators, fire was the weapon chiefly used to clear the forest, in the form of "slash-and-burn" agriculture. The trees were cut, left to dry out for a time, then burnt *in situ* and the ashes cultivated for several years until fertility fell off, when operations shifted to a new patch of forest. This system, known variously in Russia as *podsechnoye, lyadinnoye,* or *lesopol'noye zemledeliye*, by its very nature was extensive; it was also enduring and at the opening of the twentieth century was still widespread in some of the northern provinces (Semenov, 1900:137).

Equally persistent in the more remote, poor-soil provinces of the northern mixed forest and southern *tayga* was another of the earliest forms of agriculture, the *perelog*, or long fallow, system. This, like slash-and-burn, involved cultivating a plot of land for a number of years and then abandoning it to regeneration of scrub vegetation for a prolonged period, up to twenty years, but always with the intention of returning eventually. In time, the *perelog* system came to resemble the infield-outfield system of upland Britain, where one field beside the settlement received all the manure and was cropped every year. Further away, the "simple" or "visited" fields were cultivated in a long-term cycle of a few years cropping and a lengthy abandonment to fallow and natural regrowth. To these early and primitive systems one might add the similar *zalezh*, or shifting cultivation, which Smith (1959:74–87) believes was to be found in the open areas of the forest-steppe and northern steppe in pre-Slav and early Slav times.

None of these systems was especially productive; the growing population of Muscovy, and in particular the growing urban population which needed feeding, made it more and more urgent with the passage of time to maximize production from a given quantity of arable. Further possibilities were engendered by the slow development of more advanced farm implements, especially those for ploughing. When more sophisticated systems of communal farming first appeared in Russia is a matter of considerable debate, as Chapter 4 examines. Certain it is that the three-field system, even if it was no earlier, had at least begun to appear in Muscovite lands in the later fifteenth century and became widespread in the following century. It is equally certain that three-field cultivation was introduced by decree on crown lands in Lithuanian Russia in the mid-sixteenth century and that it was preceded there by forms of three-year rotations. Thus, well before the end of the sixteenth century, the three-field system had become the dominant type of agriculture, but even then it was not universal and in many regions, particularly peripheral regions, it was not even the most common system. Two-field and other variations of open, common-field agriculture also occurred, as well as survivals of the older, more primitive ways of farming. There also tended to be a distinction, especially in the early period of three-field agriculture, between the manorial estate lands and the peasant lands; the former introduced the new, more productive system with the labour made available by the enserfment of the peasantry, who on their own lands more usually employed variations of the infield-outfield system. However, as time went on, common-field cultivation in two or three fields came to be more widely adopted on the peasant lands as well.

The coming of three-field farming was a major step forward in agrarian technique. It was also the last, for a very long time. The early seventeenth century, with the "Time of Troubles", saw a severe recession in the quantity of arable land, especially in western and north-western regions, but thereafter all through the rest of the seventeenth and the eighteenth centuries as the area under the plough expanded with the advancing frontier, at the cost of the forest and steppe, the method of farming made almost no progress. Into the rich new black earth regions, landlord and peasant introduced the systems of the hearth regions, three-field, two-field, long-fallow and even, on occasion, slash-and-burn. There was little enough introduction of new crops, with rye and oats, the chief crops of Kievan times, remaining dominant still in the seventeenth century, accounting in many areas for 80–95 per cent of the arable, and indeed as much at the end of the eighteenth century; even in the mid-1880s the "grey" grains (oats, rye, and barley) were sown on 83.4 per cent of the area in twenty-three provinces of European Russia (Drobizhev *et al.*, 1973:137, 206). Industrial crops were equally unchanging and were a minor element, with the exception of flax in the north-west of European Russia, where it had been of some significance even in the sixteenth century.

Only in the nineteenth century did Russian agriculture begin to show any significant changes. Gradually new crops began to be adopted, sugar beet, sunflowers, and tobacco; even more noticeable was a tendency towards regional specialization in patterns of cropping. But any real change in practice had to await the emancipation of serfs in 1861, the breaking of the mighty fetter which held Russian agriculture chained to medieval methods. Even then the substituted bonds of redemption payments formed a severe restraint on change, until the 1905 revolution engendered the Stolypin agrarian reforms. Chapter 5 examines one aspect of the changes over the crucial half-century before the Revolution—the development of peasant land holding. But this period takes us on also to the final section of this volume, which looks at the process of economic evolution in the era, which Soviet writers designate as "capitalist"; in that section, another chapter returns to the theme of change on peasant farms.

This last half-century of Tsarism saw the weak beginnings of new techniques in farming. New crops and even new machines were being tried—in the 1860s George Hume was introducing reaping machines and steam threshers to the steppes around Khar'kov. Landownership was changing as free peasants began to buy land from the nobility, often through the intermediary of Peasant Land Bank. The Stolypin reforms opened the way to the replacement of communal farming by small-scale private farming; in some cases this led to the break-up of the village community and of the physical structure of the village itself. The first steps in co-operative organization were taken. After centuries of immobility in agriculture, where the only movement was the geographical expansion outwards by colonization, the last fifty years before 1917 were a time of ferment. But advances went hand in hand with even more significant deterioration, as landlessness, poverty, and rural discontent all increased. The failure of the relationships between man and the land, as expressed in agriculture, proved to be one of the most crucial factors in bringing about the Revolution. In due time the new socialist state would establish a new system of agriculture in collective and state farms, under close government supervision through a command economy. Even so, the relationships of man and land remain, as they have done through the long centuries as the Russians have modified their primeval environment, gradually transforming it into what we see today.

REFERENCES

Drobizhev, V. Z., Koval'chenko, I. D. and Murav'yev, A. V. (eds), (1973). "Istoricheskaya Geografiya SSSR", Moscow.

French, R. A., (1959). Drainage and economic development of Poles'ye, U.S.S.R. *Economic Geography* 35, 172–80.

French, R. A., (1964). The reclamation of swamp in pre-revolutionary Russia. *Inst. of Brit. Geogr. Trans. and Papers* 34, 175–88.

Gumilev, L. N., (1964a). Khazariya i Kaspiy (landshaft i etnos) I, *Vestnik Leningrad. Univ.: Geol. i Geog.* 6, 83–95.

Gumilev, L. N. (1964b). Khazariya i Terek (landshaft i etnos) II, *Vestnik Leningrad. Univ.: Geol. i Geog.* 24, 78–88.

Hume, G., (1914). "Thirty-five Years in Russia", London.

Kerner, R. J., (1942). "The Urge to the Sea: the Course of Russian History", Berkeley.

Kochan, L., (1963). "The Making of Modern Russia", Harmondsworth.

Komarov, B., (undated). "The Destruction of Nature in the Soviet Union", London.

Leonov, Leonid, (1966). "The Russian Forest", translated by B. Isaacs, Moscow.

Lobanov-Rostovsky, A., (1965). Russian expansion in the Far East in the light of the Turnerian hypotheses. *In* "The Frontier in Perspective", (W. D. Wyman and C. B. Kroecher, eds), pp. 79-94, Madison.

Morgan, E. D. and Coote, E. H. (eds), (1886). "Early Voyages and Travels to Russia and Persia by Anthony Jenkinson and other Englishmen", Vol. 1. Haklyut Society, First Series No. 72, London.

Semenov, V. P. (ed.), (1900). "Rossiya: Polnoye Geograficheskoye Opisaniye Nashego Otechestva. Vol III Ozernaya Oblast", St. Petersburg.

Semenov-Tyan-Shanskiy, V. P. (ed.), (1913). "Rossiya: Polnoye Geograficheskoye Opisaniye Nashego Otechestva. Vol XIX Turkestanskiy Kray", St. Petersburg.

Smith, R. E. F., (1959). "The Origins of Farming in Russia", Paris.

Tsvetkov, M. A., (1957). "Izmeneniye Lesistosti Yevropeyskoy Rossii s Kontsa XVII Stoletiya po 1914 god", Moscow.

Vernadsky, G., (1951). "A History of Russia", 3rd ed., New Haven.

Voyeykov, A. I., (1957). "Izbrannyye Sochineniya", Vol. 4., Moscow.

Wieczynski, J. L., (1976). "The Russian Frontier: the Impact of Borderlands upon the Course of Early Russian History", Charlottesville.

2 Russians and the Forest

R. A. French

The forest greeted the Russian at his birth and attended him through all the stages of his life—with the cradle of the infant and the first booting, with the nut and the wild strawberry, with the peg-top, the steam-bath switch and the balalaika, the splinter that did service for a lamp in the peasant's hut, and the painted shaft-bows at weddings, with the wild honey and the beaver, the fisherman's boat or the naval bark, the mushroom and the incense, the staff of the wanderer, the coffin hollowed out of a log and lastly, the wooden cross on the grave, decorated with fir branches. (Leonov, 1966).

THE FOREST AS PROVIDER

If the image of the Russian environment in the West European mind is not infrequently that of the steppes, it is in fact only relatively recently that Russians have occupied the wide, open, grasslands; that is, within the last three centuries. But for over 1300 years, ever since the beginnings of east Slav settlement, the forest has been the home of the Russians; even today the natural zones of *tayga* and mixed forest take up over half the enormous area of the USSR.

For the first Russian settlers, the forest was the essential provider. It gave them shelter from the onslaughts of the long series of warrior-nomads, who in turn held the steppes: Scythians, Sarmatians, Goths, Huns, Khazars, Pechenegs, Polovtsy, and Tatars. Again and again in early Russian history, after heavy defeat by the steppe peoples, above all after the Tatar whirlwind of 1237–40, the Russians were able to recuperate and build new strengths within the forests, where their foes were never happy to settle. The forest provided fuel for warmth and material for homes, barns, furniture, and

RUSSIAN HISTORICAL GEOGRAPHY VOL. 1
ISBN 0 12 081201 0

implements; it supplied the raw material for a range of industries, charcoal for iron, ship timbers, ash for potash, fuel to evaporate brine, pit-props for mines. In due turn, trees made corduroy roads for carts and sleepers for railways. The forest undergrowth provided food for man and beast, its fauna gave meat and clothing, more, it gave wealth through furs. Indeed, in the words of Leonov's Professor of Forestry, Vikhrov, in the opening quotation, the forest attended the needs of the Russians throughout their lives.

The importance of the forest to the Russian is reflected in his language. The Murzayevs' *Dictionary of Local Geographical Terms* (1959) lists some 103 words (more, if variants are counted) each of which denotes a particular forest or scrub community or ecosystem with remarkable precision. One might cite *gayëk*—a pure stand amidst other tree species; *gryadina*—a belt of oak, willow, and cork elm along the edge of a flood-plain in a wide valley; *soim*—excessively moist spruce forest along streams, with some birch and scrubby willow and rich grass undergrowth; *tayezhki*—stands of larch and spruce with a mixture of pine and birch, occurring in small patches on watershed areas along the margins of the *tayga* and forest-steppe zones. A further thirty or so terms occur in Grebenhschikov's *Geobotanical Dictionary* (1965), most denoting particular stands of trees or types of forest: *berestnyak*, elm forest; *vetlyanik*, willow grove; *ol's*, lowland alder swamp with mineralized ground water; *redkoles'ye*, sparse or open woodland. If one adds general words for forest, grove, stand and the like, together with a score or more of terms from Turkic and other languages, one ends with well over 150 words that indicate an area of land with trees growing on it. To them one can further add some fifteen terms given by the Murzayevs to indicate a clearing or open space within the forest. Perhaps only Finnish or some North American Indian languages, developed in similar environments, can match such subtlety of expression.

To the economy of the peasant household throughout all Russian history, the forest represented a major asset. In the first place, peasants normally had the right to enter the forests of their lord or of the crown, to gather dead wood for fuel, building purposes, fencing, for bast, and other domestic uses. Live timber was forbidden to them, but methods of illegally killing trees by ring-barking or drilling holes were a time-honoured tradition. Hunting game was of course strictly prohibited to the peasantry, and even on their own land only small game was allowed to be killed, but poaching still took place in defiance of the severest penalties. Fishing, on the other hand, was permissible and represented an important source of protein (Smith, 1977:60–66). Equally valuable to diet were the wild fruits of the forests: mushrooms, berries, and nuts. Smith (*ibid.*:57–59) quotes yields of 100 to 500 kilogrammes per hectare for cowberries and bilberries and of anything from 6 to 500 kilogrammes for mushrooms, but another authority has calculated that in the northern forests of European Russia the average yield of berries can be as high as 800 to 1,000 kilogrammes per hectare and of mushrooms 30 kilogrammes but rising to a ton per hectare in good years (Obozov, 1961:78). Edible and medicinal roots and plants were further botanical benefits, derived from the forests.

The right to turn out cattle to pasture in the forest and to cut hay, including fodder from the shoots and leaves of young tree growth, was very important. Smith's model of production and consumption on peasant holdings suggests that without the animal feedstuffs and pasture provided by the forest, the livestock would not survive (Smith, 1977:94). The sixteenth-century Lithuanian cadastre of royal villages in Pinsk district recorded the forest rights of the peasants and affirmed their right of access, even across private land:

> Moreover, that village of Kostichi, together with the village of Posinichi, may enjoy as of old, pastures in unmeasured oakwoods lying between those villages, and also access into the forest beyond the river Yasel'da, and the haylands which they have in swamps along that river Yasel'da, and in the forest, according to ancient custom they may enjoy bee-trees and the cutting of hay, fishing and all other usages as they enjoyed previously. And the Lords of the Osnezhitskiy estate and the Lord Mikhayl Borzobogatyy on his Mutkovichi estate, as of old, may not stop them from crossing their land by free and ancient roads, on foot and with their cattle. (*Pistsovaya Kniga* . . . , 1874, Chast' 1, 132–134).

Another major contribution which the forest made to the peasant family, was honey from wild bees' nests in natural or artificial hollows in tree trunks; the beeswax also obtained was mostly sold to make candles, the peasant households themselves usually making do with resinous wood splinters. The honey was used for sweetening and for mead. The keeping of bee-trees (*borty*), particularly in designated tracts of forest (*bortnyye ukhozhai*), occurred throughout the mixed forest zone. Numbers of bee-trees were clearly often considerable; an inventory for 1599 of the village of Oreshkovo in what is now Belorussia, listed 1044 bee-trees, of which ninety-four were oaks and 950 pines, with ninety-nine swarms in them (*Akty* . . . , 1888:644–645). In this case, the ratio of empty to occupied trees was 10:1, although Perevalov (1950:148) cites a 6:1 ratio in Putivl' district.

Bee-trees were subject to much legislation, testifying to their economic value. As early as the twelfth century, Article 1054 of the *Russkaya Pravda*, or code of laws, made it an offence to alter the blazes, which denoted ownership of the trees, punishable by a fine of twelve *grivny* (Perevalov, 1950:148). In the 1529 Statute of Lithuania, a specific clause (Section 9,

Clause 6) laid down that no one might destroy another's bee-tree or, if ploughing, approach it more closely than the ploughman could reach with the stick used to drive the oxen. Those who by ploughing, or by fire, or by other means, did harm to a bee-tree had to pay a fine of sixty *groshi*, or half if the tree was without a swarm (Yablonskis, 1960:106, 108).

If the forest was a crucial element in the economy of the peasant household, it was equally so in the economy of the boyar, the Grand Duke and the nation itself. To the nobility, perhaps the first significance of the forest was for hunting, which provided sport and meat. The privilege of hunting was jealously guarded by law. In the thirteenth century, only the Prince of Novgorod was permitted to hunt wild boar in an area sixty *versty* (sixty-four kilometres) around the town (Kirikov, 1966:24). Section 9, Clause 1 of the 1529 Lithuanian Statute stated that if anyone killed game in another's forest, that person had to pay both compensation and a fine to the owner, plus a fine to the Grand Duke, while to hunt with bow and arrow carried the death penalty (Yablonskis, 1960:104). In economic terms, of course, the animals of the forest provided the most valuable resource of early and medieval Russia—furs. The search for new supplies of furs as over-hunting depleted numbers in European Russia was the prime incentive for the advance across Siberia.

As important to crown and nobility as to the peasants were honey and beeswax; major trade goods for both Muscovite and Lithuanian Russia. Honey in the storerooms of Prince Svyatoslav of Kiev in 1146 totalled *500 berkovtsy*, some 80 000 kilogrammes (Perevalov, 1950:147). The Lithuanian peasants were required to give half the honey which they collected from their trees, as a due to the crown. Some of them were employed as the Grand Duke's beekeepers, looking after the crown's own trees and making new bee-trees, that is cutting artificial hollows. Kochin (1965:294) quotes a fifteenth-century deed, typical of many, ". . . and, lord, his beekeepers go to old bee-trees and make new bee-trees". A sixteenth-century Customs Roll, covering goods dispatched by boat down the river Neman to Königsberg over a six-week period, recorded 330 *lashti* (about 600 tons) of beeswax (*Akty* . . . , 1888:644–655). By the eighteenth century, Voronezh province alone was exporting some 55 000 poods, 900 tons, of honey a year (Rubenshteyn, 1957:295). It is hardly surprising that Muscovite landowners strove to concentrate such a valuable asset in their own, rather than the peasants', hands.

The manor houses of the aristocracy, the palaces and castles of the Grand Dukes and Tsars, needed timber for the same purposes as did the peasants' huts—for building, fencing, furniture, cooperage, cart and wheel-making, and fuel—but naturally on a vastly larger scale. Brest Castle in the 1560s was supplied by the peasant holdings within its jurisdiction with 1457 cartloads of wood each year and Kobrin Castle in 1563 received 1012 cartloads (French, 1967:176); Bobruysk Castle and manor in the early seventeenth century received ten cartloads of firewood from every occupied peasant holding on the crown lands under their control, a total of 4260 cartloads per annum (French, 1969:53).

The various needs which the forest supplied, meant that another of its roles was as a source of employment. Many peasants won their livelihood by various kinds of work in the forests and, with the coming of serfdom, they received their holdings of arable in return for such duties. There were the beekeepers, the beaver-hunters who trapped beavers along the forest rivers, and the fishermen who built fish weirs and traps on the rivers or who drew nets in the forest lakes. The *budniki* made potash in remote clearings in many areas; here and there miners of bog-iron prepared their charcoal. A considerable number were employed in the hunt. The huntsmen accompanied their lord when hunting and, between whiles, set traps and killed game for meat. Dog-keepers and grooms looked after the animals used in the hunt. In villages beside the hunting forests of the Grand Duke of Lithuania often the entire male population was engaged in these occupations; in Grodno district 159 holdings were given to hunt staff (French, 1967:177). Such people also usually went on military service when required. To protect the forests and the game needed woodwards; both the Lithuanian crown forests and the forests of the Tula defensive line developed elaborate systems of guarding, which employed large numbers.

CLEARING FOR AGRICULTURE

The deep and multifarious generosity of the forest to Russia was ill repaid. For well over a millenium, man has been attacking the forests; slowly at first, but ever more rapidly, it has yielded ground. The prime cause for human onslaught was, of course, the quest for arable land. Even in the earliest period of tribal settlement before the emergence of the first Russian state, the use of fire in the *podseka* system of slash-and-burn farming must have destroyed huge areas of primeval forest. Research indicating the effectiveness of stone axes in cutting trees has pushed back the earliest dates when *podseka* might be expected and it appears to have been the usual practice among various pre-Slav peoples such as the eastern Balts (Davydchuk, 1975:98) and the people of the Arzamas region in the last centuries B.C. (Fat'yanov, 1959:43–4).

Even though the burnt-over areas, after several years of cultivation, were abandoned, the secondary growth tended to be birch or scrub and it was a very long time, if ever, before the original climax vegetation had regenerated, especially in more northerly parts where rates of growth were slow. At best a sixty- to eighty-year process, regeneration was slowed or even prevented by the pasturing of animals (Turchanovich, 1950); Kharitonychev (1960:122) considers that "the abandonment of individual areas is not accompanied by a repetition here of the previous landscape, particularly a renewal of the former vegetation". At the same time, the use of fire frequently got out of control and destroyed far wider tracts of forest than were intended for cultivation.

The other principal early form of arable farming in Russia was equally extensive in nature and therefore inevitably widely destructive of forest. This was the "long-fallow" system, *perelog* or *perelozhnaya sistema*. In its most usual form, this involved cultivating a patch for several years, until fertility fell off (when it was abandoned for a prolonged period, perhaps twenty years or more) and moving on to another patch; eventually the cultivator would return to the first patch, by which time it would have been colonized by birch and scrub. Later, in this system, it became usual for a field beside the settlement to be continuously cultivated, receiving all the manure.

In time more sophisticated two- and three-field systems of common-field agriculture were adopted, a process which itself brought about additional clearance as third fields were carved out of the forest. In the mid-sixteenth century Lithuanian agrarian reform, geometrically regular three fields, lying side by side, were laid out, frequently including patches of forest within the new boundaries; the villages concerned were given temporary tax reliefs in order to clear and cultivate the fields.

> But since in the redrawing of the boundaries much oakwood and pinewood still unploughed was included: therefore in order that they should clear the oakwood, for three years to them all is abated one third of the *chinsh* (tax). (*Pistsovaya Kniga* . . . , 1874:322).

The spread of common-field agriculture by no means signified the end of individual, or group, clearing of outlying fields, deep within the forest. The Lithuanian cadastres of Sigismund August contain abundant evidence that the peasants were willing to add distant patches of arable, for which they paid extra tax, to their holdings in the basic three fields. Some of the villages in Pinsk district in 1561–66, where forests were particularly extensive, had large numbers of outlying fields "with forest on all sides", "with pinewood on all sides". Dovechorovichi village had eighty-two small, scattered outlying fields, beyond the fences of the main fields (*Ibid.*, 356–376). In neighbouring Kobrin district, where cadastres were compiled for 1563 and 1597, fifty-two villages increased the area under outlying fields during the intervening thirty-four years from 2337 *morgi* to 5825 *morgi* (the *morg* being approximately 0.73 hectare); one village alone, Shubichi, had increased its outlying fields at the expense of forest from a total of 41 to 870 *morgi*, more than twentyfold (French, 1968:273).

In Muscovite Russia such fields were as common and were often called *pochinki*; these frequently represented the establishment of new settlements (Cherepnin, 1960:173). Out-settlements or daughter settlements of this kind could also be known as *vystavki*. There was much peasant clearing of isolated closes (*nivy*) and small hamlets in the central Muscovite region in the fifteenth century (Smith, 1977: 122) and in the Toropets area in the sixteenth (Smith, 1973). Clearings did not necessarily involve new settlements; very frequently they were cultivated "at a distance" (*nayezdom*).

At times of severe upheavals there were recessions, when arable was abandoned and often, in the first instance, the outlying fields. Later, in calmer times, these abandoned and overgrown fields (*pustoshi*) would again be ploughed. In the fourteenth and fifteenth centuries as conditions stabilized after the Tatar invasion, as Moscow's power, area and population grew, there was intensive ploughing up of *pustoshi* in the north-west and north (Cherepnin, 1960:166). This process of reclaiming did not slow up the clearing of new arable as well, as indicated by the widespread use of such terms as *novi, noviny, chisti, roschisty*, and *sechi*, deriving from words meaning "new", "clear", and "cut" (Gorskiy, 1959:5–6).

In western areas, the Lithuanian "Forest Decree" of 1557 made it a regular practice to set aside areas of crown forest, where a site for a village and the boundaries of three fields, divided into strips, were marked out with blazes. Anyone who wished could claim a holding, clear it, and bring it into cultivation, meanwhile enjoying a period of up to ten years tax relief (French, 1967:181–182). Near Pinsk, two sites at Velesnitsa Volya and Yazvinki were so marked out with fifteen and eight holdings and seven and eight years freedom from payments respectively (*Pistsovaya Kniga* . . . , 1874: Chast' 1, 292–294; Chast' 2, 40). Both sites today have small villages, indicating that the holdings were in fact taken up. Many landowners did likewise on their own lands; some did so illegally in crown forest. The survey of royal forests, carried out for the Grand Duke of Lithuania in 1559 by Grigoriy Volovich (*Reviziya Pushch* . . . , 1867), recorded innumerable transgressions by neighbouring landowners, who settled their people in the Duke's forests.

Clearing for agricultural purposes was not solely for arable. On the Volga floodplain in the sixteenth century, forest was cut to give meadows for hayland (Kharitonychev, 1960:66). In Moldavia, the most intensive forest removal was in the fifteenth to seventeenth centuries and principally by the large estates engaged in livestock husbandry (Tkachenko, 1980:69). Even when clearing was not done primarily for animal husbandry, it was common practice to allow cattle to graze on cut-over areas, preventing any regeneration.

The early seventeenth century, during the "Time of Troubles" was again a period of land abandonment, but by no means everywhere. The defeat of the Kazan' Tatars in 1552 had led to a large influx of Russian settlers into the heavily forested Volga right-bank area and new estates were given out on service tenure and monasteries were established. Here clearing continued unabated into the following century. For example, in the *stan*, or local district, of Berezopol'skiy the ploughland increased from 4163 hectares in 1613 to 21 944 hectares in 1621–23 (Kharitonychev, 1960:50–61). Later in the century, the southward colonizing movement gathered ever greater momentum (see Chapters 3 and 6) to reach the open steppe and the southern limit of the forest. The richer soils of the southern mixed forest and forest-steppe, Grey Forest Earths and Black Earths, were a spur to very intensive clearing. The Arzamas region, at the extreme northern edge of the forest-steppe, saw its forests already significantly thinned out by the beginning of the seventeenth century (Fat'yanov, 1959:68). By the time of the "General Survey", 1776–1800, the northern forest-steppe was already 60–75 per cent under the plough and the southern part of the zone 35–36 per cent ploughed (Semenova-Tyan-Shanskaya, 1957:1403). Ploughing in these formerly forested areas brought about long-term changes in the soil itself, leading to a decrease in podzolization and increase in carbonate content (Gedymin, 1964).

By the nineteenth century the proportion of forest-steppe under the plough had reached 84 per cent in some areas and the process of clearance had become little more than a mopping-up operation. In 1847 Turgenev commented in the first of "A Hunter's Sketches": "In Orel Gubernia the last of the woods and copses will have disappeared five years hence".

NON-AGRICULTURAL DEMANDS ON THE FOREST

If the expansion of the Russian state, both in terms of area and of population, led to a steady escalation of the rate of forest clearance to win arable land, at the same time it brought about equally rapid increases in the volume of other demands made by man upon the forest, while the growing sophistication of society and economy multiplied the types of demands. In earlier periods of Russian history, the satisfaction of man's requirements of wood for heating, for building, and for a host of domestic and economic needs could usually be met without serious permanent damage to the forest ecosystems. The quantities of timber cut were matched by growth rates, with only localized and generally short-lived exceptions. Only clearing farmland made permanent inroads.

By the sixteenth century, however, many of the non-agricultural demands had reached such a large scale as to inflict irreversible damage on wider and wider tracts of forest. The growing number and size of towns stepped up requirements of wood for fuel and construction. Even by the sixteenth century, building timber had largely been exhausted in the environs of Moscow (Bakhrushin, 1952:93). The 1552 cadastre of Polotsk recorded 1200 logs and 300 "great beams" prepared and waiting for the master carpenter to float them down the Dvina to the town for the repair of but one of its towers (Lappo, 1905:8). St. Petersburg in the eighteenth century consumed thousands of rafts of timber and thousands of cartloads of firewood every year. Even the boats bringing the wood were usually broken up and sold for their timbers. In the nineteenth century, Zelenskiy in the General Staff survey of Minsk province calculated that there were 121 213 *dvory* (farmsteads and houseyards) in the province, each with its domestic and farm buildings and with an average life of fifteen years. Annual demand was for enough timber to build 8080 peasant houses, or the equivalent to cutting down about 11 000 hectares of forest (Zelenskiy, 1864:Vol. 2, 98), an example in merely one province of a universal process.

As time went on, such domestic demands were matched and overtaken by the growing needs of industry. One of the oldest wood-consuming industries was boatbuilding. Even in early Kievan times, the expeditions to Byzantium must have consisted of hundreds of boats, after heavy allowance is made for the exaggerations of chroniclers, who numbered the expedition of 907 at 2000 boats and Igor's fleet of 941 at 10 000. The fleets of river craft, which carried much of Russia's internal freight until the coming of railways, comprised thousands of all types and sizes. Tsvetkov (1953) lists a score of types, some up to 25–26 metres in length. By the end of the eighteenth century, some 5000 craft were being built annually (Rubenshteyn, 1957:187), a number inflated by the one-way nature of journeys to St. Petersburg.

Major military campaigns were mounted on boats, notably Ivan the Terrible's successful assault on Kagan' in 1552 and then down the Volga to take Astrakhan in 1556, and Peter the Great's expedition down the Don to capture the Turkish fortress of Azov in 1696. The first of these used 3500 to 4000 boats (Tsvetkov, 1953:144); the latter expedition involved the construction of 1300 river craft, thirty seagoing ships, and 100 rafts at Voronezh, while twenty-two galleys and four fireships were built at Vologda and carted overland to be reassembled on the Don (*Ibid.*: 151–152). After the fall of Azov a fleet was sent down the Don, comprising 147 river boats and a number of rafts of pine, with a total cargo of 74 396 oak timbers and 24 882 metres of sawn wood (Tokmakov, 1887:184).

Peter the Great also founded Russia's seagoing navy, thereby creating a new and hungry demand for the best quality timbers, especially oaks. Yards were set up at Arkhangel'sk, Astrakhan, and elsewhere, but the main ship-building centre was, of course, Peter's new capital of St. Petersburg, where the shipyard was second only to the Peter and Paul Fortress in construction. In all there were twenty-five yards established in Peter's reign, building between them 895 warships of all types, including 104 ships of the line. During the remainder of the eighteenth century, naval construction fluctuated in intensity with the foreign policies of Russia's rulers. Under Catherine I, Peter II, and Anna, in all twenty-four ships of the line were built for the Baltic fleet, under Elizabeth eighty-nine; it was Elizabeth who ordered that the Baltic fleet should be kept larger than that of any other Baltic power. Under Catherine the Great, a total of 1250 warships were launched, and over 1000 during the Napoleonic Wars. Altogether, from the beginning of Peter's reign to the mid-nineteenth century, some 4400 warships of all sizes had been built (Tsvetkov, 1953:153–159). By then new naval shipyards at Sevastopol, Kherson, and Nikolayev had created a Black Sea Fleet to join the Baltic Fleet and White Sea and Caspian flotillas.

As ancient an industry as boatbuilding was iron-smelting, with its needs of timber for charcoal. At first, widespread, but-small scale, iron bloomeries based on bog iron ore had only limited and localized effects on the forests; in some areas such individual workings survived to the sixteenth century at least. Near Pinsk in the 1560s lived an iron miner, called Jan, who was allotted about fifty hectares of oakwood, no doubt for his needs of charcoal (*Pistsovaya Kniga* ..., 1874: Chast' 1, 340–342). But as the industry became more concentrated in larger-scale blast-furnaces in the seventeenth century, so it began to inflict more serious damage. By the eighteenth century certain areas were suffering severely from overcutting. The Tula iron-works, established in 1632 by Vinius and boosted by the armaments factory set up by Peter I in 1712, made heavy inroads into the ancient forests of the former Tula *zaseki* (defensive line), inroads abetted by much illicit felling (Popov, 1937). By the mid-eighteenth century, small-scale iron-working in the villages of the central regions round Moscow was suppressed by law, in order to conserve forests (Lappo, 1961:34), but by then the half-dozen or so larger pre-Petrine, water-powered factories had been joined by five more, together with two works on the upper Voronezh river (Livshits, 1955:49–50).

Further north was the Olonets group of iron-works, founded by Peter with five plants, headed by Petrozavodsk. By 1716, Petrozavodsk alone was using 3131 tons of charcoal (Glagoleva, 1957:105–106). In the Urals, Peter's reign saw the start of an iron industry that was to lead the world for a time. At the beginning of the eighteenth century, the Urals factories were consuming 500 000 *sazheny* (nearly five million cubic metres) of wood annually and by the end of the century three times as much (Yastrebov, 1976a:112). By the later 1880s, even though the principal plants of that time in the Donbas were using coke, the Russian iron industry was requiring 17.5 to 20.4 million cubic metres of timber a year (*Sel'skove* ..., 1893:436). In the Urals almost all the iron-works were still operating on charcoal and continued to do so until after the 1917 Revolution; there, the privately owned iron-works in 1905 possessed about 6 500 000 hectares of forest (Livshits, 1955:247). These were often the worst offenders in improper forest management, many meeting their demands for charcoal by clear felling (Semenov-Tyan-Shanskiy, 1914:254–255). Increasing production more than outweighed the savings in timber use through improved technology, which reduced wood consumption per 1000 poods of pig iron from fifty-six *sazheny* in the eighteenth century to thirty-five in 1800 and twenty-three in 1900 (Yastrebov, *loc. cit.*).

The making of potash was no less timber-hungry than iron, but it was far more widespread, from the southern tayga to the forest-steppe and from the Urals to the Vistula. The place-name *maydan*, indicating a potash works, or a forest clearing where potash was made, occurs today all over the map of European Russia (Tsvetkov, 1957:27). The 1552 cadastre of Polotsk and its district recorded *budy popelnyye*, huts where potash was made, on almost all the private, monastic and crown estates; in this district over a two-year period, seven areas of crown forest alone produced 390 *lashti* (about 800 tons) of "ash", which the *voyevoda* (governor) had to send to Riga at his own expense (Lappo, 1905:62–63). The Lithuanian Customs Roll already cited recorded 236 *lashti* (c. 460 tons) of ash and fifty barrels of potash, similarly being sent to Königsberg (*Akty* ..., Vol. 14, 645–655). As late as the eighteenth century, these western forests were still the scene of extensive potash-making. In Brest district in 1780 there were eighty-seven potash-makers, who in that year produced 7024 barrels of good quality ash, fifty-four of medium quality and thirty of spoilage (Pokhilevich and Chugay, 1971:368).

In what is now Moldavia in 1666, 200 cartloads were produced at severe cost to the beech forests of the area and potash was being exported via Poland to western Europe. In the same period potash-making near the Belgorod Line was so damaging the forest as to endanger the defensive function of the line (Tsvetkov, 1957:27). At the other end of European Russia, Arkhangel'sk in the year 1701 alone exported 1313 tons of potash (Molchanov and Preobrazhenskiy, 1957:43).

To make a kilogramme of potash needed three cubic metres of wood, or about a thousand tons of timber to one ton of potash. In 1662–63 about 3000 tons of potash were made in Russia, about half coming from the estates of just one landowner, V. I. Morozov (Turchanovich, 1950). Morozov operated principally in the Nizhniy Novgorod and Arzamas areas; in sixty to eighty years he is supposed to have made a million roubles worth of potash, but in the process he wiped out trees suitable for its production on his estates, i.e. chiefly hardwoods, oak, elm, maple, and alder (Tsvetkov, 1957:30). As the forest in one area was exterminated the *maydany* were shifted to new sites, moving deeper into the Mordvinian forests, where in 1678 there were at least nine works, employing 497 people and producing 703 barrels, some 374 tons (Kharitonychev, 1960:66).

The production—and later export—of tar, pitch, and turpentine, was significant in many parts of the north, particularly along the Northern Dvina in the sixteenth century, and later along the Vaga as well. In 1701, 606 tons of tar (*smola*) were exported from Arkhangel'sk (Molchanov and Preobrazhenskiy, 1957:43–44). By the 1890s Arkhangel'sk was exporting annually nearly 10 000 tons of tar and up to 2000 tons of pitch, together with 4–6,000 tons of turpentine (*Lesnaya Promvshlennost'*, 1957:39).

Salt production by evaporation was well developed in certain areas from Kievan times onwards. Main medieval concentrations of salt-making were the region south of Lake Il'men centred on Staraya Russa, the middle Volga at Velikaya Sol' and in the Galich lands beyond the Volga focussed on Soligalich—the latter two placenames being examples of many indicating salt working. With the opening up of the Zavoloch'ye northlands salt extraction became extremely important along the Sukhona and Vychegda, especially at Tot'ma and Sol' Vychegodskaya, and then all round the White Sea shores, with Kargopol on the Onega river as the principal trading centre (Bakhrushin, 1952:45). From 1430 onwards the Kama region, centred on Solikamsk, Novoye Usol'ye and Cherdyn, became more and more dominant in salt production, as it has since remained. In this area the salt works of the Pyskovskiy monastery in the last eleven years of the seventeenth century, produced over 5 600 000 poods of salt at a cost of almost 450 000 *sazheny* (4 368 000 cubic metres) of timber (Yastrebov, 1976b: 103). Later still, as Russian colonization moved southwards, some of the northern centres of production declined, but yet another area of salt-working developed around Bakhmut in the Donets region.

Large amounts of wood were burnt to provide the heat for salt evapo-ration. In the fifteenth-century Kama industry, 100 *sazheny* (971 cubic metres) were consumed to make 1000 poods of salt. Although improve-ments in technology steadily reduced this quantity through time to only a tenth as much in 1910, increasing volume of production meant an overall rise in timber demand at least until the first half of the eighteenth century, when there were some 1200 salt works. By then local forests had been destroyed and timber was being rafted from over 300 kilometres. Thereafter annual timber consumption for Kama salt fell off from a peak of about

325 000 *sazheny* to under 10 000 in 1910 when coal had largely taken over as a fuel (Yastrebov, 1976b:103–110). In the Bakhmut area, on top of a coalfield, the change-over came too late and the precious forests along the rivers Bakhmut, Zherebtsa, and Krasna on the extreme southern margins of the forest-steppe had already been wiped out (Tsvetkov, 1957:35).

Medieval craft manufacture was naturally a great user of wood for a wide range of consumer goods, such as plates, bowls and spoons, sledges, carts, agricultural implements, and furniture; often whole villages were engaged in such production. But the scale of timber consumption had only very localized effects on the forest and was usually selective of certain tree species. However, as time passed rising production began to have noticeable results, especially in areas where resources were naturally more limited. The widespread distilling practised by the Ukrainian Cossack settlers in the southern forest-steppe had destroyed much of the forest there for fuel by the eighteenth century (Kirikov, 1979:107) and where in the previous century there had been 27.3 hectares of forest and meadow per head of population, by 1800 there was only 4.3 (Dolgopolov, 1961:66).

More particularly, this growth in demand was linked to the development of factory, as opposed to craft, production. For example, paper manufacture only began in a rather tentative way in the second half of the seventeenth century with the founding of two state and two somewhat short-lived private mills (Livshits, 1955:25–6). By the 1760s annual production was about 130 000 reams (*stopy*) and by the end of the century it had tripled (Yatsunskiy, 1973:209). Originally market-oriented around St. Petersburg, paper manufacture in the nineteenth century spread north to Arkhangel'sk and west into the Baltic provinces and Belorussia. By the early twentieth century, national production of paper and cardboard was running at about 310 000 tons a year (excluding Finland). From about 1800 to the Revolution factory processing of timber steadily increased. Over that period the number of sawmills rose from 500 to 1664. If the first veneer works in Russia commenced only in 1887, by World War I there were forty-five works, making 250 000 cubic metres of veneer (*Lesnaya Promyshlennost'*, 1957:52–58.

One must remember too that a general characteristic of industrial Russia in the nineteenth century was that the growth of factory manufacture, which was often in very large-scale units, was still accompanied by the persistence of great numbers of small-scale enterprises. For example, in the first half of that century, throughout the forests of Belorussia were scattered many small hut-works, making tar, pitch, and potash, each tiny but in sum representing considerable timber exploitation; for example, Minsk province produced 40 000 barrels of tar, 15–20 000 barrels of pitch and 800–1000 tons of potash (Chepko, 1966:79–80). Similarly, in Vyatka province in the period immediately before World War I, there were still over 5000 *kustari*, craft workmen, engaged in tar-making, even though the destruction of the peasant forests by their operations had already greatly reduced the numbers so employed (Semenov-Tyan-Shanskiy, 1914:283).

The long-delayed onset of the Industrial Revolution in Russia in some respects provided a respite for the forests as iron steamers replaced wooden sailing ships and as coal took over as a fuel, but these effects were only detectable in the 1870s and even then, wood remained the principal fuel for domestic, and a number of industrial, purposes. Official government estimates put the total consumption of timber by industry in the early 1890s at 7 500 000 cubic sazhens, almost 73 000 000 cubic metres a year (*Sel's-koye . . .* , 1893:437). Indeed, the coal-mines themselves formed a new demand for pit-props, while the expanding railway system needed wood for fuel, for sleepers, and for telegraph poles.

TIMBER FOR EXPORT

Russia's swelling needs for timber were matched by those of other countries, especially of such countries as England, which had even earlier squandered their forest wealth. Some mast timbers were exported from Kholmogory in the reign of Ivan the Terrible, but from the seventeenth century onwards the volume of timber exported from Russia steadily increased. At first via Kholmogory and Arkhangel'sk and the White Sea, after Peter I's conquests on the Baltic, export was also important from St. Petersburg, Riga, and other Baltic ports; finally, Catherine the Great's reign added the Black Sea ports as well.

The desperate need of the British navy in the eighteenth century for ship and mast timbers and for other naval stores, including tar, pitch and turpentine, led to Anglo-Russian commercial treaties in 1734 and 1766, and also to British participation in the despoiling of the Russian forests. The most notorious British undertaking was that of an entrepreneur called, in Russian accounts, Dzhingli Gom. In 1756, for the sum of 120 000 roubles, Gom bought the right to exploit the Onega basin forests for thirty years from Count Shuvalov, who had been granted a state monopoly. Gom was loaned 300 000 roubles over ten years by the Russian Senate and given the right to export up to 600 000 trees a year, paying twenty-five kopeks per tree. Gom set up three saw-mills and two shipyards, where between 1763 and 1779 he built many ships, which he used to export 3500 masts, almost 250 000 building logs and 2 500 000 planks.

However Gom failed to pay his debts to the Russian Government and in 1783 his undertaking was terminated. One Russian writer after another joined in condemnation of the massive forest destruction, wrought by Gom's company. Chelishchev wrote, "One must shudder to see what awful things this pernicious robber did in fifteen years" (Trofimov, 1961:83–85). A later traveller in the area, Bogoslavskiy, recorded that:

> Seventy years have passed since Gom's company ceased to operate in the Onega forests, but time has not healed, and will not quickly heal, the wounds inflicted on the Arkhangel'sk forests by Gom. (Tsvetkov, 1953:149).

Equally rapacious were the activities of another British company, Pitt and Forster, near Turov on the river Pripyat' in Belorussia. In 1793, the company was granted permission to buy inhabited estates. They then put all the serfs to work clear-felling all the timber, to the neglect of farming. The timber was sent down the Dnepr to the Kherson dockyard. The plan was that once an estate was cleared, it was to be sold for what it would fetch and a new one bought. Local landowners protested at the wholesale devastation and, after only three years, Tsar Paul took over the first estate, returning the purchase money to the English company, which thereon sold up its second estate and ceased operations (Zelenskiy, 1864: Vol. 2, 94–95).

As the eighteenth century gave way to the nineteenth, Russian state and Russian landowners alike rivalled the earlier role of the English in destroying the forests for export. In the White Sea basin, Gom's successor was the state, although foreigners were still involved. The state agency was run by one Niman, in Chelishchev's words, "by birth a Swede, by title a merchant, by office a director and by trade a destroyer" (Trofimov, 1961:86). By 1846 the English were back in business on the Onega, in the company of Clark, Hubbard, and Morgan, which in five years had exported over a million planks (*ibid.*: 87).

The construction of railways to the ports of the Baltic and Black Seas opened up swifter channels of export for landowners all over European Russia, at a time when many were seeking to recover from financial problems, deriving from the emancipation of serfs, or were wanting to raise capital to invest in industry. By the end of the nineteenth century the export of timber and timber products was on a massive scale and steadily rising (Table 2.1); about 40 per cent of the total went to Great Britain, 35 per cent to Germany, 11 to Holland, and 7 to France (Radtsiga, 1901:84). In absolute quantities, export of untreated logs rose from 1 600 000 tons in 1897 to 2 900 000 in 1908 and of saw timber from 1 616 000 to 2 720 000 tons. Between the 1870s and the end of the century the volume of timber carried on the Russian railways quadrupled (*Lesnaya Promyshlennost'*, 1957:28).

Table 2.1. Average annual value of timber-product export.

Date	Million roubles	Date	Million roubles
1860–64	6.0	1890–94	46.7
1865–69	11.1	1895–99	52.3
1870–74	22.7	1900	61.0
1875–79	29.1	1904	73.2
1880–84	34.3	1913	163.6
1885–89	36.0		

Source: A. A. Radtsiga, 1901:82–83; *Lesnaya Promyshlennost'* 1957:40.

THE DESTRUCTION OF THE FORESTS

The consequences of the sum of so many and such heavy demands made on the Russian forests were striking. The buoyant market created by the requirements of timber caused more and more landowners to raise ready capital—or simply spending money—by selling off their forests. The usual form of agreement in the nineteenth century was for a landowner to grant a contractor the right to cut trees on his estate for a set period, in return for a lump sum down; naturally it was in the interest of the contractor to cut as ferociously as possible in the time given. Moreover, the contract frequently permitted the grazing of cattle on the cut-over areas for ten years or more, thus effectively destroying any faint hope of natural regeneration. The last century before the Revolution, as a result, saw a veritable frenzy of cutting on the private estates. In the words of a contemporary, "Forest-owners strove, in every way possible, as it were to overtake each other in wiping out their forests as fast as possible" (Tsvetkov, 1957:37).

Before the Revolution, the enormous forested tracts of Siberia were scarcely touched. There forest fires did more damage than did deliberate felling by man, especially along the line of the Trans-Siberian railway, where the present-day dominance of secondary birch forest bears witness to the results of sparks from steam locomotives. Only with the establishment of a Forestry Directorate in western Siberia in 1884 was a beginning made in exploitation, and even then the value of timber produced had only reached 4 300 000 roubles by 1912. The Far East in 1895 was actually importing timber from the USA (*Lesnaya Promyshlennost'*, 1957:323).

The onslaught on the trees of Russia thus fell almost entirely on the European part of the country and there the destruction was on a huge scale. Evidence for the extent of loss is abundant. Fat'yanov (1959) has constructed maps based on the cadastres and the General Survey, showing how the Volga right bank in the Arzamas region was largely stripped of its once almost continuous dense forest, a process in which Morozov and his potash undertakings played no small part (see also French, 1963). Similar maps, demonstrating the same process, have been compiled by Gedymin (1968) for Sapozhok *rayon* of Ryazan' oblast, by Boyko (1976) for the Tatar ASSR. and by Semenova-Tyan-Shanskaya (1957) for the entire forest-steppe zone of European Russia. In the Tatar republic the percentage of the surface under forest decreased from 49 in 1800 to 31 in 1870 and only 16 per cent today (Boyko, 1976: 183). In Estonia, the 35 per cent of the surface now under arable was almost wholly derived at the expense of the forest (Isakov *et al.*, 1980: 202). In Moldavia, the period 1850–1918 saw over 130 000 hectares cleared (Tkachenko, 1980: 69). Tsvetkov (1957) cites many contemporary writers, aghast at the speed and scale of clearance.

Curiously enough, the work of Chizhova (1973) has shown a reversal of the otherwise universal trend towards ever more intensive clearance at all periods; this was in the area around Moscow, between the General Survey in 1766–81 and the mid-nineteenth century. Chizhova attributes this to the very heavy early clearance, followed by the early growth of industry in the region, leading to the abandonment of agricultural pursuits and the reversion of arable to forest. However, this seems to have been a unique exception, and even in the Moscow area the extent under forest began to fall once again after 1850. The Valuyev Commission of 1872, set up to study the state of agriculture and rural industry in Russia, reported for province after province, including Moscow, wholesale and heedless cutting, especially on private estates.

In 1894, the Forestry Department established an expedition to survey the headstreams of rivers in European Russia, including a study of the water conservation role of watershed forests. Its findings were horrific. On the upper Oka, the percentage of land under forest had fallen from 15.8 at the time of the General Survey to only 3.6 per cent, on the upper Don from 9.2 to 1.8 per cent. Individual stream basins regularly showed a decrease in the forested area of 60 per cent or more and in some cases, for example the Lyutaya basin on the upper Don, a total loss of all forests (Kharitonova, 1950).

The most thorough analysis of the degree of forest destruction in European Russia is that of M. A. Tsvetkov (1957), who calculated the area under forest for each province, at the time of the General Survey in the later eighteenth century, in 1868, in 1887 and finally in 1914, and then working back to 1725 and 1696. The results of his scrupulous calculations (Table 2.2) provide a picture of immense loss (for a cartographic representation of Tsvetkov's figures, see French, 1963).

The most northerly province of Arkhangel'sk, with its huge and remote

Table 2.2. Forests—absolute areas and as per cent of area.

Province	1696 (1725) 1000 ha	%	1796 1000 ha	%	1914 1000 ha	%
Arkhangel'sk	46 410	61.2	46 334	61.1	46 713	61.6
Vologda	38 301	95.1	37 656	93.5	31 454	78.1
Olonets	10 801	72.6	10 756	72.3	9521	64.0
St. Petersburg	(3296)	(61.3)	2957	55.0	2398	44.6
Novgorod	8258	67.5	8087	66.1	7585	62.0
Pskov	2856	64.6	2365	53.5	1132	25.6
Vladimir	2428	49.7	2355	48.2	1290	26.4
Kaluga	1556	50.3	1216	39.3	770	24.9
Moscow	1605	48.2	1459	43.8	876	26.3
Ryazan'	2029	48.2	1406	33.4	813	19.3
Smolensk	3043	54.3	2578	46.0	1367	24.4
Tver'	4953	75.8	3306	50.6	1476	22.6
Tula	749	24.2	480	15.5	241	7.8
Tambov	2697	40.5	1885	28.3	1079	16.2
Penza	2160	55.6	1554	40.0	663	16.3
Yaroslavl'	1877	52.7	1638	46.0	1015	28.5
Kostroma	6993	83.1	5882	69.9	5318	63.2
Vyatka	13 492	87.8	11 878	77.3	6073	39.6
Nizh. Novgorod	2871	56.0	2753	53.7	1917	37.4
Kazan'	4167	65.4	3358	52.7	1854	29.1
Perm	24 108	72.6	22 216	66.9	19 426	58.5
Ufa) Orenburg)	18 228	58.2	13 373	42.7	8762	28.9
Estlyand	(650)	(34.1)	543	28.5	348	17.2
Liflyand	(2559)	(58.0)	2229	50.5	931	19.8
Kurlyand	—	—	1184	43.4	824	30.2
Orel	1453[a]	31.1	1341	28.7	804	17.2
Kiev	115[a]	30.1	1250	24.5	713	15.1
Chernigov	1860[a]	35.5	1294	24.7	781	14.9
Voronezh	837	12.7	560	8.5	488	7.4
Kursk	753	16.2	572	12.3	288	6.2
Poltava	1277	25.6	858	17.2	250	5.0
Khar'kov	1117	20.5	627	11.5	441	8.1
Yekaterinoslav	90[b]	6.3	108	1.7	235	3.7
Kherson	—	—	114	1.6	121	1.7
Tavrida	—	—	361	6.0	319	5.3
Bessarabia	—	—	547[c]	12.0	256	5.6
Astrakhan	591	4.5	450	1.9	213	0.9
Voyska Donskogo	659	4.0	527	3.2	263	1.6
Stavropol'	42	0.34	38	0.31	33	0.27
Vitebsk	—	—	1816	40.2	1120	24.8
Mogilev	—	—	1903	39.6	1076	22.4
Minsk	—	—	3821	41.8	3062	33.5
Grodno	—	—	1050	29.3	804	20.8
Vil'no	—	—	2118	49.8	1008	23.7
Kovno	—	—	927	22.8	614	15.1
Volyn	—	—	3140	43.7	1825	25.4
Podol'sk	—	—	609	14.5	399	9.5
Total	213 416	52.68	217 322	44.76	172 378	35.16

[a] Boundaries as before 1792.
[b] Boundaries as before 1741.
[c] In 1812.

(Source: Tsvetkov, 1957:126–32)

reserves, showed little change in the percentage of the surface covered by trees. The southern provinces, where there was almost no forest to lose, did likewise. Elsewhere, every province evinced significant loss, with the heaviest losses tending to occur, as one might expect, in the more densely populated provinces. In most central provinces the extent of land under forest was reduced in the two centuries by a half or more and in some by nearly two-thirds. In Poltava province a mere fifth of its former forests survived in 1914. All in all, European Russia between 1696 and 1914, little over two centuries, lost almost 67 000 000 hectares, about 28 per cent of its forests (Tsvetkov, 1957:133).

Quite apart from the destruction of a great resource, there were numerous undesirable side-effects. The loss of the habitat of many species of wildlife led to their near, or total, extermination in many parts of Russia. In drier areas and areas of lighter, sandy soils, ravine development and soil erosion were greatly accelerated, with consequent silting of river courses. Yet to set against the massive destruction of the Russian "green mantle" of Leonov, the Tsarist state had little enough to put on the credit side of the balance. Some aspects of conservation were of antiquity—the protection of bee-trees, of hunting forests and, in Peter the Great's time, of naval timbers. But forest husbandry only became a matter of somewhat wider concern in the nineteenth century. Even then, despite some lead from the State in setting up a Forest Department and forestry schools and in making some plantations to fix sands or check gully erosion, private landowners did very little. By 1914, of a total 1 259 562 hectares planted, only a tenth had been accomplished by private persons (Tsvetkov, 1957:200). More significantly still, this figure of achievement by public and private efforts alike, represented 1.9 per cent of the area wiped out in the last 200 years of Tsardom. The Russians had not even begun to repay the debt they owed the forest.

REFERENCES

Akty izdavayemyye Vilenskoy Arkheograficheskoy Komissiyey dlya Razbora Drev-nikh Aktov, Vol. 14, Vil'na (1888).
Bakhrushin, S. V., (1952). "Nauchnyye Trudy", Vol. 1, Moscow.
Boyko, F. F., (1976). Izmeneniye lesistosti Tatarskoy ASSR v rezul'tate vozdeystviya cheloveka, *In* "Problemy Otraslevoy i Kompleksnoy Geografii", (N. I. Blazhko *et al.*, eds), pp. 179–184, Kazan'.
Chepko, V. V., (1966). "Sel'skoye Khozyaystvo Belorussii v Pervoy Polovine XIX veka", Minsk.
Cherepnin, L. V., (1960). "Obrazovaniya Russkogo Tsentralizovannogo Gosudar-stva v XIV–XV vekakh", Moscow.
Chizhova, V. P., (1973). Izmeneniye lesnogo pokrova v nekotorykh prirodnykh

42   R.A. French

territorial'nykh kompleksakh Moskovskoy oblasti za 200-letniy period, *Vestnik Mosk. Univ: Geografiya* 1, 106–111.

Davydchuk. V. S., (1975). Podsechnoye zemledeliye kak sredstvo vozdeystviya na landshaft, *Vestnik Mosk. Univ: Geografiya* 4, 97–100.

Dolgopolov, K. V., (1961). "Tsentral'no-Chernozemnyy Rayon", Moscow.

Fat'yanov, A. S., (1959). Opyt analiza istorii razvitiya pochvennogo pokrova Gor'-kovskoy oblasti, *In* "Pochvenno-Geograficheskiye Issledovaniya i Ispol'zovaniye Aerofotos"yemki v Kartirovanii Pochv", (I. V. Tyurin and Yu. A. Liverovskiy, eds), pp. 3–171, Moscow.

French, R. A., (1963). The making of the Russian landscape, *The Advancement of Science* 20, 44–56.

French, R. A., (1967). The historical geography of the forests of Belorussia in the sixteenth century, *Jour. of Byelorussian Studies*, 1, no. 3, 168–83.

French, R. A., (1968). "The Historical Geography of Western Belorussia, 1550–1600", Unpublished Ph.D. thesis, University of London.

French, R. A., (1969). Babrujsk and its neighbourhood in the early seventeenth century, *Jour. of Byelorussian Studies* 2, no. 1, 29–56.

Gedymin, A. V., (1964). Vliyaniye dlitel'noy raspashki na nekotoryye svoystva pochv lesostepi, *In* "Pochvenno-Geograficheskiye i Landshaftno-Geokhimicheskiye Issledovaniya", pp. 134–57, Moscow.

Gedymin, A. V., (1968). The use of old Russian land survey data in geographic research for agricultural purposes, *Soviet Geography: Rev. and Trans.* 9, no. 7, 602–24.

Glagoleva, A. P., (1957). "Olonetskiye Zavody v Pervoy Chetverti XVIII veka", Moscow.

Gorskiy, A. D., (1959). Iz istorii zemledeliya v severo-vostochnoy Rusi XIV–XV vekov, *In* "Materialy po Istorii Sel'skogo Khozyaystva i Krest'yanstva SSSR", 3, (K. V. Sivkov, ed.) pp. 5–40, Moscow.

Grebenshchikov, O. S., (1965). "Geobotanicheskiy Slovar", Nauka, Moscow.

Isakov, Yu. A., Kazanskaya, N. S., and Panfilov, D. V., (1980). "Klassifikatsiya, Geografiya i Antropogennaya Transformatsiya Ekosistem", Moscow.

Kharitonova, V. F., (1950). Ob izmeneniyakh lesistosti basseynov verkhov'yev rek Yevropeyskoy chasti Rossii, *Trudy Inst. Lesa* 5, 197–212.

Kharitonychev, A. T., (1960). "Rol' Khozyaystvennoy Deyatel'nosti Cheloveka v Izmenenii Landshaftov Gor'kovskogo Pravoberezh'ya", Gor'kiy.

Kirikov, S. V., (1966). "Promyslovyye Zhivotnyye, Prirodnaya Sreda i Chelovek", Moscow.

Kirikov, S. V., (1979). "Chelovek i Priroda Vostochno-Yevropeyskoy Lesostepi v X-nachale XIX v.", Moscow.

Kochin, G. E., (1965). "Sel'skoye Khozyaystvo na Rusi v Period Obrazovaniya Russkogo Tsentralizovannogo Gosudarstva konets XIII-nachalo XVI v.", Moscow and Leningrad.

Lappo, G. M., (1961). Nekotoryye cherty istoricheskoy geografii gorodov Moskovskoy oblasti, *Voprosy Geografii* 51, 27–51.

Lappo, I. I. (ed.), (1905). "Polotskaya Reviziya 1552 goda", Yur'yev.

Leonov, L., (1966). "The Russian Forest", translated by Bernard Isaacs, Moscow.

"Lesnaya Promyshlennost' Dorevolyutsionnoy Rossii", Moscow and Leningrad (1957).

Livshits, R. S., (1955). "Razmeshcheniye Promyshlennosti v Dorevolyutsionnoy Rossii", Moscow.

Molchanov, A. A. and Preobrazhenskiy, I. F., (1957). "Lesa i Lesnoye Khozyaystvo Arkhangel'skoy Oblasti", Moscow.

Murzayev, E. and Murzayeva, V., (1959). "Slovar' Mestnykh Geograficheskikh Terminov", Moscow.

Obozov, N. A., (1961). Pobochnyye pol'zovaniya v lesakh, *Voprosy Geografii* **54**, 75–86.

Perevalov, V. A., (1950). Nekotoryye dannyye ob ispol'zovanii lesa v istoricheskom proshlom, *Trudy Inst. Lesa* **5**, 142–70.

Pistsovaya Kniga Byvshago Pinskago Starostva sostavlennaya po poveleniyu Korolya Sigismunda Avgusta v 1561–1566 godakh Pinskim i Kobrinskim Starostoyu Lavrinom Voynoyu, 2 vols., Vil'na (1874).

Pokhilevich, D. L. and Chugay, V., (1971). Korolevskiye lesa Belorussii i Litvy vo vtoroy polovine XVIII v. (proizvodstvo, naseleniye). *In* "Yezhegodnik po Agrarnoy Istorii Vostochnoy Yevropy 1966 god", pp. 361–73, Tallin.

Popov, V. V., (1937). Tul'skiye zaseki XVI–XVV. Lesnoye khozyaystvo, *Trudy po Lesnomu Opytnomu Delu Tul'skikh Zasek* **2**, 3–47.

Radtsiga, A. A., (1901). "Les i Lesnoye Khozyaystvo v Raznykh Gosudarstvakh", Narodnaya Pol'za, St. Petersburg.

Reviziya Pushch i Perekhodov Zverinykh v Byvshem Velikom Knyazhestva Litovskom, s prisovokupleniyem gramot i privilegiy na vkhod'ye v pushchi i na zemli, sostavlennaya Starostoyu Mstibogovskim Grigoriyem Bogdanovichem Volovichem v 1559 godu, (1867), Vil'na.

Rubenshteyn, N. L., (1957). "Sel'skoye Khozyaystvo Rossii vo Vtoroy Polovine XVIII v.", Moscow.

Sel'skoye i Lesnoye Khozyaystvo Rossii, St. Petersburg, (1893).

Semenov-Tyan-Shanskiy, V. P. (ed.), (1914). "Rossiya: Polnoye Geograficheskoye Opisaniye Nashego Otechestva. Vol. 5, Ural i Priural'ye", St. Petersburg.

Semenova-Tyan-Shanskaya, A. M., (1957). Izmeneniye rastitel'nogo pokrova lesostepi russkoy ravniny v XVI-XVIII vv. pod vliyaniyem deyatel'nosti cheloveka, *Botanicheskiy Zhurnal* **42**, 1398–1407.

Smith, R. E. F., (1973). Forest cultivation in Toropets (16th century), *Forschungen zur Osteuropäischen Geschichte* **18**, 125–37.

Smith, R. E. F., (1977). "Peasant Farming in Muscovy", Cambridge.

Tkachenko, A. I., (1980). Antropogennyye izmeneniya lesistosti na territorii Dnestrovsko-Prutskogo mezhdurech'ya, *Izvestiya Ak. Nauk: Seriya Geogr.* **2**, 66–70.

Tokmakov, I., (1887). Kratkiy obzor materialov k istorii lesovodstva po dokumentam Moskovskikh arkhivov, *Lesnoy Zhurnal* **27**, no. 2, 183–89.

Trofimov, P. M., (1961). "Ocherki Ekonomicheskogo Razvitiya Yevropeyskogo Severa Rossii", Moscow.

Tsvetkov, M. A., (1953). Razvitiye lesopotrebleniya v svyazi s sudostroyeniyem, *Trudy Inst. Lesa* **10**, 138–169.

Tsvetkov, M. A., (1957). "Izmeneniye Lesistosti Yevropeyskoy Rossii s Kontsa XVII stoletiya po 1914 god", Moscow.

Turchanovich, L. F., (1950). Les Yevropeyskoy chasti SSSR v proshlom, *Zemlevedeniye* 3.

Turgenev, I., (1955). "A Hunter's Sketches", Moscow.

Yablonskis, K. I. (ed), (1960). "Statut Velikogo Knyazhestva Litovskogo 1529 goda", Minsk.

Yastrebov, Ye. V., (1976a). K voprosu o razmeshchenii prirodnykh resursov Urala i ikh osvoyenii v XVIII–XIX vekakh, *In* "Prirodnyye Resursy i Voprosy ikh Ratsional'nogo Ispol'zovaniya, (V. T. Zaychikov, ed.), pp. 111–113, Moscow.

Yastrebov, Ye. V., (1976b). Iz istorii osvoyeniya rassolov Prikam'ya. *In* "Prirodnyye Resursy i Voprosy ikh Ratsional'nogo Ispol'zovaniya", (V. T. Zaychikov, ed.), pp. 99–111, Moscow.

Yatsunskiy, V. K., (1973). "Sotsial'no-Ekonomicheskaya Istoriya Rossii XVIII–XIX vv.", Moscow.

Zelenskiy, I., (1864). "Materialy dlya Geografii i Statistiki Rossii, sobrannyye Ofitserami General'nogo Shtaba. Minskaya Guberniya", 2 vols., St. Petersburg.

3 Agriculture and Soil Erosion in the European Forest-steppe

I. Stebelsky

The European forest-steppe was, potentially, one of the Russian Empire's richest agricultural zones. It benefited from more heat and a longer growing season than the broad forest zone to the north, yet it lacked the frequent droughts and insect hazards of the southern steppes. Its rich chernozems and grey forest soils, watered by sufficient rainfall, once supported tall grasses and rich deciduous forest groves. Early settlers who cleared the land boasted of legendary yields (Kotel'nikov, 1950).

This rich farmland, however, did not remain unaltered. Throughout the eighteenth century more and more land was cleared. By the end of the nineteenth century the good earth was ploughed to its limits. Soils eroded, yields declined, and the peasantry became impoverished. Gullies carved up fields, cut through roads, and threatened railway lines. In 1890, the Eighth Congress of Russian Naturalists and Physicians appealed to the Ministry of State Property to study the gullies and take measures against them. In response, the ministry prepared a questionnaire concerning gullies which it collected from 353 correspondents in 1891 and 1893, and Prince Masal'-skiy was commissioned to analyse the results.

Masal'skiy's study (1897) encompassed the European forest-steppe and steppe zones. It revealed widespread gullying in Bessarabia, Podolya, the Dnepr Heights, and the Donets Upland, but the most intense gullying was noted in the Central Russian Upland and the Volga Upland. Subsequent studies, conducted in the recent Soviet period, largely confirmed this pattern (Sobolev, 1948; Mironova, 1971). Furthermore, the environmental degradation corresponded, to some extent, with economic decline. A Russian Government Commission, after an exhaustive study that began in 1901, established that the peasantry of the Central Russian Black Earth region suffered the most severe impoverishment since 1861 (*Materialy . . .* , 1903).

Thus, from the standpoint of both soil erosion and rural poverty, the

RUSSIAN HISTORICAL GEOGRAPHY VOL. 1
ISBN 0 12 081201 0

Central Russian Black Earth region warrants particular attention. Since the details of the environment, history of occupance, agrarian structure and evolving land use differed from one region to another, this chapter will focus on the Central Russian Black Earth region as a case study of agriculture and soil erosion in the European forest steppe.

ENVIRONMENT AND POPULATION

Located to the south of Moscow and north of Khar'kov, the Central Russian Black Earth region occupies the middle segment of the long, east–west trending European forest-steppe (Fig. 3.1). This region includes the six *gubernii* (hereafter, provinces) of Kursk, Orel, Ryazan', Tambov, Tula, and Voronezh.

From the standpoint of physiography the region may be divided into two parts. Its western half is the rolling and gullied Central Russian Upland (200–250 metres O.D.), an uplifted portion of the pre-Cambrian plate covered with layers of sedimentaries (100–600 metres thick). The upland becomes increasingly dissected to the south-east as the base level of erosion deepens until it ends, abruptly, with the high right bank of the Don river (Fig. 3.1). Beyond the Don, except for the Don-Voronezh interfluve and the Kalach Upland, stretches the flat-to-gently undulating Tambov Lowland, rising gradually to the east (100–175 metres O.D.). Unlike the upland, the lowland bears a ground moraine deposited by an ice lobe that covered it, as far as the Kalach Upland, during the so-called Dnepr advance. After the glacial retreat the upland and most of the lowland were covered by loess. Only deep ravines in the Central Russian Upland testify to the powerful water erosion that immediately followed the glacial period, when sparse vegetation could not protect the delicate surface material. Eventually, thick vegetation cloaked the land. As the powerful erosive forces abated, the surfaces acquired deep, fertile grey forest loams and chernozems.

In the sixteenth century the Central Russian Black Earth region, still very sparsely settled, was clothed in natural vegetation. Its soils and plant associations followed climatic gradients from the north-west to the south-east (Fig. 3.2). In the north-west and the north, where precipitation reached 600 millimetres per year, the grey forest loams supported extensive broadleaf forests. To the south, the chernozems nourished a parkland vegetation. Oak and lime forests, often commanding the highest points of land or protecting the steeply inclined slopes, alternated with bee-loud glades. Open grasslands prevailed on flat divides, away from major rivers. On the low terraces of the Tsna river and the southward-flowing Voronezh, Bityug, and Khoper, pine groves held the fluvial sands from wind erosion. Only in the south-east,

Fig. 3.1. Provinces and relief of the Central Russian Black Earth region.

where average July temperatures exceeded 20° Celsius and precipitation declined to 450 millimetres per year or less, the parkland gave way to open steppe. Here the tall feather-grass supported many ungulates.

For several millenia the farmers of the forested zone and the nomadic hersdmen of the steppe had contested for the European forest-steppe. The last episode of this conflict, following the Tatar invasion in the thirteenth century, resulted in a marked depopulation of the zone. In the sixteenth

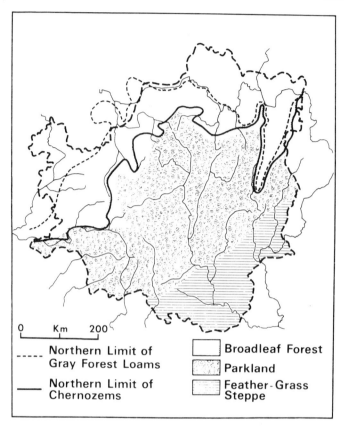

Fig. 3.2. Soils and natural vegetation of the Central Black Earth region.

century the balance of power shifted in favour of Muscovy. Its ruler, Prince Ivan IV, subdued the Tatar khanates on the Volga and secured a flank for southward expansion against the remaining Tatar khanate of Crimea. Thus, what is known as the Central Russian Black Earth region became the southern marchland of Muscovy.

The first stage of Muscovite advance into the Central Russian Black Earth region was the political acquisition and refortification of towns south of the Oka River: Tula, Venev, Yepifan, Zaraysk, Ryazan', and others. But the Crimean Tatar campaigns that involved burning, looting, and taking of prisoners for the slave markets of Turkey, prompted Moscow to construct a continuous line of wooden fortifications that became known as the *zasechnaya cherta*. This line of defence, breached only during the campaign of

Devlet-Girey (1571) provided a measure of security for the countryside. Peasant population revived around the former princely seat of Ryazan' and grew quickly near Tula, the main fort on the *cherta* (Rudakov, 1923). Other county towns, acquired from Lithuania in the upper reaches of the Oka (1494) or in the Chernigov-Severskiy principality (1523), such as Putivl' and Rylsk, remained far removed from the main Muscovite forces. Local defence measures, including patrols into the parkland, provided so little protection that the size of towns and the supporting farming population remained small (Tikhomirov, 1962).

The second stage of Muscovite advance involved not only the patrolling of the parkland to the south of the garrisoned towns, but the construction of new forts on defensible sites that the patrols had used for their encampments. These outposts, built towards the end of the sixteenth century, were located so as to observe Tatar movement and guard strategic river fords. However, within three decades, the more secure forts (especially Voronezh) had attracted farming population to the surrounding countryside. Since the latter fell prey to renewed Tatar attacks, additional measures of defence had to be undertaken.

Muscovite response, the third stage of acquisition, culminated in the construction of what became known as the Belgorod defence line. Massive earthen walls and trenches as well as palisades, abatis, and towers at regular intervals were built across Tatar trails that followed the grassy uplands (Zagorovskiy, 1969). Begun in 1637, the line became one of the largest military projects undertaken anywhere, as it skirted the parkland belt from Muscovy's western border through Belgorod, Voronezh, Tambov, and eventually to Simbirsk on the Volga. Protected by the new structures and men at arms, rural settlements expanded quickly. Servitors who were assigned to guard duty on the Belgorod line took up farming behind the defences, and runaway serfs came to join them (Aleksandrov, 1967).

Soon after the construction of the Belgorod line was inititated, another phase of occupancy began. The Ukrainian cossacks, frustrated by Poland, arrived from the west in large numbers to take up vacant land. Initially, the Muscovites hoped to disperse the Ukrainians along the Belgorod defence line towns, but their influx was so great and their desire to settle together so strong that permission was granted for them to form entire settlements. The Ukrainian cossacks, organized in their traditional regimental fashion, established towns along the south-western border of Muscovy, south of the Belgorod line and in some cases on the line itself. Subordinated to the Belgorod *voyevoda* (commanding officer of a military district), the Ukrainian cossacks provided an outer shield for the Belgorod line, and the Muscovite Tsar, in order to ensure their loyalty, offered them generous privileges (Bagaley, 1886, 1887).

The fourth stage of Muscovite advance involved the acquisition of the sparsely settled Don cossack lands south-east of Voronezh. Although in theory Moscow had long claimed these lands, in practice it had no control over them. Moreover, in the seventeenth century they experienced an influx of runaway serfs who swelled the ranks of the Don cossacks and, on occasion, encouraged rebellion among the servitors of the Belgorod line. The demise of the Don cossack *vol'nitsa* (land of the free) began with a flurry of shipbuilding and iron smelting in and near Voronezh as Peter I prepared his military for the Azov campaign (1695–96). After his forces, together with the Don cossacks, captured the Turkish fortress, the power of Crimean Tatars, the vassals of Turkey, was severely undermined. The Don cossacks were requested to vacate the Khoper and the Medveditsa river valleys and to re-settle, as mail carriers, between Valuiki and Azov (1700– 1). The remaining runaway serfs and Ukrainian cossack colonists were enumerated and their lands and villages granted to court favourites (Shul-yakovskiy, 1961).

Stemming from the history of Muscovite acquisition and military settlement of the Central Russian Black Earth region, the occupancy of the land was not even. Although old, rural populations remained dispersed among small towns and villages of the broadleaf forest zone in the north and west, two zones of higher population densities emerged in the forest steppe. These originated from the chains of towns and forts of the *zasechnaya cherta* (near Tula and Ryazan') and the Belgorod line. As security improved, the forts spun off purely agricultural villages into the nearby countryside (Semenov, 1902). Between the two defence lines the parkland was relatively sparsely settled. In the second half of the seventeenth century, with the passing of these lands to the Muscovite gentry, some hamlets were augmented and new villages planted with serfs from the adjoining forest regions or from Muscovy itself. But the new arrivals were balanced by those who fled to join the servitors on the defence line (Vaynberg, 1967). Thus population growth in this zone relied mainly on its natural increase (Yatsunskiy, 1957).

In the south-east, the feather-grass steppe was very sparsely settled by the Don cossacks. Towards the end of the seventeenth century, their number was augmented by runaway serfs from the north and Ukrainian cossacks from the west, who established new settlements along the Don and Khoper rivers, but avoided settling too close to the Belgorod line. In the eighteenth century the imposition of serfdom led to another influx of serfs and the settlement of the intervening Bityug and Vorona rivers. However, away from the rivers and their wooded banks, the open grassland steppes remained empty (Vodarskiy, 1977).

In the eighteenth century, as population doubled (from 3.1 million persons in 1719 to 7 million in 1811) the pattern of population densities among the provinces remained essentially unchanged (Table 3.1). Except for a continued small influx into the south-eastern steppes (mostly in Voronezh) and possible emigration from Orel, the migrations were mostly local adjustments, where daughter settlements were being established on remaining vacant lands. By the nineteenth century intra-regional migrations had essentially ceased. Movement to local towns was negligible as local industries remained undeveloped. The main differentiating factor in the growth of rural population densities became emigration, either to outside industrial centres (from Tula and Ryazan' provinces to Moscow, and from Voronezh and Kursk provinces to the Donbass) or to new lands in the North Caucasus and Siberia. Even so, immigration could scarcely counteract the high natural increase of rural population. As it doubled again in the nineteenth century, the increased rural density led to a profound and irreversible transformation of the land.

AGRARIAN SYSTEMS AND LAND USE

In a subsistence society, rising population densities should provide incentive for the adoption of more intensive forms of agricultural land use (Boserup, 1965). However, facets of agrarian structure, such as social obligations, political inducements, economic stimuli generating trade, advances in agronomy, and technological developments that promote regional specialization, may distort that apparent relationship. For convenience, this set of interrelationships between social, political, economic and technological conditions and agricultural land use may be called the agrarian system.

In the course of three centuries of occupance and population growth in the Central Russian Black Earth region, the agrarian system underwent considerable change. In turn, it had a direct impact on agricultural land use change. Three periods may be distinguished during which not only population densities but also the agrarian system itself changed. These periods were: (1) the military frontier; (2) expansion under bondage; and (3) stagnation after emancipation.

The Muscovite military frontier period encompassed the establishment of the *zasechnaya cherta* (sixteenth century) and the Belgorod line (seventeenth century). It involved the enlistment of peasants and artisans who, as state servitors, were obliged to defend the southern Muscovite frontier and to support themselves. In return, the state servitors obtained a generous allotment of land that they could farm. The peasants found this a convenient way to free themselves from economic obligations to their landlords or the crown. Petty gentry, too, exempted themselves from taxes by joining officers in the war zone and by obtaining title to land in perpetuity. However,

Table 3.1. Growth and distribution of population densities.

| | Persons per km² (Percentage of regional mean density) | | | | | |
	1719[a]	1762[a]	1811[a]	1857[a]	1897[b]	1914[c]
Kursk	15.6 (149)	18.0 (129)	29.3 (125)	36.9 (120)	51.0 (119)	70.1 (117)
Orel	15.1 (144)	16.0 (114)	24.9 (106)	30.2 (98)	43.5 (101)	59.1 (99)
Ryazan'	12.0 (114)	16.6 (119)	24.8 (106)	32.5 (106)	43.0 (100)	66.1 (111)
Tambov	7.0 (67)	10.1 (72)	19.2 (82)	26.7 (87)	40.3 (94)	53.0 (89)
Tula	15.6 (149)	22.1 (158)	32.5 (138)	36.3 (118)	45.8 (107)	60.9 (102)
Voronezh	3.6 (34)	8.4 (60)	17.6 (75)	27.5 (89)	38.4 (89)	55.1 (92)
Region	10.5 (100)	14.0 (100)	23.5 (100)	30.8 (100)	43.0 (100)	59.7 (100)

[a] Calculated by doubling the number of enumerated males, as given by Kabuzan, 1963:159, and dividing by area.
[b] Calculated with 1897 census data as given by Yatsunskiy, 1957:210.
[c] Calculated with 1914 population estimate as given by Rashin, 1956:61.

both had to assume military duties and bear the risks of living and sustaining themselves in a hostile frontier (Blum, 1961; Shaw, 1977).

Land on the frontier was abundant, and government allocations provided more than an individual could farm. Behind the defence lines, for example, peasant households cultivated sixteen to twenty hectares each; about as much as they could using the technology of the period (Rozhkov, 1899). By contrast, the Belgorod defence line rank and file received twenty-six hectares for cultivation and eighteen hectares of meadow (Miklashevskiy, 1894), while cossacks and officers received much more. Under peacetime conditions such land could be fully used only with the help of indentured peasants or serfs. In the war zone, however, little of the land was ploughed, for the servitors could not devote much time to farming, and methods requiring least time and effort were employed to produce food. Only as land became more secure and peasants moved in did the crop acreage significantly expand.

Cropping intensity was related mainly to the population density. The three-field system, the most intensive crop and livestock combination in sixteenth-century Muscovy, was common near Ryazan', where it not only supported the densest rural population of the Central Russian Black Earth region, but also provided grain for export to Moscow and Astrakhan. By the end of the sixteenth century the three-field system, identifiable in the land inventories of the period (*Pistsovyya knigi*, 1895) with the phrase "*a v dvu potomu zh*", was also reported behind the *zasechnaya cherta* near Tula, west of it along the Oka river, and in the south-western corner of the broadleaf forest zone near Putivl' and Rylsk (Tikhomirov, 1962). In more sparsely settled areas the annual fallow (*par*) gave way to long-term fallowing (*perelog*) (Rozhkov, 1899). Along the *zasechnaya cherta* itself the forests were preserved, at first for defence (as they constituted an integral part of the abatis and stockade complex) and later for fuel in charcoal smelters at the Tula armoury. Forests also provided honey, fruit, nuts, and berries, fur-bearing animals and fish from lakes and streams.

By the mid-seventeenth century the population had grown substantially, more forest was cleared, and more land was converted to arable. Along the new Belgorod defence line the servitors, concerned with defence, employed an infield-outfield cropping system (Miklashevskiy, 1894). Not far from the protective palisades of the settlements, where manure was applied, the more labour-demanding field crops and vegetables were grown. However, most grain was sown on distant plots of land for several years, without manuring, until the natural fertility of the chernozems declined, and then another new plot would be started. The servitors seldom visited these distant plots, except for ploughing, sowing, and harvesting; while one group of servitors worked, another group guarded against a surprise attack by the Tatars. Hayfields were located at even greater distances and sometimes in front of rather than behind the defence line. In addition, many servitors rented, from the state, rights to collect honey, trap and fish on lands they patrolled beyond the defence line. Grasslands were often set on fire—either to control scrub growth on pastures or to deprive the Tatars, in front of the Belgorod line, of a high grass cover. Thus, the natural vegetation, at least as far as the defence line, was being slowly cleared or modified.

In the second half of the seventeenth century, the Ukrainian cossacks who settled the parkland and feather-grass steppe south of the Belgorod line, brought their own technique of long-term fallow or *perelog* farming. Using teams of powerful oxen that pulled their iron Ukrainian ploughs, they were able to cut through the thick grassland sod, a feat the light horse-drawn Muscovite wooden *sokha* could not perform. Thus, not only the woodland, but also the steppe, could be transformed into ploughland (Nikonov, 1864).

Meanwhile, the state servitors near Voronezh were levied with a grain tax. Known as the *chetverikovyy khleb*, the levy required the men to produce additional rye, which the government used to pay the Don cossacks for fighting the Tatars. The tax forced the local servitors to plough their land to their capacity, and ruined many financially (Shulyakovskiy, 1961).

Russian preparations for the Azov campaign at Voronezh initiated the closing of the military frontier. Their victory at Azov allowed for the transformation of this land into a rich granary of Moscow, to be exploited by the gentry and their serfs. Thus, from the end of the seventeenth century, the rate of clearing accelerated, and ploughland grew quickly.

At first, military shipbuilding on the Voronezh river (1695–1711) speeded up the clearing of the forest. Pines were cut for ship and mast construction, hardwoods for structures and charcoal to smelt iron for tools and arms, and the exposed sandy soils were cropped to feed the massive influx of artisans and soldiers. Indeed, sandy soils were preferred, for they

ensured a good yield of rye, even in a dry year (Sobolev, 1948). For
convenience of transportation and access to water, most trees were cut
along the banks of rivers. The development of shallows on the Voronezh
and Don rivers, an early sign of soil erosion, required constant dredging.
Although Petrine legislation (1722) prohibited forest cutting along rivers
and in preserves, its objective was to retain the forests for military shipbuilding rather than for soil conservation. Later, Catherine II rescinded the law,
and rapid clearing of the river banks resumed.

The gentry, having been granted large holdings, expanded ploughland
and crop production to cater to the growing market in Muscovy. Local
distilling, provisions for the army, and opportunity for export generated
further demand (Nifontov, 1974). Thus, between 1719 and 1762, in
addition to the rapid increase of ploughland in the provinces of Voronezh,
notable gains were made in the provinces most accessible to the Moscow
market: Tula, Tambov, and Ryazan (Table 3.2). Later all provinces had a
rapid increase in ploughland, but by the first half of the nineteenth century,
only the south-eastern provinces, where some grassland still remained,
showed the most significant growth. By emancipation (1861) the provincial
percentages of cultivated land ranged from 55 per cent in Orel to 71 per cent
in Tula. Only small increments occurred after that, followed by a decline.

As the area of ploughland crested to reach its physical limits, there was no
visible re-adjustment to more intensive crop rotations or livestock improvement. An ossified social structure and economic constraints prolonged the
agony of extensive grain farming in this economically declining region. The
most profitable grain production shifted to the southern and eastern steppes,
where abundant fertile lands, enterprising colonists, modern implements

Table 3.2. Percentage of land under cultivation (Rank Order of Province).

	1719[a]	1762[a]	1796[b]	c1861[b]	1881[b]	1912[b]
Kursk	36 (3)	38 (3)	51 (2)	67 (2)	74 (1)	72 (1)
Orel	38 (2)	40 (2)	51 (2)	55 (5)	62 (5)	56 (5)
Ryazan'	30 (4)	37 (4)	47 (3)	56 (4)	56 (6)	52 (6)
Tambov	18 (5)	25 (5)	38 (5)	60 (3)	63 (4)	62 (4)
Tula	39 (1)	55 (1)	69 (1)	71 (1)	73 (2)	66 (3)
Voronezh	11 (6)	25 (5)	40 (4)	60 (3)	69 (3)	68 (2)
Region	26	34	47	61	66	63

[a] My estimates based on declining ratios of land per enumerated male, as given by Kabuzan,
1963:159.
[b] According to Yatsunskiy, 1961:126.

and direct access to the Black Sea ports and the Volga waterway offered unrivalled advantages. The construction of the new railway lines made grain even more transportable from the southern and eastern steppes. As grain prices declined, the fortunes of the grain producers in the Central Russian Black Earth region declined with them. Yet the markets for vegetables and livestock products remained undeveloped, particularly in the impoverished Central Russian Black Earth region (Smirnov, 1925).

Under serfdom, the gentry landowners could take advantage of their free labour and thus compensate for some economic disadvantages of their location. The Emancipation reforms (1861) withdrew this legal privilege, but in its place created a structure that made the peasants dependent on their landlords. Deprived of about one-third of their best allotment land, the peasants had to sharecrop or work on estates. Since there was no more land available for expansion, many peasants would have emigrated to Siberia, but the gentry, not having received new grants there, opposed the loss of cheap labour. Thus, the reduction of allotments combined with growing rural population densities decreased the peasant farmland to one-third of that which an average household tilled in the late sixteenth century.

Following emancipation, the gentry delineated their estates so as to exclude the scarce resources from peasant allotments. When peasants needed to water, graze or drive their livestock or when they needed firewood, their access to streams, meadows and forests could only be obtained for a price (Pershin, 1928). Animal husbandry became a burden, and the Central Russian Black Earth region suffered the most serious decline in livestock numbers (Nagorskiy, 1898). The peasants came to rely almost entirely on their annual grain crop, from which they could obtain an immediate return, including straw for roofing and fuel. Their land, however, suffered from lack of manuring and overploughing: even steep valley slopes and river banks were ploughed (Brzheskiy, 1908).

Although the former rank and file servitors, who later became state peasants, were never bound to gentry, they were bound to their original group land grants. As their numbers doubled and redoubled, their original allotments, interspersed among those of the officers, proved inadequate. In the meantime, the former officers, having received large individual grants, often advanced claims to the lands of the state peasants, not all of which could be refuted in courts. Thus, like the former serfs, the former rank and file servitors suffered from land shortage, landlord encroachment, and awkward land-use arrangement.

Finally, the former serfs and former servitors had to meet financial obligations to the state. In order to ensure the collection of taxes and redemption payments, the state promoted collective responsibility through the traditional Russian village community, the *obshchina*. This institution

provided a measure of common security by periodically redistributing crop-
land among households, but it also stifled incentive to improve land, discouraged experimentation with new crops, and thus maintained the antiquated three-field system. Indeed, in their concern for equity, members of
the *obshchina* laid out their strips downslope so that each household would
get each soil type. The furrows separating each strip became ideal starters
for rills and gullies (Masal'skiy, 1897).

SOIL EROSION

Evidence of factors influencing soil erosion must be examined in both space
and time. Spatial covariation of erosion features with slope, soil types,
geology, climate, etc., may provide valuable clues to the physical factors
conducive to soil erosion. Similarly, temporal co-variation of soil erosion
with changes in the environment and land use may suggest processes
responsible for increased soil removal. The more reliable and comprehensive documentation of soil erosion, the more meaningful are the conclusions.

    Evidence for the earliest occurrence of soil erosion in this region is
lacking. Although fourteenth-century Russian chronicles occasionally mentioned dust storms and gullies, none was reported for what later became the
Central Russian Black Earth region.

    Land inventories of sixteenth and seventeenth-century Muscovy, known
as *pistsovyye knigi* and compiled for the purpose of tax assessment, provided not only comprehensive information about settlements and land use,
but even noted outstanding features of the terrain (Tikhomirov, 1962). In
what later became the province of Tula, the land surveyors recorded (1578–
79), near larger settlements, the occurrence of gullies or *otvershki* (*Pistsovyya knigi*, 1895). Although some gullies were active, others were
wooded and thus testified to earlier periods of soil erosion. Similarly, in
1600, the surveyors noted the prominent denuded white chalk cliffs at
Belgorod that gave the town its name and most likely predated it (Sobolev,
1948). In the eighteenth century, as the tax base changed from land to
people, the land inventories were discontinued. Only naturalists on
geographical expeditions, such as P. S. Pallas and V. F. Zuyev, noted in their
journals spectacular cases of soil erosion. Soil erosion must have intensified,
for a number of scientists (M. I. Afonin, S. Drukovtsev, and A. T. Bolotov)
even suggested ways of fighting it.

    On the eve of emancipation the Russian Ministry of State Property was
given the responsibility of safeguarding the livelihood of the peasantry. It
began the task by initiating the preparation of provincial soil maps; between

1838 and 1868 twenty such maps were completed. The ministry also produced several editions of a soil map of European Russia that identified loose sands (an obvious manifestation of wind erosion), clay and sandy soils, and stony ground—characteristics that suggested eroded soils (Sobolev, 1948). However, soil erosion as such was neither defined nor mapped.

The post-emancipation period was marked by a growing awareness of soil erosion and increased scientific research. Following the identification of humus-impoverished chernozems along the high right banks of rivers by Grossul-Tolstoy, Dokuchaev (1883) illustrated the pattern on his soil map of the chernozem zone of European Russia. His associates produced more detailed maps of eroded soils in the Nizhegorod province and in the Balashov *uyezd* (county) of the Saratov province. Gullies were of paramount concern, and a special survey, compiled and analysed by Masal'skiy (1897) provided considerable descriptive material, but no comprehensive inventory or map was produced. Soon thereafter Dokuchaev and his associates identified wind erosion on a soil map of European Russia published by the Department of Agriculture (1900).

Detailed mapping of gullies and eroded soils began with a set of maps for the counties of Livny and Yelets in the province of Orel (Rumnitskiy and Freyberg, 1908). These were surpassed by the work of the Tula expedition, directed by A. S. Kozmenko (1913). However, a methodology for the quantitative assessment of soil outwash and deposition, a standard method of classifying soil erosion, and a comprehensive survey and mapping of soil erosion in European Russia was not attained until two to three decades after the 1917 revolution (Sobolev, 1948). Thus, the first detailed mapping of gully densities for all of the Central Russian Upland (Guzhevaya, 1945) and intensities of soil erosion for all of the Central Russian Black Earth region (Dolgopolov, 1961; Mil'kov, 1970) must be excluded from this study (see Stebelsky, 1974). The magnitude and intensity of soil erosion in the region before the Revolution of 1917 must have been enormous. Although the area of eroded soils in the entire region was not measured at the time, the area of intensive soil erosion in the province of Orel was estimated to be over one-third (Kozmenko, 1954).

More attention was paid to the area occupied by gullies. According to Ryndin (1921), the Central Russian Upland and Kalach Upland lost about 300 000 hectares to gullies (Dolgopolov, 1961), which exceeded 2 per cent of the total land area. Among the nineteen most gullied provinces of European Russia, Masal'skiy (1897) described the six provinces of the Central Russian Black Earth region first, thus implying that these provinces had even more severe gullying than those along the Volga. According to the responses from the six provinces, the percentage of land occupied by gullies in sample localities ranged from 0.5–25 per cent with 3–5 per cent of the area most commonly reported. The high figures overstated the gullied area, for careful studies during the Tula expedition revealed that many correspondents included in their count not only active gullies, but also stabilized ravines (Kozmenko, 1954).

Gullies often grew rapidly. The most intense gullying was recorded along the high right bank of the Don river, where one gully surged over 200 metres in one year. Gullies in peat bogs advanced twenty to fifty metres per year. In general, however, the more spectacular gullies of the region advanced ten to twenty metres per year, although advances of as little as two metres per year were recorded. Correspondents from other chernozem provinces indicated lesser advances: two to twenty metres per year, with spectacular cases of forty and seventy metres per year from the high right bank of the Dnepr river (Masal'skiy, 1897).

The removal of the protective plant cover, it is generally agreed, triggered wind and water erosion. In the past, thick vegetation protected the soil surface from rain and drought, delayed the melting of the snow, minimized surface runoff, and maintained high groundwater level. Generally, slow denudation processes prevailed. On steep slopes of river banks access paths trampled by animals caused the development of gullies, but the latter remained short and soon became overgrown. Occasional forest or grassland fires exposed the land to wind and water erosion, but the surface debris and short duration of the clearing reduced the rate of denudation.

Modification of the ground cover brought about significant ecological changes. Repeated burns of the steppe—first for military purposes and later for improving the pasture for cattle—eliminated the tall scrub and coarse grass species. As a result less moisture accumulated in the soil. Moreover, the grassland was not evenly grazed. The southward and eastward facing slopes, because of the prevailing winter south-easterlies, had minimal snow cover and were the first to thaw and support fresh growth in the spring. Hungry cattle thus overgrazed and trampled the grass, exposing the slope to wind and water erosion. In addition, driving the herds to village and to market created trails that served as starters for long gullies that further desiccated the land.

Clearing the forest for arable farming directly exposed the soil to erosion. Each year, the *sokha* tore through the topsoil, the harrow broke up the large crumbs, rainfall pulverized their remaining structure, and unimpeded dry winds removed the moisture that kept the soil particles together. A downpour or a strong dry wind could easily remove such particles of soil.

The switch from two-field to three-field farming increased the exposure of soil to erosion. In the two-field system, the cropped field was in part protected by a stand of grain, while the fallowed field gained protection from regenerating grasses or shrubs. However, in the three-field system, while winter rye offered some spring and summer protection, the spring-sown oats covered the soil in the summer only, and the field left in clean fallow (*par*) had no protection at all.

The establishment and growth of large settlements in the Central Russian Black Earth region—concentrated along the rivers where drinking water was available—necessitated the clearing of comparatively larger areas. As the ploughland was extended, particularly onto broad, convex valley slopes, the increasing volumes of water, moving in sheets or channels, removed successive layers of topsoil. Particularly large settlements and high population densities followed the defence lines that once fortified the northern and western banks of rivers. Settlers of these villages thus cultivated the southward and eastward facing slopes, where soil erosion became particularly acute. These slopes, thinly veiled in snow, would be the first to thaw. As the spring progressed, the snow in the upland would thaw, and meltwaters would cut rills and gullies into slopes that were not protected by their frozen soils (Kozmenko, 1954).

The physical conditions that the settlers encountered in the Central Russian Upland also were more conducive to soil erosion. Loose and soluble parent materials, such as loess and chalk, make soil much more susceptible to erosion than the sandy and moraine material, so common in the north and west (Kozmenko, 1954). Moreover, as the settlers proceeded to the south and east, they encountered steeper slopes and lower base levels of erosion, greater desiccation, and more severe torrential downpours.

Socio-economic pressures in the nineteenth century aggravated soil erosion. Shortage of land caused by rural over-population, poverty, and the power of the gentry induced the peasants to cultivate their marginal lands and overgraze the remaining steep slopes. Lack of manuring, due to livestock shortage, the distance to strips, and the uncertainty that a household would till the same strip the following year because of *obshchina* redistributions, impoverished the soil structure and resulted in a thinner crop cover. Finally, the layout of strips downslope encouraged the development of a dense gully network.

Gullies caused more than simple physical disruption. Obviously, gullies cut into roads and railway lines, interfered with cultivation and access to fields, and posed death traps to cattle who grazed too close to their brinks. They also served as conduits that aided in the removal of topsoil and water. Each spring, and especially after heavy rainfall, gullies conducted the runoff towards populated river valleys, where their silt-laden slurry clogged up mill ponds, broke dams, washed out bridges, damaged houses, ruined meadows, and waterlogged the flood-plains.

The damage, though less spectacular, was equally formidable on the watersheds, whence the gullies drew their water. By cutting deeply into the parent material and bedrock, gullies not only provided for a more efficient drainage of the surface, but also withdrew valuable ground water. In cases where gullies cut through impervious clays or shales to porous sandstones or limestones, their channels served as lengthy sinks that dramatically lowered water tables and dried up wells and sources. In winter, the deep trenches collected snow and thus deprived it from fields of rye that suffered, increasingly, from winter frost kill and spring drought (Morachevskiy, 1897).

The less obvious removal of topsoil, accomplished by means of water or wind erosion, was equally damaging. Gradual erosion of the top layer with the highest organic content meant that the soil lost its water and nutrient-retaining properties, and hence its natural fertility. Without added fertilizer, yields on such soils may have been only one-half to one-tenth of what they were before the topsoil was removed.

The response of soil scientists to the growing problem was considerable. Numerous soil conservation techniques had been suggested or tried: planting ivy and afforestation, terracing, contour ploughing, use of curtain crops, and stubble mulching (Sobolev, 1948). After the abysmal harvest of 1891, two semi-popular studies on soil erosion and desiccation of the steppe appeared (Dokuchayev, 1892; Izmail'skiy, 1893). A third scientist, E. E. Kern, not only published a book in which he advised how to control gullies (1892; 3rd ed., 1897) but also addressed conventions of landowners in Kiev (1893) and Tula (1895), thus stimulating the participants at least to make resolutions, if not to take personal action against soil erosion.

The implementation of soil conservation measures, recommended by soil scientists, fared poorly. Peasants failed to take any measures, other than fill a gully that cut through a road. Even the landlords did not employ agronomic techniques of soil conservation, although some would attempt, often with futile efforts, to stop gullies from cutting into their valuable improvements. Most landlords viewed soil erosion as an unavoidable evil that was too expensive to combat. They failed to realize the relationship between land use and gullies, and thought about corrective rather than preventive measures. The plight of the illiterate peasantry appeared hopeless. Not only did they lack information, but their initiative and ability to take action was hampered by rigid socio-economic stratification (Masal'skiy, 1897).

Concerted effort to combat soil erosion was hampered by the lack of an adequate extension service. After the emancipation, the functions of the Ministry of State Property were diffused among various departments and in part delegated to provincial and county administrations (the *zemstva*), not all of which had the funds or desire to promote soil conservation (Sobolev, 1948). The most serious gap was the lack of technicians who would bring

the scientific knowledge to the countryside, and the near absence of agricultural schools that would train them (Voyeykov, 1910).

CONCLUSION

The case of agriculture and soil erosion in the Central Russian Black Earth
region demonstrates the dynamics that operated, with some variation,
throughout the European forest-steppe. Contested between the farm-folk
and nomadic herdsmen alike, the parkland remained sparsely settled until
the demise of the nomads. The influx of farm-folk resulted in the transformation of the forest-steppe: the clearing of the forest and the burning, grazing,
and, eventually, the ploughing of the steppe. Changes in land use, depending
on a number of physical and cultural factors, led to various degrees of soil
erosion. Once initiated, erosion caused further modifications in the physical
environment that had a direct impact on yields and the well-being of the
population.

REFERENCES

Aleksandrov, V. A., (1967). Streletskoye naseleniye yuzhnykh gorodov Rossii v
    XVII v. *In* "Novoye o proshlom nashey strany", (V. A. Aleksandrov *et al.*, eds),
    pp. 235–250, Moscow.
Bagaley, D. I. (1886). K istorii zaseleniya stepnoy okrainy moskovskago gosudar-
    stva, *Zhurnal Ministerstva Narodnogo Prosveshcheniya* 245, 87–286.
Bagaley, D. I., (1887). "Ocherki iz istorii stepnoy okrainy Moskovskago gosudar-
    stva", Izdaniye Imperatorskago Obshchestva Istorii i Drevnostey Rossiyskikh pri
    Moskovskom Universitete, Moscow.
Blum, J., (1961). "Lord and Peasant in Russia from the Ninth to the Nineteenth
    Century", Princeton.
Brzheskiy, N., (1908). "Ocherki agrarnago byta krestyan. I. Zemledel'cheskiy tsentr
    Rossii i yego oskudeniya", St. Petersburg.
Boserup, E., (1965). "The Conditions of Agricultural Growth", Chicago.
Dokuchayev, V. V., (1883). "Russkiy chernozem", St. Petersburg. (Re-issued, Mos-
    cow and Leningrad, 1936.)
Dokuchayev, V. V., (1892). "Nashi stepi prezhde i teper", St. Petersburg. (Re-issued,
    Moscow and Leningrad, 1936).
Dolgopolov, K. V., (1961). "Tsentral'no-chernozemnyy rayon", Moscow.
Guzhevaya, A. F., (1948). Ovragi Sredne-Russkoy vozvyshennosti, *Trudy Instituta
    Geografii* 42, 37–74.
Izmail'skiy, A. A. (1898). "Kak vysokhla nasha step", Poltava. (Re-issued, Moscow-
    Leningrad, 1936.)
Kabuzan, V. M., (1963). "Narodonaseleniye Rossii v XVIII—pervoy polovine XIX
    v.", Moscow.

Kern, E. E., (1892). "Ovragi, ikh zakrepleniye, obleseniye i zapruzhivaniye", Moscow, (2nd ed., 1894; 3rd ed., 1897).

Kotel'nikov, V. L., (1950). Ob izmenenii geograficheskoy sredy sel'skokhozyaystvennoy deyatel'nosti cheloveka, *Izvestiya Vsesoyuznogo Geograficheskogo Obshchestva* 2, 138–151.

Kozmenko, A. S., (1913). "Gidrologicheskoye issledovaniye Tul'skoy gubernii", Moscow.

Kozmenko, A. S., (1954). "Osnovy protivoerozionnoy melioratsii", Moscow.

Masal'skiy, V., (1897). "Ovragi chernozemnoy polosy Rossii, ikh rasprostraneniya, razvitiye i deyatel'nost", St. Petersburg.

Materialy vysochayshe utverzhdennoy 16 noyabrya 1901 g. Komissii po issledovaniyu voprosa o dvizhenii s 1861 po 1900 gg. blagosostoyaniya sel'skago naseleniya srednezemledel'cheskikh guberniy, St. Petersburg (1903).

Miklashevskiy, I. N., (1894). "K istorii khozyaystvennago byta Moskovskago gosudarstva. Chast I. Zaseleniye i sel'skoye khozyaystvo yuzhnoy okrainy XVII veka", Moscow.

Mil'kov, F. N., (1970). Chernozemnyy Tsentr. *In* "Rossiyskaya Federatsiya Tsentral'naya Rossiya", (S. V. Kalesnik *et al.*, eds), pp. 619–840, Moscow.

Mironova, E. A., (1971). Ovrazhnost' territorii SSSR. *Geomorfologiya* 3, 25–35.

Nagorskiy, V. F., (1898). Oskudeniye skotom tsentral'nykh guberniy Yevropeyskoy Rossii S 1864 po 1892 god. *In* "Trudy Orlovskago oblastnogo s"yezda sel'skikh khozyayev 10–20 maya, 1898 g." Orel.

Nifontov, A. S., (1974). "Zernovoye proizvodstvo Rossii vo vtoroy polovine XIX veka", Moscow.

Nikonov, F., (1864). Byt i khozyaystvo malorossov v Voronezhskoy Gubernii, *Trudy Imperatorskago Vol'nago Ekonomicheskago Obshchestva*, 1–16.

Pershin, P. N., (1928). "Zemel'noye ustroystvo dorevolyutsionnoy derevni. I. Rayony: Tsentral'no-Promyshlennyy, Tsentral'no-Chernozemnyy i Severo-Zapadnyy", Moscow and Voronezh.

Pistsovyya knigi, (1895). St. Petersburg.

Rashin, A. G., (1956). "Naseleniye Rossii za 100 let (1811–1913 gg.), statisticheskiye ocherki", Moscow.

Rozhkov, N., (1899). "Sel'skoye khozyaystvo Moskovskoy Rusi v XVI veke", Moscow.

Rudakov, A. P., (1923). "Ocherki iz istorii Tuly i Tul'skogo kraya", Tula.

Rumnitskiy, M. G. and Freyberg, I. K., (1908). "Pochvy vodosbora srednego i nizhnego techeniy reki Sosny (uyezdy Livenskiy i Yeletskiy)", Orel.

Ryndin, F. A., (1921). "Nash kray", Voronezh.

Semenov, V. P. (ed.), (1902). "Rossiya. Polnoye geograficheskoye opisaniye nashego otechestva. Tom 2. Sredne-Russkaya chernozemnaya oblast", St. Petersburg.

Shaw, D. J. B., (1977). Urbanism and economic development in a pre-industrial context: the case of southern Russia, *Jour. Hist. Geog.* 3, 107–122.

Shulyakovskiy, Ye. G., (ed.) (1961). "Ocherki istorii Voronezhskogo kraya s drevneyshikh vremen do velikoy oktyabr"skoy sotsialisticheskoy revolyutsii", Vol. I., Voronezh.

Smirnov, V., (1925). Oskudeniye Chernozemnogo Tsentra i puti k yego vosstanovleniyu. *In* "V bor'be s zasukhoy i golodom. Neurozhai v zasushlivykh rayonakh SSSR i bor'ba s nimi", (A. I. Rykov, ed.) pp. 142–177, Moscow and Leningrad.

Sobolev, S. S., (1948). "Razvitiye erozionnykh protsessov na territorii Yevropeyskoy chasti SSSR i bor'ba s nimi", Moscow and Leningrad.

Stebelsky, I., (1974). Environmental deterioration in the Central Russian Black Earth region: the case of soil erosion, *Canadian Geographer* **18**, 232–249.

Tikhomirov, M. N., (1962). "Rossiya v XVI stoletii", Moscow.

Vaynberg, Ye. I., (1967). Bor'ba krest'yan protiv krepostnichestva na yuzhnoy okraine Russkago gosudarstva v pervoy polovine XVII v. *In* "Novoye o proshlom nashey strany", (V. A. Aleksandrov *et al.,* eds). pp. 251–263, Moscow.

Vodarskiy, Ya. Ye., (1977). "Naseleniye Rossii v kontse XVII—nachale XVIII veka", Moscow.

Voyeykov, A. I., (1910). Zemel'nyye uluchsheniya: ikh sootnosheniye s klimatom i drugimi yestyestvennymi usloviyami, *Yezhegodnik Otdela zemel'nykh uluchsheniy,* **1909**, 27–53. (Reprinted in "Vozdeystviye cheloveka na prirodu", pp. 87–110, Moscow, 1963).

Yatsunskiy, V. K., (1957). Izmeneniye v razmeshchenii naseleniya Yevropeyskoy Rossii v 1724–1916 gg., *Istoriya SSSR* no. 1, 192–224.

Zagorovskiy, V. P., (1969). "Belgorodskaya cherta", Voronezh.

4 The introduction of the Three-field Agricultural System

R. A. French

ARGUMENTS AND ANTECEDENTS

In the history of agricultural evolution in the Russian lands from the sixth century to the twentieth, there have been very few periods of major, significant, technological change. Undoubtedly, one such development, as in much of Europe, was the adoption of common-field arable farming based on a crop rotation including fallow. Various forms of common cultivation existed in different areas at different times, various crops were grown and different cycles of rotation were employed. As Smith (1977:27) has pointed out, the term "three-field" (in Russian, *trekhpol'ye*) is itself as imprecise in Russian as in English usage. However, the most frequently met version, which for centuries dominated agricultural practice over a huge area of northern and central Europe from the English midlands to the Urals, was a three-year rotation including one year of fallow, carried out in three equal-sized fields. Russia, like the rest of Europe, had its variations, but its basic, most widespread agricultural practice for a very long period of its history was this "classic" three-field system. It is in this classic sense that the term is defined for the purposes of this chapter.

The introduction of the three-field system is thus a matter of considerable importance in agricultural history and historical geography, "a factor of first degree importance in the history of productive forces" (Yurginis, 1964:95). In the Russian context, the date at which it occurred has been a subject of prolonged and often sharp debate. In particular, a number of Soviet historians have attributed an early date to the first appearance of *trekhpol'ye* as a replacement for the more ancient and primitive agricultural methods of *podseka* (slash-and-burn) and *perelog* (long fallow), described in Chapter 2.

RUSSIAN HISTORICAL GEOGRAPHY VOL. 1
ISBN 0 12 081201 0

Dovzhenok was convinced that the system existed in the Dnepr region in Kievan times, in the eleventh and twelfth centuries, on the basis of the existence then of a wheeled plough with coulter and mould-board, together with references to spring and winter grains and an assumed increase of agricultural productivity, compared with earlier times (Smith, 1959:88–90). Kir'yanov reckoned the same period saw the system in the Novgorod lands, also on the basis of spring and winter crops and on the claimed presence among seed finds of certain weeds, which slash-and-burn would supposedly remove (Kochin, 1965:80). Doroshenko (1959:59), in quoting Kir'yanov and also the view of Łowmiański that the system long pre-dated the thirteenth century, clearly approved. Grekov (1959:64) thought "very possibly" the eleventh and twelfth centuries, from two chronicle references to spring and winter crops.

Lyapushkin believed that some sort of crop rotation was practised even earlier, in the eighth or ninth centuries, based on archaeological finds of winter rye together with spring grains, wheat, barley, and millet, although he admitted that it was not possible to say whether there was a two- or three-field system. "It is only clear that a fallow system replaced *perelog*" (Lyapushkin, 1968:137). Slobodin argued that the first stage in the transfer from *podseka* and *perelog* to a fallow system dated from the second half of the first millenium A.D. and considered that by the ninth and tenth centuries the latter was dominant in the most developed areas of Novgorod, Kiev, and the Baltic, as well as among the Volga Bulgars (Slobodin, 1965:162). Blum (1964:22–23), although saying that indisputable evidence of the three-field system can only be found in the last part of the fifteenth century, presumed two- and three-field practices were dominant in the second half of the ninth century.

These different authorities have concluded that three-field cultivation, or something very close to it, existed before the thirteenth century and even in the very early Slav period, on grounds that, to say the least, are shaky. Smith (1959:88–89) effectively pointed out both the error of Dovzhenok in assuming an early date for the wheeled plough and the lack of any necessary correlation between an improved plough and three-field system. Kochin (1965:80–82) was even more ruthless in demolishing Kir'yanov's hypothesis on the presence of weeds, pointing out the absence of solid investigation of types of weeds found on early fields and on *podseka* clearings; slash-and-burn patches, contrary to Kir'yanov's view, rapidly acquire weeds. Kochin quoted the work of A. R. Rasin'sh on weeds, which showed that in Latvia and adjacent regions one cannot use evidence of this nature to demonstrate the presence of the three-field system before the thirteenth century. This is supported for Russia more generally by Shapiro (1977:44–49), who concluded that in the context of weed pollen analysis, "so far laboratory research does not provide a basis for talking of a fallow-grain system, and still less of its dominance, up to the fourteenth century". Many authors have pointed out that references to both spring and winter crops do not, by themselves, give any proof of three-field agriculture, since they could and did occur with two-field or other systems (Gorskiy, 1959:15–16; Yurginis, 1964:100). The same objection is equally valid to using references to "fallow".

There is therefore no hard evidence at all that a three-field system, properly speaking, was practised anywhere in the Russian lands before the Tatar invasion. One of the reasons, which various writers have put forward, for assuming the wide operation of *trekhpol'ye* at an early date, is the need to account for increased agricultural production, as population (including urban population) grew. It is generally agreed that *podseka* was probably the initial form of cropping in most areas within the forest zone and that this was a very extensive system of low productivity. The *perelog* system of a few years cultivation and twenty or more years abandonment to long-fallow is also accepted as being widespread in the earliest Slav period, but it was not significantly more productive per unit area than *podseka*. The same was true of the similar *zalezhnaya* system of long fallowing in the open, unforested parts of the forest-steppe zone.

However, it has often been pointed out that it is not necessary to assume that a regular three-field cultivation was the direct successor to *podseka* and *perelog*. Shapiro (1977:38) saw a progression from the form of *podseka* where the primeval forest was burnt (*lyada*) to the burning of scrub (*syroseka*), with an implication that this was the burning of secondary growth; Shapiro called this "forest *perelog*". In true *perelog*, presumably, there is from the start the intention to return to an area after a sufficient time has elapsed. The Polish historian, Łowmiański, distinguished what he called, in contradistinction to the "classic", the "archaic" three-field system, where there were not three regular, equal-sized fields, but a number of interspersed holdings, each element of which was cultivated on a three-year rotation. Yurginis believed this to be misconceived and commented, "that which he (Łowmiański) called the 'archaic' three-field system was a three-field system without rotation, or a two-field system" (Yurginis, 1978:16).

In fact Łowmiański appears to be nearer the truth than his critic. Surviving documents from the Grand Duchy of Lithuania—the area with which he was concerned—do not indicate the classic three-field system before the reforms of Queen Bona and her son Sigismund August in the mid-sixteenth century. They do, however, indicate the use of some type of three-year rotation on a number of scattered plots. Thus the inventory of Radosh-kovichi castle (near Minsk) in 1549 describes in detail the arable.

First they sowed this year on the field behind the alder wood 31 barrels (*bochki*) and behind the town nearby on a second field by the meadow 9 barrels of rye are sown, on a third field at Chaplevshchyna at a verst from the barn on the river Serebrenka they sowed 40 barrels. By that field is hayland for 100 cartloads. For the second year there is a field by the barn; this field is for eighty barrels. To that field and for that year at Chaplevshchyna are being sown 20 barrels. By that field is forest for 15 barrels, which can be cleared for arable. For the third year there is a field at the new lands one verst from the manorial farm, this field is for 40 barrels; by that field is birch scrub for 40 barrels. For the same year at Chaplevshchyna is a field for 40 barrels; to the same field by the old town is Gorodishche field on which they sow 10 barrels. For the spring crops on manured land by the manorial farm—20 barrels' (*Dokumenty* . . . , 1897: Vol. 1, 93–94).

The reference to a three-year cycle is clear, but there are eight separate fields described, plus the manured field by the manor (no doubt sown every year), plus two further areas fit for ploughing up. The totals for each of the three years were 80, 100, and 90 barrels, only a very rough parity. This example seems to illustrate Łowmiański's "archaic" system very precisely and certainly demonstrates at least one intermediate practice between long-fallow and classic three-field methods.

Yurginis himself saw his postulated two-field system in two forms. In the first form, the arable was in two equal areas, one fallow and one divided in half between spring and winter crops. In the second form, there were three equal divisions, two under fallow and the third divided between spring- and winter-sown grains. Thus, in this second variant, there were two consecutive fallow years (Yurginis, 1964:100). Yurginis postulated that for the western areas with which he is concerned, such two-field systems were the intermediate stage between primitive cultivations and the classic three-field practice. It is certainly easy to see how the second form could be rapidly transposed to the classic system. Other authors too have seen the two-field arrangement as an intermediate stage. In particular, Shapiro (1977:51) and Gorskiy (1959:17–20) saw the three-field system developing by the addition of a third field to earlier pairs of fields, not before a relatively late date in the fifteenth century. Certainly there is no reason to doubt that forms of two-field cultivation were adopted, both before and contemporaneously with, the three-field system. One can also accept, on the evidence of the Radoshkovichi cadastre, that a three-year rotation on many scattered plots was used. It may well be the case, however, that both these intermediate practices were primarily adopted on estate lands, rather than on peasant lands.

Few authors seem to suggest that there was a very usual intermediate stage, which corresponded to an infield–outfield system, that is to say, where the *perelog* arrangement of a period of cultivation followed by a long period of fallow, was combined with an "infield" of constant cultivation, to which all the available manure was applied. Yet this appears to have been the case very widely, especially on peasant lands. Such a situation was well exemplified in the Lithuanian lands before the agrarian reform of the 1550s. The 1545 inventory of Myadel' *volost'* (district) listed for each peasant household the quantity of *navoz*, manured land, and *prostoye*, "ordinary" or unmanured land (*Dokumenty* . . . , 1897: Vol. 1, 75–85. On average the area of "ordinary" field was approximately ten times that of the manured field, but the ratio of manured to unmanured varied very widely between holdings, from 1:2 to 1:30. Presumably all the areas listed as "ordinary", were cropped at the time of the inventory, which also listed twenty-five abandoned areas (*pustovshchiny*).

This inventory did not indicate whether the "ordinary" field was in one or (more probably) several plots. However, the exceptionally detailed cadastres compiled to record the agrarian reform also included descriptions of village lands, which for one reason or another escaped reform and reorganization. Such was the case for a large group of villages in the extensive swamps of Poles'ye, in the Lithuanian districts of Pinsk, Kobrin, and Brest (in present-day western Belorussia). For these villages the cadastres gave the size and location of every individual plot of arable. In addition to the manured plot by the settlement, a holding had commonly up to twenty parcels, occasionally up to forty or more and in one extreme case, sixty-four parcels (*Pistsovaya kniga byvshago Pinskago* . . . , 1874: Vol. 2, 380–82). Seldom were there fewer than ten. These scattered plots, of very varied size, were intermixed with those of other holdings in the same village, with those of other villages and with those of other estates; often they lay isolated, deep in tracts of forest or swamp. In the case of the holding in sixty-four plots, the size of the parcels ranged from 66.43 hectares to 0.14 hectares. Usually there was only one manured plot per household, very rarely two or three, but always the manured plots were small. At Voroche-vichi village, near Pinsk, there were four settlement plots, ranging in size from 0.4 to two hectares and lived on by six named persons, that is families. Three were described as "with kitchen gardens". The village had thirty-nine arable plots, varying from 0.175 to 15.25 hectares, dispersed among the lands of minor gentry, the forests and the swamps (*Pistsovaya kniga byv-shago Pinskago* . . . , 1874: Vol. 1, 410–420). Unfortunately, in all such cases of unreorganized villages operating on this "infield–outfield" system, the cadastres do not indicate which of the scattered, unmanured parcels were under cultivation at the time of the survey.

These examples of manured "infield" and unmanured "outfield" occurred in the western parts of European Russia, but similar situations existed very commonly on peasant lands in central Muscovite regions in the fifteenth and sixteenth centuries, where many households had small clearings scattered through the forests, in addition to a settlement plot receiving all the available manure (Smith, 1977, passim). Perhaps of all the various agrarian practices, which appear to have preceded the three-field system, it may well be that what has been called here for convenience a form of "infield-outfield", but which is a natural, indeed obvious, development from a "pure" *perelog* of shifting cultivation, was the most widespread on peasant lands. On their lands it continued to exist long after the general appearance of the *trekhpol'ye* and in some areas was still to be found in our own century.

THE DATE OF THE THREE-FIELD SYSTEM

As the previously cited authors have claimed, "classic" three-field agriculture may have existed in Kievan times, even early Kievan times. If there is no firm proof that it did, equally there is no firm proof that it did not. Nevertheless, it seems a not unreasonable assumption that one can relate its appearance on the Russian scene to the presence of solid evidence. Such evidence as is presently available is almost all documentary. As already indicated, the limited research on pollen analysis points to a later rather than an earlier date. Field evidence, such as ridge-and-furrow, has not been investigated in Russia; it may not even exist, although it is certainly still to be seen in central Poland. Lacking such information, what material is there to give one fair confidence that a three-field system existed at a particular time?

In the first place, as both Shapiro and Yurginis have commented, there should be, not just a reference to both spring and winter crops, but a balance of crops. Yurginis (1964:97–98) cited an inventory of a private Lithuanian estate, dating from 1542 (i.e. before the agrarian reform), where there was considerable variation in the areas sown to winter rye and spring grains, whereas later inventories from the post-reform period showed a close correspondence. Shapiro (1971:345) worked back from the known correspondence between winter and spring crops on three-field lands in the nineteenth century, to postulate three-field cultivation in the Novgorod lands of the late fifteenth–early sixteenth centuries, when also there was correspondence. In fact, of course, a crop balance is still not enough evidence, since it would exist in a two-field system, but it is possible to say that a proper three-field system could not exist without a balance.

Secondly, and more surely, there are specific references to a "third field". In a number of cases such a third field is distinguished from the other two and bears a separate name, or may have a separate location, characteristics which lead Shapiro (1977:51) to conclude that the explanation has to be a comparatively late addition of the field to the earlier pair. This process is exemplified in a will of 1505, cited by Gorskiy (1959:19): "to my grandson, to have land beyond the pond . . . two fields, but he will not get a third field on his side, and he is to have for a third field at Ternovo". Even clearer indication is given by phrases such as "arable in all 3 fields for 8 *korob'i*" (Danilova, 1955:26; Gorskiy, 1960:32). Gorskiy (1959:18–19) tabulated seventeen references specifically to a third field between 1454 and 1505. The number is not large, although it must be remembered that the period is one of few enough surviving documents.

From the late fifteenth century in the Novgorod lands and from the early sixteenth century onwards in other Russian territories, one meets with ever greater frequency phrases on the lines of: "in one field so many *cheti* and in two as much"—the *chet* being the most usual measure of grain or the amount of land on which that grain could be sown, a "quarter". Even quite early in the sixteenth century this phrase has become the standard formula for the assessment of arable area, occurring over and over again in documents. It certainly appears to be incontrovertible evidence of three equal-sized fields, but even the widespread, indeed almost invariable, use of this formula is not without its drawbacks as an indicator of the three-field system. Both in the sixteenth century and later one finds the phrase used for arable known to be worked under other methods of cultivation, for waste or abandoned land and even for forest. A document of 1597 refers to "*perelog* and overgrown forest for 50 *cheti* in the field and in two as much" (*Akty feodal'nogo* . . . , 1961: Vol. 3, no. 115, 167). Kharitonychev (1960:63) cited the general use of the formula in the Volga right bank area south of Gor'kiy during the sixteenth and seventeenth centuries, when *perelog* was there the most common system.

Under such circumstances, one must agree with Shapiro (1977: 53), when he says:

> The universal nature of this formula in the late fifteenth–sixteenth centuries absolutely does not allow one to speak of the general and universal division of arable into three equal fields, of the transformation of three-field rotation into the single type of agricultural economy in Rus.

Nevertheless, the use of the formula, perhaps especially its use for other land-uses, does indicate beyond any doubt that a system of three regularly sized fields was very much a norm in people's minds; it was unlikely to have been employed unless the system was generally comprehended and thus very common.

It is therefore generally accepted that the three-field system was wide-spread in the sixteenth century and that in many central areas it was the dominant form of arable farming. During that century it spread into new regions of Russian colonization, notably the lands of the former Tatar khanate of Kazan', captured in 1552, where it "undoubtedly dominated in the main agricultural regions" (Mukhamed'yarov, 1959:118). In the north, the same period saw the three-field system on the Karelian isthmus (Grigor'yev and Ivanov, 1956:122). It is also common ground that the system was well established in the last two or three decades of the fifteenth century, at least in the Novgorod lands.

For the existence of *trekhpol'ye* before about 1470 there is little to go on. There are the handful of references to third fields, already mentioned. Additionally, there are the recorded testimonies of the *znakhari*, the knowledgeable people, or rememberers, who gave witness in legal disputes. They claimed to recall third fields forty or more years beforehand, in some cases up to eighty years, thus suggesting that the system was in existence in the early part of the fifteenth century or even the end of the fourteenth (Shapiro, 1977:50). Such sparse pieces of evidence suggest that the earliest, sporadic adoptions of the three-field practice were occurring throughout the fifteenth century, to become commonplace after 1470.

Finally, the point needs to be stressed that even in the sixteenth century, the wide use of three-field agriculture in the territories of Muscovy seems to have been principally on the demesne arable of crown, church, and boyar estates. Then, and for some time to come, the lands of the peasants were more often than not scattered in outlying fields, often deep in forest and cultivated individually or on the "infield-outfield" system (see particularly, Smith, 1977). These "closes" were cultivated *nayezdom*, literally "by riding", that is at a distance. Frequently, such patches were termed "waste" or "empty" in documents; commonly, this term must have meant abandonment to long-fallow, rather than total desertion. Only later, as population density increased, as average settlement size increased, giving greater labour resources per settlement, and as the amount of intervening forest shrank, did the majority of peasant lands adopt the basic three fields, which demesne lands had laid out long before.

THE LITHUANIAN CASE

In most of the western Russian lands, which in the sixteenth century still lay largely within the Grand Duchy of Lithuania, the introduction of classic three-field agriculture was a remarkable, indeed unique process. There the previously existing systems, principally forms of infield–outfield operation, were swept away on crown lands by royal decrees in the 1550s. In their place was established a highly uniform, regular version of the *trekhpol'ye*, known as the *voloka* system, from the term *voloka* (or in Polish *włoka*) used for a peasant holding or tenement in the three fields. The state-introduced nature of the agrarian transformation and the consequent scrupulous documentation, which has in part survived, means that this particular instance of three-field adoption is not only precisely dated, but is also more clearly described than for any other part of present Soviet territory and in all probability than for any other area in Europe (French, 1969a; French, 1970).

The Grand Duchy of Lithuania in the sixteenth century was united under the Jagiellon dynasty with Poland. In Poland, classic forms of the three-field practice were widespread well before the fifteenth century and might well be considered to have been derived from Brandenburg, where they were found in the thirteenth century. The eastward diffusion continued in the fifteenth century into Podlasia, the westernmost province of Lithuania, where there was extensive introduction of the three-field system on land being colonized by Poles (a process which led to the transfer of the province to Poland by the Union of Lublin in 1569). In the first half of the sixteenth century, the Grand Duke Sigismund I extended three-field agriculture throughout royal lands in Podlasia province (Lyubavskiy, 1910:226).

In the next stage, Sigismund's widow, Queen Bona, in 1552 introduced a regular three-field system to her estates in Lithuania proper, in the districts of Pinsk, Kletsk, Kobrin, Kremenets, and Gorodets. Her reform involved the consolidation of estates by exchange with neighbouring landowners, the laying out of three equal-sized fields divided into strips and the allotment to her peasants of a holding of one strip in each field, to give a total tenement of thirty *morgi* or some 22 hectares (*Pistsovaya kniga Pinskogo i Kletskogo . . .*, 1884).

Queen Bona's son, Sigismund August, no doubt as a result of the success of her reform, five years later in 1557 made her new system (with only most minor modification) mandatory on all crown lands throughout Lithuania, by issuing his *Voloka* Decree (*Ustava na Volok: Russkaya Istoricheskaya Biblioteka*, 1914:542–85). The ever-present need of the Grand Duchy to support its unending series of wars with Muscovy, Sweden, the German knightly orders, and the Tatars, together with the growing export market for grain via the Baltic to Germany, provided the necessary financial stimulus to reform the antiquated agrarian regime and to raise agricultural productivity.

The old system was one of chaotic, intermixed holdings. Reorganization of the crown estates into three equal-sized fields could only be achieved after exchanges of land with neighbours to establish consolidated blocks of territory. To allow this essential prerequisite, the *Voloka* Decree enforced compulsory exchange of land and established a qualitative ratio for exchange of 1 good: 1½ medium: 3 bad. The result was that the neighbours often also ended up with compact holdings and they too followed the royal example and introduced the new *voloka* three-field system. Inventories of private estates in the post-1557 period almost always show them organized on the *voloka* pattern, e.g. the Ponevezh estate of Prince Oginskiy in 1563 (*Akty izdavayemyye* . . . , 1888:77–79).

Von Loewe (1973) has disputed the primacy of the Lithuanian crown in introducing the three-field system, on the grounds that the weak monarchy followed the lead of the large, independent, hereditary landowners, rather than vice versa. This is always possible, but examination by the present author of very many primary sixteenth-century cadastres, inventories and other documents has not so far established a single private estate where the *voloka* system existed before Sigismund August's 1557 decree, nor did von Loewe himself put forward any such primary evidence. On the contrary, there is documentary record of private estates where the land was organized on the *voloka* system only after the 1557 crown reform; this was the case on the lands of the peasants of Putroshki village on the Rusota estate of the powerful Volovich family, which was inventoried in 1556 and again in 1581 (*Akty izdavayemyye* . . . , 1888:20–23; 227–231).

However, it is fair to say, in view of the great paucity of surviving documents earlier than 1557, that the question of the prior existence of the *voloka* system on private estates remains open; all one can say is that there is no contemporary evidence for it, despite von Loewe's categoric statement that the crown applied "methods already in use on the estates of the nobility" (von Loewe, 1973:35). It may very well be that von Loewe was confused between the three-field system and forms of three-year rotation on a number of scattered parcels. The latter certainly did exist in Lithuania earlier in the sixteenth century, as described above for Radoshkovichi Castle (see also French, 1970:107). Indeed it is hard to imagine that there could be any widespread introduction of the true three-field system without the prior consolidation of estates by exchange, a process generally facilitated only by the *Voloka* Decree. It is certainly the case that post-1557 inventories and surveys demonstrate near universal conversion to the new regime.

The system prescribed by the decree was applied throughout the principal Lithuanian provinces with most striking uniformity. Within the newly consolidated royal estates, or manors, the formerly hopelessly intermixed arable, together with intervening forest patches now cleared, was laid out anew as three equal-sized fields, lying side by side and all divided into parallel strips of identical length, breadth, and area (Fig. 4.1). Although the length and breadth could vary from one village to another (and very

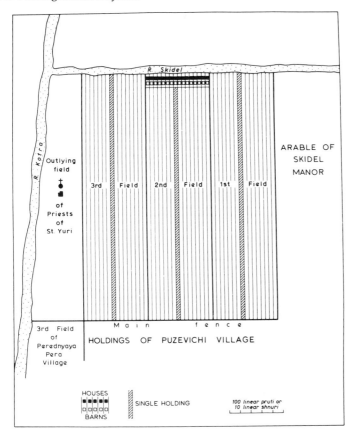

Fig. 4.1. The standard three-field layout of the *voloka* reform, Nekrashevichi village, Grodno District; reconstruction based on the cadastre of 1558.

occasionally between fields), the area was the standard enjoined by the decree, eleven *morgi* or roughly eight hectares. One peasant holding, or *voloka*, which was worked by one to four or more households, consisted of one strip in each field, in contrast to the characteristic "bundle" of strips in much of England and central Europe. Only where there were special reasons—poor soil, stony land, the presence of swamp—were the overseers of the reform permitted to establish larger strips, without any corresponding increase in taxation. Where land quality varied within a field, the size of individual strips could vary accordingly.

At the same time as the arable was transformed, the previous village itself was uprooted from its old site and reconstructed along a single street, with a house at the end of each middle field strip "in one line, with the threshing barns opposite", as the contemporary cadastres record for village after village. A pattern of street villages was then established, which remains to this day a feature of the region's settlement geography.

The field and village lay-out illustrated in Fig. 4.1 was created for the overwhelming majority of crown villages. Of the exceptionally detailed cadastres, compiled by the crown to record the newly organized land, its holders and tax dues, there are four principal ones which have survived; they give field descriptions for 436 reorganized villages and of these 292, or 67 per cent, adhered precisely to the decreed "blue-print". The remainder showed only relatively minor departures from the norm, for example, one field set at the end of the other two, or one field with its strips not parallel to those of the other two, or the village accommodated in an end field to be nearer a water supply (for a fuller account of such variations, see French, 1969a).

This highly standardized new dispensation was introduced with great rapidity. Within a dozen years the reform was complete in central provinces of Zhmud, Vil'no, and Troki. Only in the east, along the war-torn borders with Muscovy, did implementation drag on into the next century; indeed, in the east the new system was rarely set up in its full, decreed form (French, 1969b).

A fundamental part of the reform, one of its primary causes, was a very considerable increase in the extent of crown demesne arable, cultivated for the financial benefit of the Treasury by royal stewards, or bailiffs. New manors with new sets of three fields were carved out of the better quality lands, the former owners being compensated with larger areas of poorer lands in the remote forests and swamps. A reconstruction of such a newly founded manor is seen in Fig. 4.2. Unlike the usual situation on the English common-fields, manor and village in Lithuania each had its own geographically separate set of three fields.

At the time of the reform, the immediately attached manor servants, who had previously been slaves, were given freedom and small plots of land as *ogorodniki*, or "gardeners"; their responsibility was to work in the manor and its farm buildings and to tend its kitchen gardens and orchards. Their numbers were never great and, in consequence, the work-force needed for the extensive new fields of crown and private manors had to be provided by the village peasants. They now received their new *voloka* holdings in return for their labour, fixed by the decree at two days per week, with three weeks of annual holiday at mid-Lent, Easter, and Christmas (French, 1970:112).

Holdings surplus to the needs of the manor and those too remote for convenient access were allocated for a money rent. In both cases, there were additional dues in kind, which varied in accordance with land quality and which could be commuted for cash (French, 1970:120). The two methods

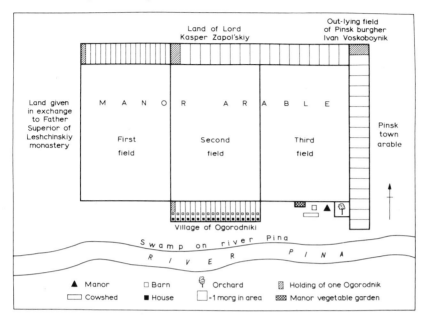

Fig. 4.2. The layout of a crown manor, Selets, Pinsk District.

by which the peasants held their land were known in Lithuania as *tyaglo*, for labour, and *osada*, for cash and corresponded exactly to the *barshchina* and *obrok* of Muscovy. The stewards could reallocate the holdings of peasants who left, indicating that the former rights of peasant land ownership were now abrogated. In other words, the transmogrification of agrarian practice was part and parcel of the social transformation to serfdom. The Third Lithuanian Statute of 1588 made this final, by removing the peasants' right to leave the land and making it a legal requirement to return runaways.

The new fields were cultivated on a three-year rotation of winter-sown rye, spring-sown oats, and fallow. Seldom were any other crops grown; if any were, they were always on the spring field. What, barley, peas, and flax were grown in usually small quantities on the lands of the manors, but there is an almost complete lack of evidence for such crops on the village lands, apart from a little flax, probably grown on outlying fields.

In addition to the highly standardized holdings in the standardized three fields, carrying standardized dues of work, money, and kind, the peasants could, and did, clear additional plots of arable in the surrounding forests, for which they paid supplementary taxes. Comparison of subsequent surveys with the cadastres compiled at the time of the reform indicates that this process of assarting proceeded very actively. These remote plots "beyond the fences", which often numbered up to a score or more for one village, were no doubt cultivated on an outfield system of several years cropping and prolonged fallowing, making them very comparable to the peasant "closes" described by Smith (1977) for various districts of Muscovy. Moreover, in some remote and particularly swampy regions, especially in the Poles'ye marshes along the river Pripyat', the reform overseers found themselves totally defeated by the difficult conditions and there the old, more primitive system continued unchanged, providing yet again a parallel with parts of the Muscovite territories.

CONCLUSIONS

It is tempting to see in the development of three-field agriculture a smooth process of eastward diffusion from thirteenth-century Brandenburg to fourteenth-century Poland to fifteenth-century Podlasia, reaching Novgorod in the latter part of that century and completing the process in the bulk of Lithuanian and Muscovite lands during the sixteenth century, thereafter moving desultorily eastwards into Siberia with Russian settlers of the seventeenth century. In Lithuania at least, the use of terms such as "gardeners" for the manor servants, or fol'vark (cf. vorwerke) for the manor farm itself, or morg for the new areal measure replacing the traditional bochka or "barrel" of land, all suggest links back to Brandenburg.

However, although there certainly does seem to have been a leisurely eastward progression in the spread of the system, it was of course far less orderly than such a simple pattern would infer. For example, the three-field development had already begun to take root in parts of Muscovy up to a century before the Voloka Decree brought so much of Lithuania into line with the lands surrounding it. It may well be that the source region for Muscovy was the Baltic, where the creation of three fields on manorial demesne was commonplace by the sixteenth century, although there too, according to Doroshenko (1959:65), were to be found "the most varied modifications, often departing a long way from 'correct' three-field operations".

It is also clear that, whereas in Lithuania the state-controlled introduction of the voloka system on its lands meant that demesne and villenagium alike experienced the change, in Muscovy proper the initial stages of the new development were largely confined to the lands of the great owners, whether monasteries, nobles or the crown. On the peasant lands, even when the standard formula "in one field so much and in two as much" does occur, "in reality it is various fields, patches and clearances in the forest which predominate" (Smith, 1977:27). When the peasants moved east to colonize

Siberia in the seventeenth century, the formula was used to measure their lands, but forms of long-fallow were widespread; only later towards the end of the century, when shifting to a new site became less practicable was there greater development of a three-field system, based on manuring (Shunkov, 1946:121–122).

In all parts of Russia, the ancient practices of *perelog* and even *podseka* continued side by side with three-field cultivation for some considerable time, especially in peripheral regions. In Moldavia these early systems could still be found in the nineteenth century (Byrnya, 1969:144); in the north of European Russia they were being used on the eve of the Revolution. Nevertheless, with the passing of time, the three-field system became more and more widespread, both from land-owners' arable to peasants' arable and geographically outwards into more recently colonized territories.

It was, if not an agrarian revolution, an agrarian transformation and an advance in efficiency, and for three or four centuries no significant advance in agricultural technology appeared to take its place. The serfdom, which was to so large an extent a concomitant of *trekhpol'ye*, was only ended in 1861. An enclosure movement, breaking up the three big commonfields and ending co-aration, only took place after the Stolypin reforms of 1906 and, as Chapters 5 and 15 indicate, the time left before World War I and the Revolution was so short as to limit severely the degree of change. In western areas, which have remained in Poland, there are still today surviving three fields, cultivated on the same three-year rotation as in 1557. It is not unreasonable to say that the next agrarian transformation on a scale comparable to that of the introduction of the three-field system, was the collectivization of the Soviet period.

REFERENCES

Akty Feodal'nogo Zemlevladeniya i Khozyaystva, Vol. 3, Moscow (1961).
Akty izdavayemyye Vilenskoy Arkheograficheskoy Komissiyey dlya Razbora Drevnikh Aktov, Vol. 14, Vil'na (1888).
Blum, J., (1964). "Lord and Peasant in Russia from the Ninth to the Nineteenth Century", New York.
Byrnya, P. P., (1969). "Sel'skiye Poseleniya Moldavii XV–XVII vv.", Kishinev.
Danilova, L. V., (1955). "Ocherki po Istorii Zemlevladeniya i Khozyaystva v Novgorodskoy Zemle v XIV–XV vv.", Moscow.
Dokumenty Moskovskogo Arkhiva Ministerstva Yustitsii, Vol. 1, Moscow (1897).
Doroshenko, V. V., (1959). Sel'skoye khozyaystvo feodal'noy Liflyandii (Vidzeme) v XIII–XVI vekakh. *In* "Materialy po Istorii Sel'skogo Khozyaystvo i Krest'yanstva SSSR", (K. V. Sivkov, ed.) Vol. 3, pp. 41–88, Moscow.
French, R. A., (1969a). Field patterns and the three-field system—the case of sixteenth-century Lithuania, *Inst. of Brit. Geog. Trans. and Papers* 48:121–134.

French, R. A., (1969b). Babrujsk and its neighbourhood in the early seventeenth century, *Jour. of Byelorussian Studies* **2**, No. 1, 29–56.

French, R. A., (1970). The three-field system of sixteenth-century Lithuania, *Agri. Hist. Review* **18**, Part II, 106–125.

Gorskiy, A. D., (1959). Iz istorii zemledeliya v severo-vostochnoy Rusi XIV–XV vekov, *In* "Materialy po Istorii Sel'skogo Khozyaystva i Krest'yanstva SSSR", (K. V. Sivkov, ed.), Vol. 3, pp. 5–40, Moscow.

Gorskiy, A. D., (1960). "Ocherki Ekonomicheskogo Polozheniya Krest'yan Severo-vostochnoy Rusi XIV–XV vv.", Moscow.

Grekov, B., (1959). "Kiev Rus", Moscow.

Grigor'yev, A. A. and Ivanov, A. V., (1956). "Karel'skaya ASSR", Moscow.

Grossman, Yu. M., (1962). Polozheniye krest'yan Lezhayskogo starostva (vtoraya polovina XVI—nachalo XVII v.), *In* "Materialy po Istorii Sel'skogo Khozyaystva i krest'yanstva SSSR", Vol. 5, pp. 21–60, Moscow.

Grossman, Yu. M., (1964). Kmeti, zagrodniki i komorniki zapadnoukrainskoy derevni vo vtoroy polovine XVI–pervoy polovine XVII v. *In* "Yezhegodnik po Agrarnoy Istorii Vostochnoy Yevropy 1963g." (V. K. Yatsunskiy, ed.) pp. 167–178, Vil'nyus.

Kharitonychev, A. T., (1960). "Rol' Khozyaystvennoy Deyatel'nosti Cheloveka v Izmenenii Landshaftov Gor'kovskogo Pravoberezh'ya", Gor'kiy.

Kochin, G. Ye., (1965). "Sel'skoye Khozyaystvo na Rusi v Period Obrazovaniya Russkogo Tsentralizirovannogo Gosudarstva Konets XIII—nachalo XVI v." Moscow and Leningrad.

Lyapushkin, I. I., (1968). Slavyane vostochnoy Yevropy nakanune obrazovaniya drevnerusskogo gosudarstva. *Materialy i Issledovaniya po Arkheologii SSSR* **152**.

Lyubavskiy, M. K., (1910). "Ocherk Istorii Litovsko-russkago Gosudarstva do Lyublinskoy Unii vklyuchitel'no", Moscow.

Mukhamed'yarov, Sh. F., (1959). K istorii zemledeliya v srednem Povolzh'ye v XV–XVI vekakh. *In* "Materialy po Istorii Sel'skogo Khozyaystva i Krest'yanstva SSSR", (K. V. Sivkov, ed.), Vol. 3, pp. 89–122, Moscow.

Pistsovaya Kniga Byvshago Pinskago Starostva sostavlennaya po Poveleniyu Korolya Sigismunda Avgusta v 1561–1566 godakh Pinskim i Kobrinskim Starostoyu Lavrinom Voynoyu, 2 vols., Vil'na (1874).

Pistsovaya Kniga Pinskago i Kletskago Knyazhestv, sostavlennaya Pinskim Starostoyu Stanislavom Kh'valchevskim v 1552–1555 g., Vil'na (1884).

Russkaya Istoricheskaya Biblioteka (1914), **30**.

Shapiro, A. L. (ed.), (1971). "Agrarnaya Istoriya Severo-zapada Rossii: vtoraya polovina XV—nachalo XVI v.", Leningrad.

Shapiro, A. L., (1977). "Problemy Sotsial'no-ekonomicheskoy Istorii Rusi XIV–XVI vv.", Leningrad.

Shunkov, V. I., (1946). "Ocherki po Istorii Kolonizatsii Sibiri v XVII—nachale XVIII vekov", Moscow and Leningrad.

Slobodin, V. M., (1965). O vozniknovenii i razvitii parovoy sistemy zemledeliya na territorii Rossii v period feodalizma. *In* "Yezhegodnik po Agrarnoy Istorii Vostochnoy Yevropy 1963g.", (V. K. Yatsunskiy, ed.) pp. 158–166, Vil'nyus.

Smith, R. E. F., (1959). "The Origins of Farming in Russia", Paris.

Smith, R. E. F., (1977). "Peasant Farming in Muscovy", Cambridge.

von Loewe, K., (1970). Commerce and agriculture in Lithuania, 1400–1600, *Economic History Rev.* 26, no. 1, 23–37.

Yurginis, Yu. M., (1964). O zemledel'cheskoy sisteme predshestvovavshey trekhpol'yu. *In* "Yezhegodnik po Agrarnoy Istorii Vostochnoy Yevropy 1962g." (V. K. Yatsunskiy, ed.), pp. 95–100, Minsk.

Yurginis, Yu. M., (1978). Vliyaniye agrarnoy reformy serediny XVI v. na proizvoditel'nyye sily Litvy. *In* "Problemy Agrarnoy Istorii", (V. L. Yanin, ed.) Vol. 1, pp. 12–18, Minsk.

5 The Development of Peasant Land Holding from Emancipation to the Revolution

J. Pallot

In Chapter 4 the establishment of the three-field system was discussed. In this chapter the focus shifts to the nineteenth and early twentieth centuries when Russian peasant farming was forced to adapt to new pressures. These arose for two main reasons: firstly, from the middle of the nineteenth century population growth accelerated sharply and, secondly, the peasants were drawn increasingly into the market economy. Both these changes meant that peasant households somehow had to increase their income. This could be done by expanding output from the land or by developing alternative or supplementary livelihoods. For the geographer it is interesting to see if, and how, these changes were reflected in the way in which the land was settled; that is, in the layout of farms and settlements and in the disposition of fields. At the same time, the patterns observed can give some insight into the forces at work in peasant society in late nineteenth and early twentieth century Russia.

As a starting point, 1861 has been chosen, for it was in that year that proprietal serfs in Russia were granted their legal freedom in the Grand Statute of Emancipation. For economic and political reasons the government provided in the statute for the continued existence of the peasant commune (*obshchina*) and household (*dvor*). Indeed, as G. Robinson has shown (1969:75–78) it was made very difficult for peasants to disentangle themselves from either institution. As the century wore on official opinion began to turn against the commune. The objections were both economic (the commune was believed to inhibit agricultural progress) and political (it was thought to be a seed-bed of revolution). By the beginning of the twentieth century, therefore, a policy was emerging to phase the commune out of rural Russia. Some form of individualized land-holding was the

RUSSIAN HISTORICAL GEOGRAPHY VOL. 1
ISBN 0 12 081201 0

preferred replacement for the communal system. Individualization, it was believed, would enable peasants to introduce modern systems of farming onto their land and the resultant increases in prosperity would benefit everyone in society.

The assault on the commune was given an impulse by widespread peasant participation in the revolutionary uprisings that swept through Russia in 1905. In 1906–10 a series of legislative acts was introduced that enabled the heads of peasant households all over Russia to take out title to the land and to demand that this land be consolidated into a single parcel. In an obvious way this legislation, known as the Stolypin Land Reform, was designed to help along the process of capitalist development in rural Russia. In withdrawing from the commune and becoming the inalienable owner of land, each household head adopting the Stolypin Land Reform, at least as far as the law was concerned, transformed his relationship with his neighbours and also with the members of his household. According to official figures, between 1906 and the outbreak of war and revolution about ten per cent of all peasant households in Russia withdrew from the commune and consolidated their land, and a further fifteen per cent withdrew without consolidating.

To the officials charged with recording for the government the number of secessions from the commune, the distinction between the various species of farm that now could exist in rural Russia was no doubt quite clear. Certainly in law there was no way of confusing peasant households that had taken out title to their land with those that continued to hold their land in the commune. Thus, as far as officialdom at the time was concerned, the farms set up under the provisions of the Stolypin legislation were something new and different in the Russian countryside. Moreover, each additional household that adopted the Stolypin Reform was taken both as further proof that the commune was indeed in decline and as a vindication of the government's policy.

Analyses of the Stolypin Land Reform have been conflicting* and it is doubtful whether anyone today would deny that the processes involved in the adoption of the reform were complex and the results difficult to interpret. The image of the enclosed farms set up after 1906 as a novelty in the

---

* Western writers on the reform tend to divide into those who believe the reform was on the road to success and, had war not broken out, would have brought prosperity and stability to the Russian countryside, and those who believe it was introduced too late and could make little impact on rural poverty. An exposition of the first view is found in Pavlovsky (1968) and of the second in Mosse (1965) and Robinson (1969). Soviet and Marxist historians focus on the role the reform played in peasant class formation. See, for example, Dubrovskiy (1963).

Russian countryside and their spread as signalling a new departure in the development of land-holding run through much work dealing with the reform; but there are grounds for questioning this, essentially the official, view. Journeying back to rural Russia before the Revolution, an observer would no doubt be surprised by the variation to be found in peasant land holding. By the first two decades of the twentieth century, different forms of land-holding were developing in every province of Russia in response to particular combinations of political and economic forces and the demands of the physical environment. Between the two extremes of, on the one hand, highly fragmented holdings in repartitional communes and, on the other, the model version of a consolidated owner-occupied unit, there was a wide spectrum of different types of farm among which those formally falling into the category of enclosed farm overlapped considerably with others.

LAND HOLDING IN THE COMMUNE

The commune which the Tsarist Government sought to eliminate from the Russian countryside had a long history. Its origins are controversial but by the nineteenth century it had come to control many important aspects of the Russian peasant's life. It bound peasant households together in a complicated web of economic, social, and legal relationships but it was a self-governing institution with elected officials and general meetings. Two main types of commune were recognized at the time of the serfs' emancipation, the distinguishing feature being land ownership. First, there were communes in which rights in land were held in common by all the member households (*obshchinnoye zemlevladeniye*): these were the most numerous type of commune in Russia and they dominated land-holding in the central provinces of both forest and steppe. Secondly, there were communes in which rights in land were vested in the individual member households (*podvornoye zemlevladeniye*): the largest concentrations of these were in the south-western and western provinces. In the simplest situation, communes co-incided physically with single settlements but this did not have to be the case as communes covering only part of a settlement or, alternatively, embracing several, were to be found in provinces in different parts of Russia.

Farming in communes with communal and hereditary tenure was based in most provinces on the use of a number of fixed categories of land. Normally these were the house and adjoining allotment (*usad'ba*), the arable (*pashnya*) abutting onto the occupied area, natural hayland or meadow (*senokos* and *lug*), natural pastureland (*vygon*), and woodland and scrub (*les* and *kustarnik*). Every member of a commune had the right to use each of these categories of land found within the boundaries of the commune. The distribution of the land between households and the rules and regulations pertaining to its use were, however, laid down by the commune of peasants as a whole. The chief way in which communes with communal tenure differed from hereditary communes was in their right to redistribute land between member households. In most, but by no means all, such repartitional communes it was usual for the house and garden allotment to be allocated to individual households in perpetuity (once assigned their location could never be changed), for arable and natural hayland to be subject to repartition and for natural pastureland, woodland and scrub to be held undivided for common use.

The rationale behind repartitioning was to maintain equality over time between households by adjusting the amount of land they had for their use to their size. It was obviously an important task and one for which each commune developed its own rules and procedures. For example, the frequency of repartitioning varied. In some communes there was a regular interval between repartitions but in others repartitions took place only when the need arose, while in yet others the practice had virtually ceased altogether by the second half of the nineteenth century. The most radical type of repartition (*korennoy peredel*) involved the removal of all field boundaries and a change in the number and size of allotments. Repartition "by lot" (*zhereberka*) and "re-ordering" repartition (*pereverstka*) were less radical; the size, number, and location of allotments remaining the same, but entitlement to their use being redistributed between households. Sometimes repartition involved all the members of a commune but at other times only a few households, this latter type of repartition (*svalka-navalka*) usually taking place in response to a sudden change in household size.

In addition to the purely quantitative aspect, repartitioning sought to equalize peasant land-holdings in terms of quality and accessibility. The way this was done was by allocating households their share of land in different places so that everyone could use at least some of the best and most accessible land the commune had to offer. As a result of this practice few peasant households in the commune held their land in a compact unit; instead, it was usual to hold land in several parcels which were separated from each other by the land parcels of other households. Households worked their farms independently but the intermingling of a large portion of their land compelled them to follow a common cropping cycle and, if it was the practice locally, to open their arable when free of crops to the neighbours' livestock for grazing. Decisions relating to rotations, pasturing rights and the agricultural calendar affecting all members were made by the commune as a whole.

In the essentials of land use and farm layout, communes in which land was held in hereditary ownership were similar to repartitional communes with the familiar pattern of an area of pasture and sometimes woodland or scrub in common use and discrete blocks of arable, hayland, and the settled area in individual use. As in repartitional communes, the arable and hayland in hereditary communes were parcelled out in interlocking fragments between households, but these parcels were not subject to redistribution. Fragmentation in these communes went back to the original land settlement and was sustained by the practice of gavelkind. It meant that households in an hereditary commune, like those in repartitional communes, had also to develop their farming system in common.

By the end of the nineteenth century, relative land shortage meant that few households could depend upon their commune land alone for a livelihood. In the quest to increase production peasant land-holding expanded onto the estates of the nobility and crown. In the 1880s over one-third of Russian peasant households were renting land, often from their former lords and on very unfavourable terms. For every six *desyatiny* of commune land the peasants held one *desyatina* of rented land by the end of the century. Land purchase by peasants grew steadily in the second half of the century with eight times as much land passing into peasant ownership in the 1890s as in the 1860s (Robinson, 1969:99–100). The establishment by the government of the Peasant Land Bank in 1883 to provide credit to purchasers was important in the development of land sales. Where both rent and purchase were concerned individual or collective transactions could be made. Individual purchase tended to be the privilege of the wealthier members of the community and the land acquired stood separate from the commune holdings. In collective purchases the fate of the land varied but it is certain that some ended up absorbed into the commune land and being repartitioned. On the eve of the Stolypin Land Reform the peasants in a single commune could thus hold their land under more than one ownership system. The differences were not always apparent, however, in the way the land was treated.

THE DISLOCATION OF LAND

Of the various features of land-holding in the commune, it was the parcelling of peasant farms that had changed most obviously by the end of the nineteenth century from being a source of some advantage to a weakness. The problem was, quite simply, that land fragmentation became excessive and therefore, costly to the peasants in terms of lost output. Just how severe was fragmentation is clear from central and local government surveys. Peasant land was particularly fragmented in provinces belonging to regions such as the mixed forest belt, which had a long history of settlement and in which soil and physiographic conditions were varied. In Tver province north-west of Moscow, for example, peasant households in more than half the communes held their land in forty or more separate parcels by the second decade of the twentieth century. In two *uyezdy*, Vishnevolotskiy and Ostashkovskiy, the average number of parcels per household exceeded fifty. The individual land parcels were small and it was rare for them to exceed one-fifth *desyatina* in size (*Sbornik Materialov* . . . , 1913–1920).

Regional variations in the degree of land fragmentation were marked as was shown by a government investigation of farms that subsequently enclosed their land (*Zemleustroyennyye Khozyaystva* . . . , 1915). The contrast between the situation in Mologskiy *uyezd* in Yaroslavl province and · *uyezdy* such as Berdyanskiy, Kremenchugskiy and Bogodukhovskiy in the eastern and southern steppes is obviously great, as Table 5.1 illustrates, and was presumably related to the differences in the length of settlement, physical conditions and land availability.

The steppe provinces were, however, adversely affected by the problem of distance between fields. In the conditions of rural transport in Russia distances of 3–3.5 *versty* (one *versta* = 1.067 kilometre) were considerable and it was rare for fields situated this far from a peasant's dwelling to be cultivated intensively, if at all. But in the eastern and southern steppe provinces the land of some communes extended tens of *versty* across often

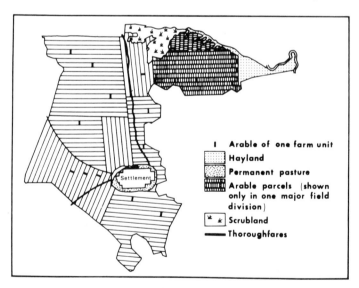

Fig. 5.1. Fragmentation in Borma village, Samara province, with nine fields, where each of 286 households had a number of parcels.

Table 5.1. Land Fragmentation in eleven *uyezdy* of European Russia.

Uyezdy	Percentage number of households with their allotment land in *n* number of parcels:									
	1	2	3	4–5	6–10	11–20	21–40	41–60	61–100	100
Berdianskiy (Taurida)	0.4	0.1	0.1	31.3	64.5	1.4	1.3	0.7	0.1	0.1
Bogodukhovskiy (Kharkov)	0.4	0.9	3.2	28.6	50.6	10.9	5.3	0.0	—	—
Krasnoufimskiy (Perm)	0.5	0.6	2.5	10.8	40.8	31.2	12.2	1.3	—	—
Kremenchugskiy (Poltava)	23.4	17.4	22.4	19.5	14.6	2.6	0.2	—	—	—
Mologskiy (Yaroslavl')	—	—	—	—	—	—	24.3	56.1	17.5	0.7
Nikolayevskiy (Samara)	—	—	0.1	13.5	22.5	58.9	4.7	0.1	—	0.2
Orlovskiy (Orel)	0.9	0.1	5.5	6.7	10.8	27.4	33.9	7.9	5.9	1.0
Ostrovskiy (Pskov)	0.3	—	0.1	—	0.3	4.4	10.9	23.7	36.1	24.1
Rzhevskiy (Tver)	2.2	—	—	—	0.2	13.0	50.7	25.0	8.8	0.2
Sichevskiy (Smolensk)	1.7	—	0.3	0.4	4.0	13.0	36.5	27.1	15.3	1.8
Troitskiy (Vil'no)	5.5	0.3	1.6	4.0	12.9	43.8	29.6	1.6	0.9	—
Total	3.9	2.1	3.8	14.5	26.9	20.2	16.1	6.6	4.4	1.5

Source: *Zemleustroyennyye Khozyaystva*, St. Petersburg (1915). Totals of −/+ 100 per cent due to rounding.

completely arid land and the distances peasants had to go to get to their land were very great (Table 5.2). The Samara province year book reported, for example: "In the southern *uyezdy* some allotment land extends 45 *versty* across completely arid land . . . the peasants often have their land 30, 40 or more *versty* from their village" (*Pamyatnaya Knizhka* . . . , 1910:63).

Table 5.2. Distant land in the eleven *uyezdy* of European Russia.

Uyezdy	Percentage number of households with their most distant allotment at *n versty*						
	Adjacent	0.25	0.251–0.5	0.51–1.0	1.01–3.0	3.01–5.0	5.01
Berdianskiy	—	0.1	—	0.7	5.7	18.5	75.1
Bogodukhovskiy	0.4	1.1	2.2	5.1	10.0	11.8	19.5
Krasnoufimskiy	0.5	—	0.2	3.0	52.0	26.1	18.4
Kremenchugskiy	8.8	1.1	3.5	7.0	37.7	28.0	14.0
Mologskiy	—	—	0.4	5.4	35.7	32.1	26.4
Nikolayevskiy	—	—	—	—	1.3	—	98.7
Orlovskiy	0.9	—	2.6	5.3	33.4	15.7	42.2
Ostrovskiy	0.3	2.6	20.0	34.6	33.2	5.8	3.5
Rzhevskiy	2.2	0.8	10.0	35.4	51.8	—	—
Sichevskiy	1.7	0.9	9.8	43.1	43.6	0.4	0.5
Troitskiy	5.5	0.8	4.8	27.7	49.6	10.7	1.0
Total	2.4	0.8	4.2	14.7	28.9	12.6	36.5

Source: *Zemleustroyennyye Khozyaystva*, St. Petersburg (1915). (Totals of −/+ 100 per cent due to rounding.)

The fragmentation of individual farms was only one aspect of the dislocation of peasant land in Russia, for in some provinces land belonging to separate communes was fragmented. Also it was often intermingled with land of private landowners. The problem was most widespread in the noble strongholds of Russia, in the central Black Earth provinces and further north in the forest provinces. In Tula province in the Black Earth centre, 27.5 per cent of all communes held their land in more than two places in 1902 and in some cases these were fifty *versty* apart (Kashkarov, 1902: ch. 2). An example can show how complicated arrangements could be. In Rozhdestvenyy *sloboda*, Yepifanskiy *uyezd*, 4828.5 *desyatiny* of land were

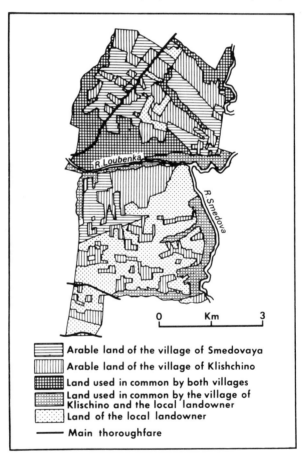

Fig. 5.2. Land held by Smedovaya and Klishchino communes and by a private landowner before their adoption of the Stolypin reform. Meadow, forest, and pasture of the two villages were shared.

occupied in 1899 by thirteen peasant communes and 141 private land-owners but were divided into no less than 2110 separate parcels (*Itogi Otsenochno-Ekonomicheskogo Issledovaniya*, 1903:60). A less extreme version, with two communes and one private landowner, is shown in Fig. 5.2. In this case not only was land intermingled but some was also held in common by the three parties. The arrangements for using land in such situations varied. Sometimes the land was divided into a series of parcels equivalent to the total number of households in the communes sharing the land and repartitioned at intervals, or it could be used in rotation by each commune, or again, in the case of pasture, it could simply be thrown open for the use of all.

The frustrations associated with trying to farm highly fragmented hold-ings must have been considerable. One important impact was the reduction of the amount of land in effective use and this served to worsen the problem of land shortage which, in the nineteenth century, the peasants identified as the cause of their difficulties. Where fragmentation was severe, land that could have been used for crops was taken up in boundary furrows and some parcels abandoned because they were too distant or because there was simply not the labour available to work them all. Again examples, this time from reports of the Tver *zemstvo*, will help to make the point. Writing about Bezhetskiy *uyezd* one investigator noted:

> Thanks to the fragmentation of land in these parts, the peasants waste a lot of time to no purpose. The peasants from Lyubin village, for example, have to travel one day some four *versty* beyond the village of Fedorovo to harvest just one *desyatina* of hay . . . and on the next day the peasants from Fedorovo might have to undertake the same journey to their hayland beyond Lyubin. (*Sel'skokhozyaystvennyy Obzor*, 1910:ch. 3).

Sometimes communes were able to rent out their distant land parcels to other communes but such land could also be left to waste. Trostino village held one parcel fifteen *versty* from the settlement but, reportedly, "this land was never visited by any of the peasants". It was given "in return for vodka" to peasants in a nearby village (*Statisticheskoye Opisaniye Rzhevskogo Uyezda*, 1885:21). Another village, Svistalov, received an allotment in 1861 of twenty-nine *desyatiny*, fifteen *versty* from the settlement but "where it is exactly has never been discovered" (*ibid.* 21). Tula province was similarly affected by fragmented communes and despite having among the smallest land-holdings in European Russia, whole portions of peasant land were abandoned. In Yepifanskiy *uyezd*, in 1899, even the smallest communes had abandoned 10 per cent of their land, and the larger communes much more.

Apart from exacerbating an already difficult situation with regard to land

Table 5.3. Abandoned land in Yepifanskiy *Uyezd*, 1899.

Area of land (in *desyatiny*) per commune	Percentage of land partially or completely abandoned
100.0	10.5
100.01–300.0	11.9
300.01–500.0	31.8
500.01	38.6

Source: "Itogi Otsenochno-Ekonomicheskogo Issledovaniya Tul'skoy Gubernii", Vol. 1. Yepifanskiy Uyezd, 1899.

availability, fragmentation also put some constraints on farming practice, although this aspect of the problem was probably exaggerated by the legislators in 1906. Fragmentation certainly prevented individual peasant households from experimenting with alternative systems of farming but whole communes, if they so desired, could vote to change. Shortage of capital and ignorance of modern methods were more likely inhibitors in the development of Russian peasant agriculture than tenure and farm layout. More important where farming practice was concerned was the effect fragmentation and distance had upon the peasant's ability to take manure to the land and to cross-plough.

ADAPTATIONS AND ADJUSTMENTS IN THE COMMUNE

Land fragmentation was an obvious source of problems for peasant farmers in nineteenth century Russia. Yet, interestingly, the practice of repartition-ing and partitioning between heirs does not seem to have abated as the situation worsened (Robinson, 1969:122). Indeed, a government act intro-duced in 1893 to restrict the frequency of repartitions to every twelve years, was ignored by some communes. Had peasant households in the commune been in a position to take a long-term view of their situation no doubt they, like the officials in St. Petersburg, would have admitted the irrationality of further subdividing their land. The consequences of fragmentation were, after all, understood at first hand by the peasants. But faced with increasing pressures on a land resource base that was not expanding fast enough, the importance of making sure that they got all the land due to them, and that at least some of this was of good quality, became an issue of vital importance for all peasant households. It was an issue that had to be resolved at once, whatever the longer term consequences might be, for what was at stake was the survival of the household through the next agricultural year. Viewed in this way, the continuing redistribution of land was a rational response to the pressures in the nineteenth century to produce more. Where the problem of population pressure on the land was concerned, the paradox was, of course, that there was every reason to keep birth rates high, as additions to the household meant increased allocations of land on the next repartition. This stimulus to population growth must have been particularly great in those communes in which the unit used for calculating the amount of land due to each household was the number of "consumers" (*yedoki*).

Some experiments were made before 1906 with alternative forms of land-holding. Their fate shows that there was a strong commitment to the practice of subdividing land among the peasants. A useful illustration is a programme introduced in 1846 to settle Russian peasants on former cossack land east of the river Volga in Samara province, described in a contemporary report of 1910 (*Podvornoye i Khutorskoye khozyaystvo* . . . , 1910). Under this programme, eleven villages were established in Stavropolskiy *uyezd* and 142 in Samarskiy *uyezd* and in each thirty-eight *desyatiny* of land

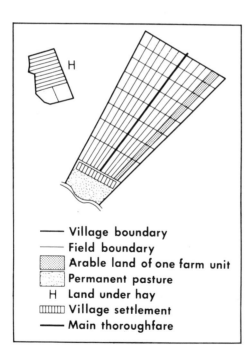

Fig. 5.3. Vvedenka, with hereditary family farms, organized in "ribbons".

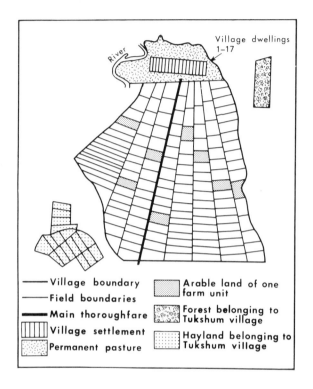

Fig. 5.4. Tukshum, with hereditary family farms, organized in "squares".

were allocated to every household in hereditary ownership (*semenoye pod-vornoye vladeniye*). Figures 5.3 and 5.4 show how the farms were laid out with the arable fields arranged either in "ribbons" (*lenti*) or "squares" (*karti*). Each household received eight parcels in the arable, plus a plot of hayland and the right to use pasture in common. The eight-fold division is explained by the fact that a long fallow system, in which one-eighth of the land was used at any time, was thought most appropriate for the arid conditions of the two *uyezdy*. The subdivision of these farms was prohibited, provision being made in the settlement for them to be passed on to a single heir. This provision was not in force for long, however, as it was cancelled in 1861 under the Statute of Emancipation. Thereafter, the farms were subdivided between successive heirs and the farms by the twentieth century had become fragmented some into twenty or more parcels.

A later experiment in the same province had a similar outcome. In 1895 the Administration for Appanage Lands decided to rent land in two appanage estates to migrants from central Russia. Forty-one villages were formed in which the arable was laid out in three fields consistent with the winter–spring–fallow rotation practised over much of Russia. Each household received a parcel in each field and, in addition, the usual parcel of hayland and rights in the common pasture. Figure 5.5 shows the position in one of the villages thus laid out. Twenty-four-year contracts were signed with the peasants on condition that the layout of farms remained unchanged and no subdivision took place. Provisions were made for the extension of the contract indefinitely if a number of restricting covenants were adhered to and for the transfer of the farm to a single heir should the original tenant die or retire from farming. As half a century before, however, legal restrictions were no proof against custom and farms had within fifteen years of the settlement become fragmented. According to the chairman of the Samara Land Settlement Committee this occurred

> as a result of attempts by several settlers in the hamlets to equalise their land holdings through repartitioning the land annually under a voluntary agreement of the tenants themselves . . . This has led to some groups of rented farms

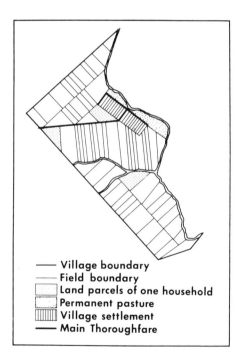

Fig. 5.5. Mekkerovskiy hamlet on rented appanage land.

becoming barely distinguishable from farms in the commune. (*Pamyatnaya Knizhka* . . . , 1910:30).

There were obviously compelling reasons for the continuing fragmentation of peasant land in Russia. Nevertheless, before 1906, attempts were made by some communes to improve farm layout. Tver province again provides an example. In Kashinskiy *uyezd*, in an attempt to reduce the number and increase the size of households' parcels, some communes began allotting land at repartitions in standard units of one quarter, one-sixth and one-ninth *desyatina* in size. Previously it had been the custom for parcels to be equivalent in width to the number of allotment units due to individual households, a system that had resulted in small households receiving very narrow parcels of land. The use of standard-sized units helped to reduce the total number of land parcels in a commune and made each a workable size. By 1902 the new system had apparently begun to spread rapidly through the *uyezd* (*Trudy Mestnykh Komitetov* . . . , Vol. XLII). It is not possible to discover just how widespread were such initiatives by communes as no systematic records were kept. At the higher scale, however, there is evidence from petitions to the Ministry of Internal Affairs, of which there are many in the archives, of attempts by the peasants to unravel shared and fragmented land belonging to communes. In 1896, for example, the villages of Kholma and Desna in Tver province asked the Ministry of Internal Affairs for permission to effect an exchange of land: part of Kholma's land lay seven *versty* from its settlement and adjacent to Desna, while some of Desna's land was only one-half *verst* from Kholma. The exchange was permitted with Kholma village having to pay thirty-three roubles per *desyatina* to Desna as compensation for the inferior quality of its land. (*Delo o Razreshenii Krest'yanam Prodat' Zemli* . . . , 1896–97, No. 622).

Redistributing land between communes produced immediate results, increasing the amount of land that could be put to productive use. It is not surprising therefore that when the machinery was set up to transform peasant land-holding in 1906–10, the demand for this type of consolidation was very great. Group Land Settlement (*gruppovoye zemleustroystvo*), as it was called under the Stolypin legislation, did not involve any tenure changes as did enclosure proper and it did not alter the fundamentals of farm layout (although it helped to reduce the number of land parcels each household held). What it did involve was a range of tasks from unravelling the land of separate communes and different categories of land owner, to dividing land held in common and demarcating the boundaries of communes. Between 1906 and 1914 nearly one-half of all the projects carried out under the Stolypin legislation were such group settlements and the number of peasants touched by them far exceeded the number that withdrew from the commune onto enclosed farms (Fig 5.6). Group Land Settlement was most developed in the central provinces and the west where it was, in fact, most needed (Fig. 5.7).

Despite its appeal for the peasants, group land settlement did not have much support in the government, and local committees charged with carrying out the Stolypin Reform were directed to give this type of work low priority; it was to be undertaken only when a more radical solution proved impossible (Yaney, 1961:235–237). Sometimes group projects had to be carried out as a first stage in the process of enclosing land of individual peasant households but group work was not encouraged as an end in itself and applications for it were often turned down. The Samara province directory for 1909 reported, for example, that, "in view of the necessity of directing all energy towards the fullest and most complete fulfilment of the aim of Land Settlement (the formation of enclosed farms) applications for Group Land Settlement are always turned down" (*Pamyatnya Knizhka . . .*, 1910:62). The government did not want "improved" communes in Russia—it wanted a completely different system of land-holding.

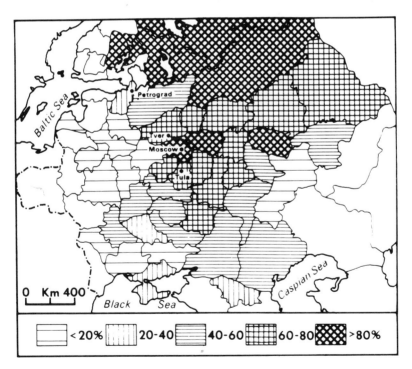

Fig. 5.6. Group land settlement as a share of all land settlement work, 1907–1914.

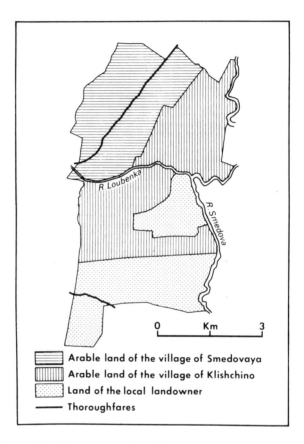

Fig. 5.7. The results of Group Land Settlement in Smedovaya and Klishchino (see Fig. 5.2).

It would be wrong to suppose that all peasant farms existing in Russia prior to the Stolypin legislation were highly or even partially fragmented. Owner-occupied consolidated farms were widespread in the north-eastern provinces and in all provinces there were some households that had been able to enclose under the provisions of the Emancipation Statute, although they were few in number. But even within the commune farms could be consolidated. This occurred where land was relatively abundant and settlement recent. In Novouzenskiy *uyezd*, Samara province, peasant households in some communes held their land in a single parcel which sometimes they occupied or settled for part of the year. Isolated from their neighbours and not obliged to follow a common rotation, the peasants were able to work the land as they chose (*Podvornoye i Khutorskoye Khozyaystvo* . . . , 1910). Such farms, although not the inalienable property of the occupiers, in almost every other respect resembled the type of farm favoured by the government after 1906.

THE STOLYPIN FARMS

The plan that the enactors of the 1906–10 legislation had for the development of land-holding in Russia was ambitious. Nothing short of the elimination of the commune was thought necessary if Russia's agricultural backwardness was to be overcome and political instability averted. A social revolution in the countryside transforming the peasant mode of production was put on the agenda. The legislators had a clear image of the farm that would signify this change. The model was the *khutor*, a fully consolidated unit of land on which the proprietor's dwellings and farm-buildings were situated. On such a farm, it was believed, the peasant would be able to reap the benefits of close proximity to the land and have the freedom to innovate. A lesser type of farm, for which, in fact, the authorities had to settle most often, was the *otrub*. In *otrub* formation, land, as on the *khutor*, was consolidated, but the owner's dwellings and out-buildings remained separate, for example, in the existing village. Figure 5.8 shows the two forms in one of the government's successful enclosures (nos. 7, 23, 4, 18, and 15 are *otruba*).

The 1906–10 legislation provided for *khutora* and *otruba* to come into being in a variety of ways: by individual households leaving the commune, by whole communes deciding to consolidate or by new settlement on land purchased from the Peasant Land Bank. More than three-quarters of all enclosed farms were formed on consolidated commune land and two-thirds of these by the action of whole communes. Regionally, the pattern of adoption was complex. The greatest number of farms was found in the eastern and southern provinces and on the western borderlands stretching in a broad belt from St. Petersburg to the Ukraine. In the provinces lying in the heart of the coniferous forest and in the centre of European Russia the number was small (Fig. 5.9). The paradox of the Stolypin Reform is that it failed to take off in precisely those regions in which the dislocation of peasant land in the commune was most severe.

DEPARTURES FROM THE MODEL

Among the one million and more enclosed farms formed after 1906 there were those that corresponded closely to the model envisaged by the legislators and, moreover, went on to develop commercial systems of farming. Agricultural improvement was not the sole privilege of the enclosed farm, however, as a later chapter will show. Among the one million there were

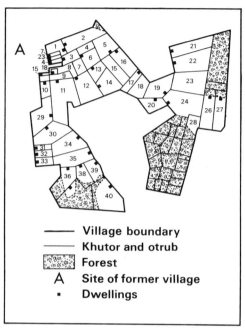

Fig. 5.8. Stupino, after consolidation.

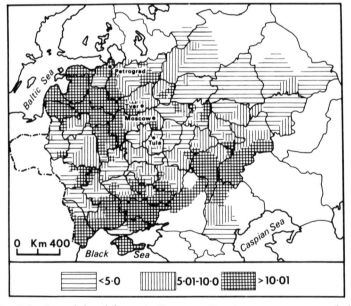

Fig. 5.9. Consolidated farms in European Russia as a percentage of all peasant farms.

also farms that fell short of the model *khutor* or *otrub*. In some instances it was simply a case of incomplete consolidation, farm land remaining divided in several parcels, but in other instances the short-fall from the model was in how the peasants reacted to the change in the legal status of their land. Not all the peasants that adopted the reform seemed to perceive land law in the way intended by the legislators.

The degree of land consolidation achieved on enclosure was recorded in a sample of *uyezdy* in a government survey conducted in 1913 (*Zemleustroyennyye Khozyaystva . . .*, 1915). The results are shown in the Tables 5.4 and 5.5. In all the *uyezdy* investigated, enclosed farms consisting of two to five land parcels were the norm. Some of the land parcels could be located very considerable distances from the peasants' dwelling places. *Khutora* were out-numbered in all cases by *otruba*. But there were differences between *uyezdy*. These in large measure must have been related to physical conditions.

Table 5.4. Degree of land consolidation achieved on enclosure.

| | Percentage no. of households with allotment land in *n* number of parcels | | | | | Percentage of *khutora*[b] to total number of consolidated farms | |
| | | | | | | On allotment land[a] | On Bank and state land |
Uyezdy	1	2	3	4–5	6–10		
Berdianskiy	5.4	66.5	28.1	0.1	—	2.1	100.0
Bogodukhovskiy	2.9	55.7	23.5	16.8	1.6	5.0	15.5
Krasnoufimskiy	29.2	49.0	17.3	4.6	—	32.3	12.8
Kremenchugskiy	12.2	64.6	14.2	8.6	0.6	13.6	40.6
Mologskiy	29.6	33.9	22.1	14.3	—	30.7	100.0
Nikolayevskiy	0.3	57.7	39.1	2.6	0.3	7.4	1.4
Orlovskiy	41.0	48.8	10.2	—	—	42.7	66.7
Ostrovskiy	77.2	19.9	2.6	0.3	—	84.0	64.3
Rzhevskiy	27.0	56.8	11.8	3.8	0.5	37.9	—
Sichevskiy	24.5	48.0	21.3	5.9	0.3	39.2	—
Troitskiy	66.0	27.5	4.8	1.5	0.3	99.2	—
Yepifanskiy uyezd	—	—	—	—	—	—	25.5
Total	26.5	48.9	17.7	6.4	0.5	34.0	31.4

[a] This does not include households that divided their land or sold on enclosure.
[b] This includes *khutora* onto which the peasants' dwellings were moved and those formed by land being consolidated next to the existing dwelling place. It does not include *otrub*-settlements on bank and state land.
Source: *Zemleustroyennyye Khozyaystva*, St. Petersburg (1915).

Table 5.5. Distant land on enclosed farms in eleven *uyezdy* of European Russia

Uyezdy	Percentage number of households with their most distant allotment at *n versty*						
	Adjacent	<0.25	0.251–0.5	0.51–1.0	1.01–3.0	3.01–5.0	>5.01
Berdianskiy	4.6	1.7	3.3	11.0	35.3	26.3	17.9
Bogodukhovskiy	2.9	3.5	3.9	7.4	25.0	22.3	35.0
Krasnoufimskiy	29.7	3.3	7.1	14.4	46.0	9.9	4.2
Kremenchugskiy	10.6	3.5	8.1	14.2	44.1	15.5	4.0
Mologskiy	29.6	6.8	11.1	18.9	26.4	3.2	3.9
Nikolayevskiy	0.3	0.2	0.1	0.9	9.2	15.4	73.3
Orlovskiy	41.0	5.1	10.3	9.7	14.3	8.0	11.5
Ostrovskiy	77.2	7.0	7.0	6.1	2.5	0.1	—
Rzhevskiy	27.0	17.1	25.0	21.0	8.0	0.5	1.4
Sichevskiy	24.5	20.7	19.9	18.3	12.5	1.5	2.7
Troitskiy	66.0	3.6	6.0	10.1	10.7	2.5	1.1
Total	26.2	5.5	7.5	10.7	21.0	12.2	17.0

Source: *Zemleustroyennyye Khozyaystva*, St. Petersburg (1915). Totals of +/− 100 per cent due to rounding.

In the arid southern and eastern provinces, *khutor* formation was particularly difficult because it required a well to be sunk on every new farm. The separation of dwelling and land parcels in the *otruba* that were formed instead was, inevitably, considerable, since villages were large in the steppe. Observe the distance recorded in Nikolayevskiy, Bogodukhovskiy and Kremenchugskiy *uyezdy* in Table 5.5. One compromise that was devised in such situations was to resettle groups of peasant households from large villages in new settlements surrounded by consolidated parcels. Households moving to these otrub-settlements (*otrubnyye poselki*) had jointly to dig a well.

Apart from problems associated with water provision, the consolidation of land from several to only a few parcels was fairly easy in the southern and eastern steppe provinces since physiographic and soil conditions were relatively uniform. Where land capability varied, consolidation in contrast often proved to be difficult. Tver was one such province and the Witte commission had reported in 1902 that while some reordering of peasant land was desirable:

> the complete elimination of fragmentation is impossible because of differences in the fertility of the soil and drainage . . . it is possible only to reduce the number of fields to five–eight per household. (*Trudy Mestnykh Konitetov* . . . , Vol. XVI, 214)

It is, perhaps, a digression to note that in a province like Tver, when complete consolidation was achieved in a commune, some households inevitably had to be allotted their *otrub* or *khutor* on poor land. In the Chief Administration of Land Settlement archive there are many petitions from peasants complaining of having an enclosed farm made up largely of unworkable land. The equivalent in Samara province was the peasant who found all his land, instead of only part of it as before, more than five *versty* from where he lived. Even with compensation, either in additional land or cash, peasant households receiving poor-quality enclosed farms must have faced serious difficulties in the first years of farming.

Although one point of the Stolypin Reform was to create the conditions appropriate for transforming peasant agriculture to a higher system, when it came to enclosure, concessions had to be made to the existing systems of farming. Peasant farming, after enclosure as before, depended upon the complementary use of arable, hayland, pasture, and woodland or scrub. It simplified matters on enclosure to retain the existing blocks of these different types of land and allot each household a parcel, or rights, in each. This, then, was another reason why there was incomplete consolidation and the plan of Borma village shows the pattern of land use that could result. The previous disposition of its land is shown in Fig. 5.10.

An interesting feature of Borma village is that adjacent to each new hamlet formed an area of pastureland in which all households held rights was laid out. The retention of common pasture was not peculiar to Borma but was encountered in villages throughout the provinces of Russia. It was encountered also on the estates that the Peasant Land Bank that were divided for sale into consolidated farms, where there were ideal conditions to create model *khutora*. The Chief Administration for Land Settlement

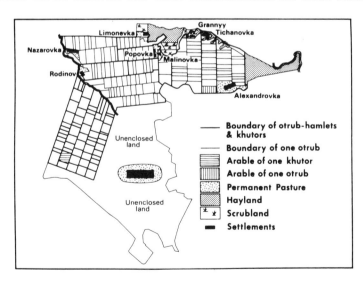

Fig. 5.10. Borma, after enclosure of part of the land.

viewed the retention of common pasture as a temporary measure, necessary during the transitional period to a higher form of farming. Whatever the expectations for peasant agriculture, in outward appearance consolidated villages with their common pasture, separate arable, hayland, and wood and concentration of dwellings, must have retained something of the former commune. And perhaps the points of similarity went deeper than appearance alone.

Stolypin farms were defined not just by their layout. Tenure also was a distinguishing feature with ownership of the land passing from commune or household to the head of the peasant household. The transfer of title in land was supposed to put an end to repartitioning, where this had been practised, and give owners the incentive that comes from security to sink capital into their land. It also, of course, gave the new owners the right to sell. It is not possible to find out to what extent the peasants understood the changes in tenure. However, there were some instances recorded of the carry-over of communal practices onto consolidated farms. These may, of course, have been isolated instances.

An investigation of farms in Bogoroditskiy *uyezd* in 1912–13 brought to

Table 5.6. Land ownership among consolidated farms in eleven *uyezdy*.

| | Per cent of consolidated farmers' land in: | | | Per cent of all households retaining rights in common land |
	Individual ownership (consolidated)	Communal ownership	Other (unconsolidated)	
Berdianskiy	82.3	9.4	8.4	61.6
Bogodukhovskiy	75.8	11.3	13.0	81.8
Krasnoufimskiy	71.7	16.8	11.5	88.8
Kremenchugskiy	55.7	0.1	44.2	0.6
Mologskiy	68.6	18.9	12.5	40.6
Nikolayevskiy	74.4	18.0	7.7	75.9
Orlovskiy	77.3	9.3	13.4	49.3
Ostrovskiy	68.9	2.2	28.8	12.6
Rzhevskiy	63.1	3.9	33.0	25.5
Sichevskiy	78.1	3.0	18.9	31.1
Troitskiy	92.7	2.2	5.1	14.1
Total	76.9	9.8	13.3	45.4

Source: *Zemleustroyennyye Khozyaystva*, St Petersburg (1915). Totals of +/− 100 per cent due to rounding.

light several cases. In one, a group of peasants settling in Nikolayevskiy hamlet, a settlement that had been prepared by the Land Settlement Committee in a series of separate *otruba*, apparently destroyed all the boundaries between the *otruba* and divided the land into three fields, allocating several parcels in each to every household; they then reverted to communal practices of grazing livestock on the stubble and repartitioning at set intervals. Again, two brothers in Taushevka village moved onto neighbouring *khutora* but decided to amalgamate them; three arable fields were created in which each brother held one parcel and also an area of hayland and common pasture (Mozzhukhin, 1917:302–303).

The government survey of 1913 found that in most *uyezdy* there was a small number of households that some time after consolidation had undergone division, partitioning land between the new smaller units. In a minority of cases the partitioned land was intermingled, as in the case of the two brothers from Taushevka, but more often the partitioned land was held in discrete parcels. Although the percentage of households partitioning was small, 2.2 per cent of the total enclosed, it is perhaps significant that the partition was not made at the time of enclosure; it is therefore unlikely that it was a motive for withdrawing from the commune. The possibility that there could have been more partitions in the future as families grew and heads of households died cannot be ruled out. Indeed, experiments with various forms of hereditary tenure, such as those in Samara province, showed that a change in the system of land ownership was not a sufficient guarantee against land fragmentation.

The pattern of land tenure in Russian villages after consolidation under the Stolypin legislation was less straightforward than perhaps the legislators envisaged. The retention of common pasture meant that some householders, while having the greater part of their land in private ownership, could continue to exercise rights of communal ownership. A situation of "dual ownership" was encountered most frequently among peasants purchasing Peasant Land Bank *khutora* and *otruba*, for the majority of them held on to their land in the commune. It was possible for the amount of land held by such peasants in the commune to exceed the amount purchased. The question that arises is whether a peasant who purchased an *otrub* from the Peasant Land Bank but remained living in his village as before can legitimately be included among the ranks of the consolidated. Before 1906, individual peasants in the commune had begun purchasing land from the Peasant Land Bank but nobody suggested that they were "otrubyanini".

The situation of Peasant Land Bank *khutora* was also not always clear. The Bank's definition of a *khutor* seems to have been broad. According to the Peasant Land Bank's own records, a *khutor* was taken to have come into being so long as any building, be it only a simple shed for storing equipment,

Table 5.7. Land ownership among consolidated farms on Peasant Land bank and state land in nine *uyezdy*.

Uyezdy	Per cent of consolidated farmers' land in:			Per cent of all households that retained:	
	Individual ownership (consolidated)	Commu-nal ownership	Other (uncon-solidated)	Rights in common land	Uncon-solidated land
Berdianskiy	75.0	19.4	5.6	73.8	34.3
Bogodukhovskiy	73.8	0.1	26.2	0.6	79.2
Yepifanskiy	70.2	2.0	27.8	24.0	91.5
Krasnoufimskiy	49.5	14.3	36.1	60.4	83.0
Kremenchugskiy	77.7	1.9	20.5	18.5	61.3
Mologskiy	94.2	—	5.9	—	19.3
Nikolayevskiy	61.6	15.5	23.0	91.5	52.0
Orlovskiy	79.0	0.2	20.8	4.7	67.4
Ostrovskiy	75.0	0.3	24.7	2.1	70.4
Total	65.7	8.7	25.6	37.0	72.4

Source: *Zemleustroyennyye Khozyaystva*, St. Petersburg (1915), Totals of +/− 100 per cent due to rounding.

had been placed on the land. Land also was sold as *khutora* on the understanding that at some time in the future the purchaser would move onto it. In the 1911 census for Yepifanskiy *uyezd*, Tula province, it was recorded that only 69.4 per cent of purchased *khutora* were occupied on a permanent basis—the rest were occupied periodically or not at all (*Materialy dlya Otsenki Zemmel'* . . . , Vol III). There must be some doubts about the validity of official figures of numbers of *khutora* and *otruba* on Bank land.

CONCLUSION

The intention here has not been to suggest that the end of the nineteenth and beginning of the twentieth century did not witness any changes, or even very significant changes, in peasant land-holding in Russia. On the contrary, the period was one when the whole framework of the peasants' existence was being transformed and there is no reason to suppose that any system of land holding should have remained immune from the impact of the changes. It is probably a mistake, however, to think in terms of the emergence of over one million new farms (with more ready to follow suit) in the period 1906 to the war, or of a transformation of the Russian cultural landscape. To do so is to accept a number of propositions which, as the previous pages have tried to show, cannot easily be upheld. First, it would be necessary to accept that the farms that the government counted as consolidated corresponded in their essentials to the model put forward. Secondly, in much the same way, it would be necessary to accept the government's presentation of the state of land-holding in the commune, and thus to ignore its variety. Thirdly, it would be necessary to accept that individual peasant householders, used where land relationship were concerned to the rule of custom, had the same understanding of, and respect for, land law as the legislators in St Petersburg. Finally, a point that has not been discussed here, it would be necessary to ignore the fact that differences in the economy of peasant householders before the Revolution were not especially related to farm type, as defined by the government.

The development of land-holding in late nineteenth and early twentieth century Russia was the outcome of reasoned decisions on the part of peasant households, however mistaken some of these decisions may have seemed to outsiders. The picture of a peasantry trapped in the feudal institution of the commune, released in 1906 to become farmers on their own isolated parcels of land is an over-simplification of what happened. It ignores the fact that communes were dynamic institutions and could accommodate change. It also exaggerates the importance of the Stolypin Reform. Land reform was needed, but it is clear that among the peasants who did adopt Stolypin's measures there were those who simply adapted the reform to suit their own requirements, as well as who viewed it in the same way as the original authors. The enormous variety in peasant land-holding in Russia in the decades before the Revolution seems to be another testimony to the complicated and often contradictory tendencies that develop within the peasantry in a society undergoing modernization.

REFERENCES

Delo o Razreshenii Krest'yanam Prodat' Zemli Ts.G.I.A.L., Fond 1291, opis 71, 1896–97, No. 622.
Dubrovskiy, S. M., (1963). "Stolypinskaya Zemel'naya Reforma," Moscow.
Itogi Otsenochno—Ekonomicheskogo Issledovaniya Tul'skoy Gubernii, Tom I. Yepifanskiy Uyezd, Vypusk II; Otsenka Ugod'ya, Tula (1903).
Kashkarov, M., (1902). "Statisticheskiy Ocherk Khozyaystvennogo i Imushchest-vennogo Polozheniya Krest'yan Orlovskoy i Tul'skoy Gubernii," St. Petersburg.
Materialy dlya Otsenki Zemel' Tul'skoy Gubernii, Tom III Yepifanskiy Uyezd, Vypusk 1. Krest'yanskoye Khozyaystvo (1911).

Mosse, W. E., (1965). Stolypin's villages, *Slavonic and East Eur. Rev.* 43, No. 101.
Mozzhukhin, I. V., (1917). "Zemleustroystvo v Bogoroditskom Uyezde", Moscow.
Pamyatnaya Knizhka Samarskoy Gubernii za 1909, Samara (1910).
Pavlovsky, G., (1968). "Agricultural Russia on the Eve of the Revolution", New York.
Podvornoye i Khutorskoye Khozyaystvo v Samarskoy Gubernii, Samara (1910).
Robinson, G. T., (1969). "Rural Russia under the Old Regime", Berkeley and Los Angeles.
Sbornik Materialov dlya Otsenki Zemel' Tverskoy Gubernii, Tver, Vols. 1–7 (1913–20).
Sel'skokhozyaystvennyy Obzor Tverskoy Gubernii za 1909 god. Vypusk II, Tver (1910).
Statisticheskoye Opisaniye Rzhevskogo Uyezda, Tver (1885).
Trudy Mestnykh Komitetov o Nuzhdakh Sel'skokhozyaystvennoy Promyshlennosti, Vol. XLII, Tverskaya Guberniya (1903).
Yaney, G. L., (1961). "The Imperial Russian Government and the Stolypin Land Reform", unpub. PhD., Ann Arbor, Michigan.
Zemleustroyennyye Khozyaystva. Svodnyye Dannyye Sploshnogo po 12 Uyezdam Podvornogo Obsledovaniya Khozyaystvennogo Izmeneniya v Pervyye Gody posle Zemleustroystva, St. Petersburg (1915).

Part II

The Frontier

Introduction

R. A. Pierce

More than any other European or Asian country, Russia is the product of her frontiers. In the usual sense a frontier is "a demarcated boundary between settled states". From the ninth century, coincident with the beginning of their recorded history, the eastern Slavic tribes were united by the grand princes of Kiev, drove westward, and contested for territory with the Teutonic Knights, Poland, and Hungary. Though adjusted frequently by war and diplomacy, the nation's western frontier soon followed the fairly well-defined borders of neighbouring developed states.

But Russia for centuries had a greater frontier, in the sense of "a shifting or advancing zone or region that marks the margin of settled or developed territory". For Russia this open frontier, involving a large territory devoid of natural boundaries, a vague perimeter inhabited by less-developed peoples, and providing a stage for her "unique, enormous and continuous expansion", has been characteristic from very early times. It has taken many forms and has exerted a deep influence on Russian life.

For the Slavic tribes of ancient Russia such a frontier lay all around. Situated on the eastern periphery of Europe, in a great flat land of forests and rivers, close to nature, they lived off the land by hunting, fishing, and a little agriculture, remote from the cultural and economic changes taking place among more advanced peoples to the south and west.

During those nearly silent centuries, the frontier milieu must have done much to set the attitudes and responses that make up the Russian national character. Though impossible to measure, and with many exceptions, a whole complex of traits have been noted and speculated upon by Russians and foreigners alike, and have usually been associated with environmental factors. Thus in the opinion of the eminent Russian historian Klyuchevskiy, the swamps and forests of early Russia confronted the settler with risks, difficulties and hardships, so he learned to observe nature closely. He became resourceful in dealing with perils and difficulties, and inured to

RUSSIAN HISTORICAL GEOGRAPHY VOL. 1
ISBN 0 12 081201 0

misfortune. Although cautious and careful in the forest, he also learned to live with it and off it. He used it as a defence against invasion, as a source of products for trade, and he made it and its creatures figure in his jokes, proverbs, songs, and folk-tales. He became imbued with a profound love of the land.

The relatively flat terrain made the eastern Slav a natural colonizer and pioneer, borne far and wide on the network of slow-flowing rivers. The absence of barriers permitted an identical culture to spread easily, and prevented the development of local peculiarities. The plain was open to invaders, but they themselves were thereby easily displaced or absorbed after their initial strength had passed.

The short growing season made the eastern Slav work in prodigious bouts, but once he had put forth his effort, he was inclined to be philosophical about the outcome. Patience and fatalism became part of his nature. The long cold of winter made him stay indoors reflecting on the problems of his existence and pondering the vagaries of nature, giving rise to a speculative disposition. The changeability of the climate may likewise have caused a lack of restraint, and quick changes of mood.

The rigorous climate and a sparse population developed in the inhabitants a communal spirit, a readiness to work together and co-operate, an openhanded hospitality, and gregariousness.

Fortunately, no one is likely to possess all of these characteristics. They are controversial by their very nature, but the fragmentary evidence of the past produced by the archaeologist, the philologist, the folklorist, and the ethnographer, make it seem likely that over many centuries the terrain which set the Russian apart from the rest of Eurasia did help to form a national character as distinctive as the land in which it grew.

Even after the formation of a Russian state this uncertain frontier remained a predominant influence. In the north, east, and south, the Russians faced tribes and nations which were semi-sedentary and scattered in small groups over vast areas; or nomadic, sometimes very large, but constantly shifting their grazing grounds in the steppe. It was not a fixed frontier; it lacked sharp demarcation; there was a large no-man's land which facilitated infiltration by both sides. On this uncertain, flexible periphery, Russia traded, colonized, built forts to ward off hostile raiders or to protect portages and other key points, and took new areas to protect what had already been acquired. Thus immense gains in territory were made, and experience accumulated which could be applied in governing what had been annexed, or in making new advances.

The Mongol conquest halted the process for a time, but as the Mongol hold waned, Moscow became a dominant force in liberating and "regathering the Russian lands". In 1478, Moscow took over Novgorod and its vast territories to the north-east; in 1552 she took the Khanate of Kazan', and in 1581, through Yermak and his cossacks, crossed the Urals. During the next seventy years, Russian private traders and government forces advanced rapidly, by rivers and portages, across Siberia, reached the Pacific at Okhotsk, gained a foothold on the Amur River, and probably rounded the east cape of Siberia. By the end of the seventeenth century Kamchatka was secured, and in 1741 Bering and Chirikov crossed the sea to North America, opening up yet another frontier. In quest of sea otter pelts, the *promyshlenniki* explored the Aleutian Islands, and in 1786 founded a permanent settlement on Kodiak Island. Other settlements followed, the coasts and parts of the interior were explored, and efforts were made to acquire the coast as far south as Spanish California.

The conquest of the southern steppes meanwhile proceeded slowly, sometimes with long pauses, but was finally completed in the eighteenth century with the annexation of the Crimea. Thereafter, the Caucasus region was taken over, followed by the conquest of Central Asia. The Soviet seizure of Afghanistan is merely a late phase in this process, under a new guise.

The methods utilized were as diverse as the course of the expansion. In the southern steppes, defence lines were developed to hold what had been gained or to provide bases for further advances. Fortified posts were established across Siberia and in Alaska. The cossacks, evolving from bands of fugitive serfs and border ruffians into free frontier communities, became an arm of the state for operations in the Kuban region, Siberia, and Central Asia. At need, to guard and colonize new areas, additional cossack hosts were formed. Bribery, trickery, treachery, and hostage-taking all appear repeatedly in the long chronicle of operations. The time-honoured method of "divide and rule" was employed, as in the setting of the Bashkirs and Kazakhs against one another, weakening both. Rebels were dealt with vigorously, but generous treatment was accorded after surrender. Thus the Caucasian leader Shamil was settled on an estate in the interior of Russia, on a pension. Other native chieftains were showered with presents and given trips to Moscow and St. Petersburg to impress them with Russian power, and their sons were educated at Russian military schools. Trade was sought not only for profit but as a means of gaining the adherence of native tribes. The church was helpful as a russifying medium, and non-Russians were accepted as equals if they were converted to Orthodoxy. Thus many old Russian noble families bore names derived from Tatar princelings who received lands and preferment upon conversion and change of their allegiance to Moscow.

Numerous reasons have been put forth for this expansion. It has been ascribed to innate qualities in the Russians such as an "age-old longing," lemming-like, to reach the sea, and a "tendency" towards migration and colonization. Some have laid it to the lust of individual rulers for power. Others have alleged special qualities in the participants themselves—tough, adventure-loving frontiersmen, always called by the unknown, and avid, like the conquistadores, for personal gain. Cultural factors have been suggested, such as a feeling of superiority, or a messianic drive to bring enlightenment to neighbouring, less-advanced peoples. The role of terrain has already been mentioned, facilitating the flow of traders, settlers, and the military along rivers and over great plains. Economic motives have been present in the quest for furs and the desire for trade. Private initiative, government policy, and pure chance have also been evident. Excluding the alleged innate qualities, it would appear that at one time or another all of these causes have been involved, reflecting the varied nature of the expansion involved.

The effects of this succession of frontiers upon the Russians and upon the peoples overrun have been as numerous and complex as the causes of the movement. Strategically, Russia gained buffers against neighbouring tribes and states, though usually each gain only led to yet another advance. Economically, Russia gained income for the present and resources for future generations. Thus Siberian furs were an important part of Muscovite state income and foreign trade, while the mineral wealth being used today lay undreamed of. Furs were the motive for the spread of Russian rule to North America, and the decline of the fur tade there was the principal reason why Russia abandoned her holdings. The conquest of Central Asia, accomplished at low cost, secured Russia a ready supply of cotton and the varied mineral wealth exploited in Soviet times.

Politically and socially, the effects of the frontier on Russia as a whole are more obscure, but existence of an open frontier over such a longer period may have held back internal development by draining off national energies which might otherwise have been directed toward the solution of internal problems. Within the community of nations the effect of empire on Spain may afford a parallel.

For the population on the frontier itself, some of the factors pointed out by Frederick Jackson Turner in his well-known essay on the influence of the frontier on American life may have been in operation. As in the United States and other countries with a similarly advancing line of conquest and settlement, the Russian frontier was the edge of the wave, "the meeting point between savagery and civilization", where social development was continually beginning again, amid primitive conditions. Born of isolation, a rude democracy developed, and populations evolved which were of a different stamp than their docile, down-trodden European Russian counterparts, sometimes inter-marrying with the native Finns, Buryats, Yakuts, Kamchadals, or other peoples; or, as in Siberia in the late pre-Revolutionary period, going so far as to develop separatist tendencies.

Upon the conquered peoples, the frontier imposed modern ways with a Russian flavour. Some resisted change, some were overwhelmed by it, all tried to select certain traits—not always the best—and reject others. In Imperial times the conquerors took up a Russian variant of "the white man's burden", rationalizing their intrusion by self-congratulation for the benefits bestowed. At first professedly critical, the Soviets later took over these ideas. The "conquest" restated as "annexation", was first declared to have been a "lesser evil" and then a positive good, a "progressive step" which established the Russian as the "elder brother" of the conquered peoples, who were placed under prolonged tutelage and protection.

To sum up, the complex history of the Russian frontier can reveal much about the country as a whole. Its study requires not only careful reconstruction of events, but close attention to methods, causes and effects. Generalization may help to set the course, but the diversity of the process makes it necessary to test hypotheses through detailed examination of specific regions and periods.

6 Southern Frontiers of Muscovy, 1550–1700

Denis J. B. Shaw

During the 1550s the Tatar khanates of Kazan' and Astrakhan' fell to Tsar Ivan the Terrible, opening the middle Volga region to Russian settlement and allowing penetration into Siberia. Yet the Crimean khanate, situated far to the south across the often waterless steppe, was to elude the Russian grasp for another two centuries. Such were the military skills of the nomadic steppe peoples, especially the Crimean and Nogay Tatars, that expansion and settlement in this direction were possible only in the context of appropriate military and defensive measures. These measures frequently meant that the Russian Government itself became intimately involved in the process of colonization.

Since the nineteenth century scholars of Russia's southern frontier have debated whether the state or the free movement of settlers played the primary role in Russia's southward expansion after 1500. A major participant in this debate was the Ukrainian scholar D. I. Bagaley (1857–1932) whose major thesis was that, while Ukrainian settlement in the south was largely free and spontaneous, that of the Great Russians was in essence state controlled. He wrote of the Great Russian settlement process:

And thus the government played an exceedingly important role in the colonization of the steppe frontier . . . it established and fortified the towns and villages, settled them with its servitors, provided the settlements with all things needful—with land and with sustenance, appointed their *voyevoda* (governor) and their local administration, and took an immediate interest in the agricultural and general economy. With full justification, therefore, it is possible to call the Great Russian colonization of the steppe frontier of Muscovy state colonization.

RUSSIAN HISTORICAL GEOGRAPHY VOL. 1
ISBN 0 12 081201 0

In conclusion, Bagaley emphasized "how little personal initiative or enter-prise remained to the local population" (Bagaley, 1887:131–132). Even in his own day Bagaley's thesis attracted criticism, focusing especially upon his misconception of the role of free settlers in the Great Russian movements, the product of the Ukrainian bias in his scholarship (for example, *Russkaya Mysl'*, 1887). In the present century many Soviet scholars have also been critical. To M. N. Tikhomirov, for instance, Bagaley's position was a "veritable anthem to the Tsarist administration" (Tikhomirov, 1962:420), while V. P. Zagorovskiy has characterized Bagaley's view as one which "abases the creative energies and abilities of the Russian people" (Zagorovskiy, 1969a:22).

The main argument of the present paper is that such generalizations as that of Bagaley and others are difficult to square with the complexity of the processes that were operative in the south over the 150-year period under consideration. For one thing, the very terms "colonization" and "settle-ment" require closer definition. Russia's southward expansion involved first the acquisition of territory, which meant the provision of security against outside threats, and secondly the actual peopling and settlement of the new territories. In both these processes both the government and the "free" individual played varying roles in different times and places. It is therefore the case that no neat model or generalization will accurately describe the state of affairs during this period. For ease of exposition, the colonization movements are here divided into a series of "frontiers". However, the divisions proposed are little more than broad guidelines adopted for con-venience. In reality, the frontiers coalesced and the process of settlement was both uneven and discontinuous.

One of the major hindrances to scholars of Russia in the period in question is that of sources. Many sources available to scholars of the nineteenth century are now either lost or buried in Soviet archives. Fortu-nately, however, a wealth of material has been published either by nineteenth-century archive commissions and local enthusiasts or, though less frequently, by the Soviets. Incomplete and inadequate as these materials often are, they are notable for their variety and complementary nature. Particularly important are the official materials compiled by the government and its officials, including the local *voyevody*, providing information on military works, preparations and supplies, settlement and landholding, taxation, general administration and economic activity (see, for example, Shaw, 1973). Such materials are supplemented by travel accounts and the works of Russian and Soviet scholars. In this way, a reasonably comprehen-sive picture can be constructed, though one which necessarily lacks the rigour which other historical periods and situations allow.

THE FOREST-STEPPE AND STEPPE IN THE SIXTEENTH CENTURY

In the sixteenth century the huge area lying south of the Oka valley and east of the valley of the Dnepr was still sparsely settled and the natural vegetation was thus relatively unaffected by permanent human settlement and agriculture. In the north that vegetation primarily consisted of broad-leaved forests, especially oak, with pine woodlands on the sandy river terraces (Fig. 6.1). Towards the south-east the forests were gradually superseded by a mixed landscape of oak woodlands, meadows and steppe grasslands. Beyond this zone, again to the south and south-east, there lay the more or less continuous feather grass steppe and finally, by the lower Volga, the semi-arid *polyn* steppe. This vegetational transition closely followed the diminishing availability of moisture. In detail, however, the natural vegetation was much affected by local environmental conditions. Thus, accord-

Fig. 6.1. Southern Muscovy and adjacent territories in the late sixteenth century.

ing to Dokuchayev (1940:198–199), forests had extended over much wider areas in former times, even as far south as the Black Sea. In the sixteenth century they were still to be found far to the south in river valleys, on sandy river terraces, on the steep valley sides of the Central Russian Uplands and the Volga Heights, and occasionally on higher watersheds. The Shipov Forest, on the high right bank of the Osered' River in the southern Voronezh Province, remains to this day. In 1599 the builders of Tsarevborisov, close to the confluence of the Oskol and Severskiy Donets Rivers in the steppe zone, utilized oak and pine to construct their palisades and buildings (Bagaley, 1886:5–13). Kirikov has listed some of the fairly extensive forested areas to be found in the central part of the forest-steppe zone in the following century (Kirikov, 1979:67–8).

   In similar fashion the steppe grasslands in the sixteenth century often extended far to the north. The steppe particularly characterized the watersheds which provided the natural routeways (*shlyakhi*) for Tatar incursions into Russia and Poland. Indications of its significance and extent derive from sixteenth century documents citing incidences of Tatar groups wintering close to Russian and Polish towns at this period (*Pamyatniki*, 1895: 377). Evidence also derives from lists of instructions to Russian guards and patrols to burn the steppe grasses as a defence against the Tatars (Kirikov, 1979:35–36). Even in the sixteenth century areas of steppe still existed in close proximity to such towns as Tula and Shatsk (Kirikov, 1979:65).

   Movement across the forest-steppe and steppe-lands was not difficult in the sixteenth century although severe winters, such as that of 1560–61 when numerous Tatars and their horses perished, naturally impeded mobility (Skazaniya, 1868:54). Available evidence seems to indicate that many more rivers were navigable than would be the case today (see, for example, Answers to the Academy of Sciences questionnaire in Veynberg, 1885–90, Vols. 15, 16), and the steppe nomads were certainly hindered in their wanderings by the necessity of crossing rivers only at well-defined points. This factor later influenced the defensive techniques employed by the Russians. The Russians for their part valued the southern lands because of their natural wealth. Hunting, fishing, fowling, and beekeeping had been practised in favourable locations from an early period. Permanent settlement was eventually encouraged by the natural fertility of the soils, the forest-steppe and steppe-lands largely coinciding with the humus-rich black earth (chernozem) soils. In the northern part of the region climate was in general no hindrance to agriculture, although the occasional drought precipitated harvest failure in certain years. Where the tough steppe grasses were discontinuous, as in river valleys or the lower slopes of valley sides, cultivation was relatively easy and in such locations agriculturalists also had the possibility of utilizing local meadows, haylands and forests. This situation, for example, was the case at Voronezh in 1615 (*TsGADA*, f 1209, d. 614, 2ff). Russian settlement also paid heed to local relief for reasons of defence. Thus the town of Voronezh was built in 1585 on the high right bank of the Voronezh River, with a commanding view over the Oka-Don plain to the east, while Korotoyak was constructed in 1647 in a "strong place" on the right bank of the Don, with a view of twenty *versty* to the east and fifteen to the south (*Stroyel'naya Kniga goroda Korotoyaka*, 1647).

The nomads who wandered across the steppe grasslands in the sixteenth century were descendants of the Tatars of the Golden Horde. By this period they had subdivided into numerous separate groups, the most significant being the Crimean Tatars, living on the Crimean peninsula and on the steppes to the north, and also the various groups belonging to the Lesser Nogay Horde, living on the southern and Volga steppes and in the Kuban. The Nogays were an off-shoot of the Greater Nogay Horde inhabiting areas to the east of the Volga. Most eventually fell into dependence upon the Crimean khan. Although the Tatars seem to have practised a certain amount of agriculture in some areas (Bagaley, 1887:73–74), their basic economy was pastoralism, supplemented by the fruits of trade and of plunder. A major objective of raids directed against settled agriculturalists was the capture of slaves who were then sold via the port of Kaffa on the Black Sea throughout the Middle East. While alternate raiding and trading had been an integral part of the life of the steppes for centuries, the assertion of Ottoman suzerainty over the Crimeans late in the fifteenth century added a new political dimension to the struggle on the steppes. Henceforward, this struggle formed part of the international competition between Russian and Turk, a competition complicated by the intervention of Kalmyks and other steppe peoples after 1600.

In the sixteenth century the sole supremacy of the Tatars over the steppes began to be challenged by the appearance of the cossacks. The cossacks may have originated as off-shoots of the Tatar hordes but by the middle of the sixteenth century the majority were Slavs who had fled to the steppes to escape economic and social distress in the dominions of the Tsar and of Poland. On the frontier the cossacks adopted the economy and life-style of the Tatars. Eventually, the most organized groups consolidated themselves as autonomous "Hosts", notably that at Zaporozh'ye on the lower Dnepr and a similar one on the lower Don. Numerous cossacks, however, lived an independent life in various parts of the steppe and the forest-steppe, and refused to acknowledge the authority of the Hosts. Some of them were recruited by the Tsars for military service and many took up residence in the frontier towns. At the same time the Tsars attempted to cultivate the political and military allegiance of the organized Hosts. However, the Tsars' policy was frequently frustrated by the lawlessness of these steppe peoples.

Thus when, in 1578, the Sultan and the Crimean khan demanded that the Tsar evacuate his cossacks from the steppe, the latter was obliged to explain that there were no "state cossacks" in the area, but only robbers and outlaws (Pronshteyn, 1967:171).

THE SOUTHERN FRONTIER IN 1550

With the gaining by Moscow of the lands lying to the west of the upper Oka at the end of the fifteenth century, and her final annexation of the Principality of Ryazan' in 1521, the whole of Russia's southern frontier came under a single political authority. Though long fortified by strong towns and military posts, the southern frontier area was still weakly settled in the middle of the sixteenth century. Nevertheless, by that stage settlement had already begun to creep southwards. Thus soon after 1500 the Oka itself ceased to be the southern defensive frontier of Muscovy with the fortifying of Tula between 1509 and 1521. By 1550, together with the other so-called "Ukrainian" (*Ukrainnyye*, literally "frontier") towns, Tula defended the most direct Tatar raiding routes into Muscovy. The less direct routes were guarded by other groups of fortified towns which flanked Tula to east and west. To the east, and protected by dense forests and by tributaries of the Don and Oka, were the Ryazan' towns, guarding the Tatar routes to eastern Muscovy and along the valley of the Tsna. To the west were the Zaotskiy towns, and to the south-west, in a very exposed position, stood the Severskiy towns and Putivl' (Fig. 6.2). Both of the latter groups of towns had formerly enjoyed semi-autonomy under the suzerainty of Lithuania (Bakay, 1892:7ff). They were protected from Tatar and from Polish incursions by extensive areas of forest and swamp (Platonov, 1898; Tikhomirov, 1962:370–414).

In view of the frontier character of the southern towns and their surrounding districts in the mid-sixteenth century, an important element of their populations consisted of state servitors who held areas of land from the Tsar in return for military and ancillary services. Already by this period a southward movement of people towards the frontier was taking place, partly in response to the opportunities in terms of land and service which the frontier provided. In the case of Tula, for example, the lesser servitor class, whose major duties consisted of guarding the walls and fortifications of the town and surrounding districts, formed an important constituent of the population (Chechulin, 1889:258 ff; Sokolova, 1975:13). The same was true of other towns. Outside the towns, in the Tula and Ryazan' districts, the population was largely formed by middle-ranking servitors, including junior boyars, holding small service landholdings (*pomest'ya*). Some larger

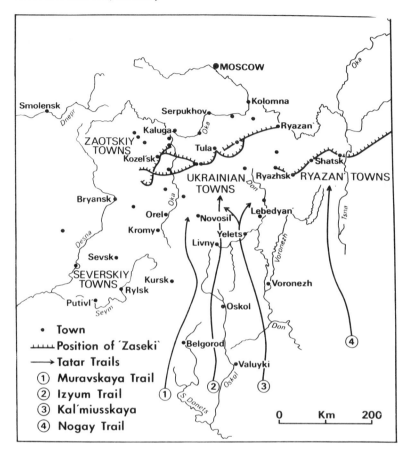

Fig. 6.2. Muscovy's southern frontier and the *zaseki* at the end of the
sixteenth century.

monastic estates were also be found and, well to the south, one or two large
hereditary estates (*votchiny*) in the hands of the higher nobility (Chermenskiy, 1917:43–81; Tikhomirov, 1962:380–381, 387–390, 395–397). In the
Zaotskiy and Severskiy areas, but especially in the former, larger hereditary
and monastic estates were more in evidence, though here also servitor
landholders predominated. *Pomest'ya* were often large but weakly settled
(Tikhomirov, 1962:374–375, 410–412).

By the middle of the century the frontier defensive system was becoming
very sophisticated. Linking the towns together, and taking full advantage of
such natural obstacles as rivers and areas of forest, were the *zaseki*, or
fortified lines, consisting of felled trees and supplemented by earthen ram-

parts and trenches. While the basic system in the 1560s stretched from Kozel'sk in the west by way of Tula to Ryazan' in the east, a distance of 300 *versty*, there is evidence for other lines to the north and the south (Margolin, 1948; Razin, 1955–61: Vol. 2, 342; Nikitin, 1965:116–213). Their actual disposition, however, probably varied through time (Fig. 6.2); see, for example, Yakovlev (1916), for their positions in 1638. The *zaseki* were designed not merely to cut off the major Tatar routes into Muscovy but also any alternative paths. Manning was undertaken by the local servitors and more especially by the large cavalry armies of the middle class of servitors which gathered in the south each summer. Down to 1598 these armies were divided into two: those "on the bank" (i.e. of the Oka), and those "beyond the river" guarding the Tatar routes and *zaseki* further south (Novosel'skiy, 1948:66).

The armies of servitors along the *zaseka* system could only be really effective against the hit-and-run techniques of the Tatars if they were provided with early warning of possible attacks. This end was served by the system of guard posts and frontier patrols which dated back to the four-teenth century (Belyayev, 1846). The guard posts were situated some four to five days' journey to the south of the frontier towns and perhaps ten to twelve kilometres apart. They were manned by six to ten guards, often recruited from the cossacks or even from Tatars who had entered the Tsar's service. The guards were required to conduct regular sorties within a defined zone. The frontier patrols were posses of servitors and cossacks who, at regular intervals, set out from the towns and followed pre-determined routes before returning to base. The whole purpose of this system was to give advanced warning to the frontier towns and their populations of the approach of Tatar raiders. Patrols and guards were generally operative from early spring until the beginnings of heavy snow.

ADVANCE AND RETREAT, 1550–1613

Such threats to Russian security as the Tatar attack on Tula in 1552 acted as a spur to the more careful regulation of defence on the frontier. However, the building of new *zaseki*, the fortification of already existing towns, and the founding of certain new ones such as Orel in 1566, soon proved inadequate. The Tatar-Turkish attack on Astrakhan in 1569, followed by the sack of Moscow itself by the Tatars two years later, prodded the Russian Government to more decisive action. The system of frontier guard posts and patrols was thoroughly overhauled under Prince M. I. Vorotynskiy, a sys-tem of "state" guard posts was inaugurated, and the burning of the steppe grasses, designed to deny provender to the Tatars' horses, was carried out on a more systematic basis.

Not until the end of the exhausting Livonian War (1558–83) was the Russian Government prepared to adopt further measures. These included the building of a series of towns to threaten the three Tatar routes—the Muravskaya, the Izyumskaya, and the Kal'miusskaya—which ran along the watersheds between the valleys of the Donets, Oskol, Don, Voronezh, and Tsna, and penetrated the gap between the Severskiy towns to the west and the open Volga steppes to the east (Fig. 6.2). Two of these towns—Livny, fortifying the Bystraya Sosna, and Voronezh, close to the Voronezh River's confluence with the Don—were completed in 1585. With another Tatar attack on Moscow in 1591, Boris Godunov resolved to strengthen these southern outposts by completing Yelets (1592) on the Bystraya Sosna, securing the Oskol valley through the foundation of (Staryy) Oskol (1596) and Valuyki (1599), and overawing the Muravskaya route by building Kursk and Belgorod (both 1596). Finally, way to the south, Tsarevborisov was constructed in 1599 (Zagorovskiy, 1969a:24–25).

This official policy of advance was much encouraged by the incidence of peasant flight to the frontier which seems to have increased in the latter part of the sixteenth century. This factor has already been alluded to as the origin of the cossacks. A document of 1570, for example, refers to "Oskol cossacks" many years before the founding of that town (*Razryadnaya Kniga*, 1966:234). Zagorovskiy has shown that Voronezh in 1585 was soon populated by servitors who had formerly been local cossacks or runaway serfs (Zagorovskiy, 1968:22–23), and the builders of Tsarevborisov in 1599 were instructed to invite the "Donets and Oskol cossacks" into the service of the Tsar (Bagaley, 1886: No. II, 10). There seems little reason to doubt that the more northerly of the new towns, such as Livny and Yelets, were quickly settled by volunteer cossacks, runaways, and also the sons or relatives of already-established servitors living further north. The more exposed towns, such as Valuyki and Tsarevborisov, were much slower to develop.

The documentation on the new southern towns in the late sixteenth century is sparse (but see Anpilogov, 1967, for one collection), but several cadastres and related materials date from the early years of the following century (see, for example, Veynberg and Poltoratskaya, 1891; Miklashevskiy, 1894:103–109). From these it is clear that the overwhelming population of the new southern towns and their districts (*uyezdy*) consisted of servitors. In and immediately around the towns lived the lesser, "contract" servitors, whose duties primarily consisted of manning the walls and fortifications of the towns themselves. Such servitors, as well as being agriculturalists, frequently engaged in trading and handicrafts since, unlike the older and more northerly towns, the southern towns possessed few traders (*posadskiye lyudi*) at this period. The middle-ranking servitors generally lived in villages in the districts and included junior boyars (*deti boyarskiye*) and higher-ranking cossacks. Almost all servitors held only relatively small areas of land and few had more than a handful of serfs. A striking feature of this new frontier is the number of servitors who possessed no serfs, and who therefore cultivated their lands by their own labour and by that of their families alone. With one or two exceptions in the more northerly districts such as Yelets and Lebedyan' there was a complete absence of larger estates, and in the most exposed towns such as Valuyki the middle class of servitors was also lacking (Veynberg and Poltoratskaya, 1891:143–185; Sokolova, 1975). Numbers of serfs were to be found on small estates belonging to the few frontier monasteries, such as Uspenskiy in Voronezh and Borshchev on the Don below Voronezh, while Belgorod district contained several villages of crown peasants belonging to the extensive Komaritskiy *volost'* (i.e. an area inhabited by crown or state peasants) which had developed in the Severskiy area (Zagorovskiy, 1969a:45–46). But these were relatively minor exceptions in a sparsely peopled landscape of small-scale land tenure.

   The so-called "Time of Troubles", ushered in by the seventeenth century, was a time of retreat for the new frontier. Tsarevborisov disappeared completely at some undisclosed date, and much damage was wrought by cossacks and Tatars (Zagorovskiy, 1969a:25; Kargalov, 1974:167–168). The 1615 cadastre for Voronezh lists several settlements damaged or destroyed by the cossack leader Ivan Zarutskiy (Veynberg and Poltoratskaya, 1891:119). Even after the accession of Michael Romanov to the throne in 1613, the disruption continued for several years. In 1617 Oskol was burnt by the Poles, and in 1618 the towns of Livny, Yelets, and Lebedyan' were sacked by the Hetman Sagaidachniy, leader of the Dnepr cossacks. But under the more settled conditions introduced by the Romanov dynasty, frontier advance was to continue in a gradual, if not unfaltering, manner.

THE SOUTH-CENTRAL FRONTIER AND THE BELGOROD
LINE, 1613–1658

Peace with Poland and Sweden in 1618 and improved relations with the Crimean Tatars brought Russia a relatively less troubled period on her southern frontier. Documents of the 1620s (for example, the cadastres for Voronezh in 1615 and 1629, and that for Valuyki in 1626) testify to the gradual, if unspectacular settlement then taking place around the frontier towns (Veynberg and Poltoratskaya, 1891). The progress of settlement was undoubtedly more rapid in more secure regions. However, the re-opening of hostilities with Poland in 1632 brought devastating Tatar raids in succeeding years as the Crimean khan sought to take advantage of this situation. According to Zagorovskiy (1969a:73), the Russian response was at first conservative, not wishing to undertake the expense of a whole new defensive frontier and preferring to fortify the *zaseka* line in the traditional manner. Nevertheless, the building of the town of Kozlov and an earthen rampart to seal off the so-called Nogay trail (*shlyakh*) between the rivers Voronezh and Tsna in 1635–36, became the signal for similar treatment to be applied to the other trails or routes used by the Tatars on their raids. Down to 1645, eleven fortified towns and defensive networks were constructed—Kozlov 1635, Bel'skiy 1636, Chelnovoy 1636, Yablonov 1637, Userd 1637, Korocha 1638, Khotmyzhsk 1640, Vol'nyy 1640, Kostensk 1642, Ol'shansk 1644, and Usman' 1645. However, the severe Tatar raids of the early 1640s proved the inadequacy of these measures and led to more decisive action, especially after the accession of Tsar Alexis in 1645. In the next few years a further eleven fortified towns were built and the remaining gaps between defensive works ramparts and forests were plugged (i.e. Karpov 1646, Bolkhovets 1646, Orlov 1646, Novyy Oskol 1647, Korotoyak 1647, Verkhososensk 1647, Dobryy 1647, Sokol'sk 1647, Uryv 1648, Ostrogozhsk 1652, Nezhegol'sk 1654). By the mid-1650s a continuous fortified line ran through the forest-steppe lands from the upper Vorskla valley in the west to the basin of the Tsna in the east, a distance of some 800 kilometres (Zagorovskiy, 1968:3; Fig. 6.3).

As in the previous century, government policies were greatly aided by the fact of peasant flight to the frontier, which seems to have become even more important during stable periods such as the 1620s and later 1630s (Novosel'skiy, 1948:161–166). The government also recruited among the cossacks. In the case of many southern towns there are extant decrees inviting local "free people" into the service of the Tsar (e.g. Vtorov and Aleksandrov-Dol'nik, 1851: no. 37; Veynberg and Poltoratskaya, 1887:35, 99, 113, etc.). But in several places along the Belgorod Line the government seems to have had great difficulty in attracting any settlers at all. This was true of such vulnerable towns as Yablonov, Userd, Korocha, Verkhososensk, Novyy Oskol, and Korotoyak. In these cases the state now resorted to the compulsory settlement of servitors from districts lying further to the north. The 1630s and 1640s also witnessed much greater social mobility in the south than was characteristic of earlier or later frontiers. Entrance into the ranks of the junior boyars by "free" people and others seems to have been comparatively easy at this period. No doubt this was because of the lack of members of the middle servitor class ready to settle in the more vulnerable regions—the lesser servitors were now in the van of the colonization movement. Many southern servitors at this period lost their serfs, as these ran away to join the ranks of servitors in the newer towns (Shaw, 1977:114 footnote 1; see also Bagaley, 1890: no. 13, 49–74, for numbers of serf-owners settling at Karpov in 1648).

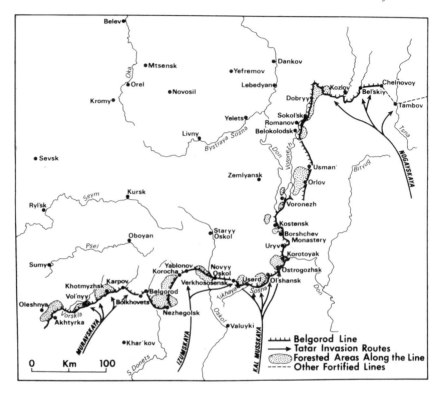

Fig. 6.3. The Belgorod Line in the mid-seventeenth century.

In order to settle and to defend its new frontier, the government resorted to some rather uncharacteristic policies at this period. A decree of 1637 listed twelve southern towns and districts where higher-ranking (i.e. "Moscow" ranks) servitors were forbidden to have land (*Ukaznaya Kniga*, 1889). This measure was no doubt designed to preserve the land along the line for occupation by the lesser and middle-ranking servitors who were the backbone of the defensive system. Then, as part of its policy of recruiting new regiments to guard the frontier, the government also resorted to the "militarization" of some of the few estates of peasants then to be found in the south. This happened in the 1640s to the crown peasants of Komaritskiy *volost'* north of Belgorod, and to various hereditary and monastic estates situated on the upper Voronezh and its tributaries. The peasants in question retained their land but were henceforth to serve as dragoons. The effect of these policies was to reinforce further the pattern of small-scale service tenure which was already characteristic of this frontier in the early seventeenth century.

Russia's southern frontier formed the setting for the initial formation of Russia's new army which appeared in the middle years of the century (Hellie, 1971). From 1646 the armies of cavalry which had previously met on the Oka and the northern *zaseki* each summer began to gather on the Belgorod Line instead. These armies were soon augmented by regiments of dragoons, cavalrymen, and infantrymen (*soldaty*) which the government began to recruit among the southern peasants, cossacks and the families of servitors from the late 1640s. At first it would seem that the government intended these regiments to form a permanent standing army but the expense quickly proved prohibitive. In the south many of the soldiers and other formations were soon granted land in the traditional manner. In 1658 the new regiments, which included many of the traditional servitors, were formed into a unified Belgorod Regiment under the control of the *voyevoda* of Belgorod. Henceforth, his military and civil jurisdiction embraced much of the south which now became known as the Belgorod Military District (*Belgorodskiy razryad*).

Despite the completion of the Belgorod Line in the 1650s, large regions behind the line were not settled until the latter part of the century. This gradual settlement stands in marked contrast to the western part of the line itself which was rapidly colonized and soon proved obsolete as a military entity. The reason for this situation was the Ukrainian colonization movement which began in earnest in the 1640s.

THE SOUTH-WEST FRONTIER AND THE SLOBODSKAYA UKRAINA, 1638–1700

The mass migration of Ukrainians or Little Russians into the southern frontier area was a product of the religious and social problems of the Polish territories which they had previously inhabited. Religious persecution, enserfment and increasing government control were grave causes of resentment on the part of the Ukrainian cossack agriculturalists and peasants of the forest-steppe fringes, as well as the freebooting Zaporozh'ye cossacks of the open steppe. The Ukrainian cossacks, or *Cherkasy*, had been active on the Russian frontier since the sixteenth century and were to be found among the builders of Tsarevborisov in 1599 (Bagaley, 1886:5; Apanovich, 1954). The first mass migration occurred in 1638 when a party of *Cherkasy* settled at Chuguyev south of Belgorod. In the 1640s and 1650s they were settling as servitors along the Belgorod Line in such towns as Ostrogozhsk and Korotoyak. Their numbers were soon augmented by mass migrations in the wake of the Ukrainian uprising of Bogdan Khmel'nitskiy beginning in 1648, and the Russo-Polish War over the Ukraine which began in 1654. At first the Ukrainians were settled on the land on the same basis as the

Russians and served the Tsar in the normal way. Soon, however, so desirous did the Russian Government become of peopling its southern frontier that it began to grant special privileges to the new settlers.

The settlement of Ukrainians at Chuguyev in 1638 was the first step in the peopling of the vulnerable forest-steppe lands to the south of the Belgorod Line. No doubt the government decided to agree to this measure because of the defensible nature of these forest-steppe lands and because of its need for significant areas of land on which to establish the large influx of Ukrainian settlers. Though the settlement at Chuguyev was not entirely successful, from the 1650s, with the founding of Sumy in 1652 and Khar'kov in 1656, and the reoccupation of Tsarevborisov in 1654, the colonization of the area which became known as Slobodskaya Ukraina began in earnest (Fig. 6.4).

A number of features help to distinguish the Ukrainian colonization movement from that of the Great Russians at this period. Among the privileges that the Ukrainians enjoyed, those of free trade and of the free distillation of liquor applied to many towns and districts and turned the Ukrainians into major traders, often to the disadvantage of the Great Russians. Morover, in Slobodskaya Ukraina particularly, there soon developed systems of land holding which were rather different from those of the Great Russian towns. Whereas in the latter the amount of service land held

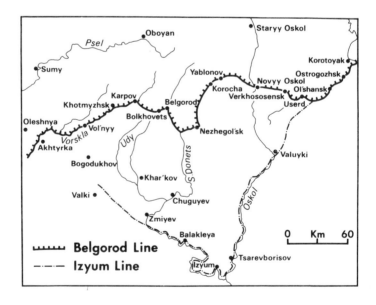

Fig. 6.4. Slobodskaya Ukraine in the late seventeenth century.

by each servitor or group of servitors was generally strictly limited according to a scale of norms and surveyed and recorded in *chetverty* (one *chetvert* = 0.546 hectare), the Ukrainians brought with them the cossack tradition of tilling the land "wheresover each wishes" (*gde khto pokhochet pakhat'*). This tradition of individual or small group tillage in the wild waste (*dikoye pole*), of claiming "intakes (*zaimki*) wherever the *Cherkasy* had a mind, often led to the establishment of fairly large holdings in the hands of individuals. It also produced a more uneven and irregular pattern of farming than that typical of the Great Russian towns. Later on, however, as land became scarcer, the pattern of land holdings became more and more like that of the Russians and, according to Vazhinskiy (1974:ch. 3, 4), often the only difference was that the *zaimki* were not surveyed and recorded in *chetvert*.

The *Cherkasy* on the frontier brought with them a further tradition which distinguished them from the Great Russians—that of cossack administration. In the south they were settled in five cossack regiments—the Ostrogozhsk, Sumy, Khar'kov, Akhtyrka, and Izyum—and enjoyed a limited autonomy from Moscow and its *voyevody* and a certain degree of official, internal democracy. Bagaley postulates that the two systems of administration in the south (the Great Russian with its *voyevody* and the cossack) and the two forms of colonization (the Russian state colonization, and the Ukrainian free colonization with its privileges) often led to conflict between settlers and between them and the government. However, the antiposing of Ukrainian and Russian settlement in this way is almost certainly an oversimplification and often even forms of administration were probably not very different in practice.

In view of the exposed position of the Slobodskaya Ukraina, it is hardly surprising that, as it developed, it suffered from the full onslaught of Tatar raiding. Especially severe were the raids of 1680 and 1691 when large numbers of people were taken or died and much livestock was lost (Bagaley, 1886:84–93, 157–163; 1890:92–101). By the late 1670s, when the Ukrainian settlement was reaching the outer reaches of the forest-steppe zone, it was becoming clear that a new defensive line was required. This, the Izyum Line, was largely built and settled by both Russians and by the *Cherkasy* themselves and was completed in the early 1680s (Zagorovskiy, 1980:ch. 1–2). It formed a triangle, south of Belgorod and the Belgorod Line, and followed the valleys of the Severskiy Donets and the Oskol, thus guarding the heart of Slobodskaya Ukraina (Fig. 6.4). However even this line quickly proved inadequate as the *Cherkasy* and others continued to spread south and east. This successful movement is testimony to the growing power of the agriculturalist over his nomadic adversary.

THE VOLGA BASIN AND THE SOUTH-EAST FRONTIER, 1552–1654

Ivan the Terrible's conquest of Kazan' in 1552 and of Astrakhan four years later established Russia's hold over the entire length of the Volga. But for over a century that hold remained tenuous. The reason for this state of affairs lay in the constant menace posed by the Nogay Tatars, occupying the steppes both to the east and west of the river, aided on occasions by other warlike groups such as the Kalmyks and the Bashkirs. Hardly less troublesome were the Volga cossacks who were active from the sixteenth century. Unlike their cousins of the Don and Dnepr, these cossacks had no organized Host. They included many unruly elements, and frequently harried Russian communications or complicated the Tsar's relations with the Tatars and Turks. In the period 1606–7 during the Time of Troubles, and again under Stepan Razin's leadership (1667–71) the Volga cossacks played a leading role in the rebellions against Moscow's rule.

Russia's policy on the Volga at first took the traditional form of organizing patrols and guard posts to look for Tatar movements and threats to the Russian lines of communication along the Volga and across the steppes. The guard posts and patrols were especially designed to keep an eye on places where the Tatars were able to cross the river, and the system was reorganized and improved under Prince Vorotynskiy in the 1570s (Osipov, 1976:11). In the late 1580s, in accordance with the more aggressive southern policy adopted by the government of Fedor Ivanovich and his minister Boris Godunov, the defence of the Volga was further enhanced. In 1586 the construction of Samara was begun where the Volga turns sharply to the east, and in 1588 Tsaritsyn was built close to a major Tatar fording place. These measures were completed by the building of Saratov in 1590 (Osipov, 1976:14–19). For many decades, the three 'lower towns' led a marginal and precarious existence on the very edge of the Russian domain. Their servitors seem to have been provisioned from afar because of the difficulty or even impossibility of local agriculture in a situation of continuing insecurity. However, the inhabitants did raise cattle and the towns played a notable role in trade along the Volga and with the nomads of the steppe (Osipov, 1976:25–36).

The gradual Russian settlement of the middle and lower reaches of the Volga began soon after the conquest of Kazan'. A significant feature of this settlement frontier was the role played by non-Slav peoples—the Tatars, Chuvash, Mordva, and others. In part this movement was encouraged by the displacement of Tatars and others from lands in the old Kazan' khanate after the Russian conquest (Gritsenko, 1948:15ff; Smith, 1977:202–203). In part it was also furthered by the willingness of the Tsarist Government to accept the settlement of Christianized non-Russians as servitors on the frontier on the same terms as its own people. From the middle of the sixteenth century settlers from districts to the north and north-west began to take up lands on a *pomest'ye* basis on the west bank of the middle Volga (Peretyatkovich, 1882:22–70). Many of these settlers owned serfs and belonged to the middle class of servitors. An important role was also played by the monasteries which possessed fishing and hunting rights along the Volga from an early period and gradually occupied estates in the area (Peretyatkovich, 1882:67–72). Settlement was protected by fortified towns such as Vasil'sursk (1522), Sviyazhsk (1551), Cheboksary (before 1553), Tetyushi (1574) and Tsyvil'sk (1590) (Fig. 6.5). Though *zaseki* were also constructed, their exact disposition is now difficult to trace. That along the River Sviyaga, however, played an important role in guarding the Tetyushi area which was settled from the 1590s (Zertsalov, 1896:51–52; Gritsenko, 1948:16–17).

As on other parts of the southern frontier, the Time of Troubles proved to

Fig. 6.5. The settlement of the Volga basin and the Simbirsk Line.

be a major setback to the colonization of the middle Volga. But the return of a more stable period in the 1620s witnessed a revival of activity with many districts such as those near Tetyushi and Cheboksary being rapidly occupied at this time (Peretyatkovich, 1882:67–72). There is also evidence of the occupation of the less-protected lands to the south and south-west and also the establishment of claims to hunting and fishing rights (Peretyatkovich, 1882:71–72; *Nizhegorodskiye*, 1848 no. 7; *Deystviya*, 1905; Zertsalov, 1900: nos. 1, 2). Eventually, with the continuing settlement of lands to the west of the Volga, the government felt able to take more decisive defensive measures, spurred on by the nomad raids of the 1630s and 1640s. The building of Kozlov in 1635 was rapidly followed by that of Tambov on the Tsna in 1636. The area was quickly settled by servitors, especially migrants from the Ryazan' towns such as Ryazhsk and Shatsk, and also by Tatars (Chermenskiy, 1911; Shvetsova, 1966). A significant role in the settlement of this region was additionally played by court peasants who inhabited Verkhososensk *volost'* in the northern part of the Tambov district (*Pistsovaya kniga*, 1890; *O vladeniyakh*, 1893).

In the late 1640s the government resolved to augment the fortification of the west bank of the Volga by extending the newly completed Belgorod Line to the east. This extension, the so-called Simbirsk Line, was constructed in several sections between 1647 and 1654 and ran from Tambov on the west and by way of Nizhniy and Verkhniy Lomov, Insar, Saransk, Karsun, Tagay and Yushansk (Peretyatkovich, 1882:73–78; Vereshchalin, 1968:12 ff.). Its terminal point, Simbirsk on the Volga, was completed in 1648. Documents of the period describe the settling of the line. Thus the town of Karsun, built in 1647, was settled by servitors from Kumysh, including serving Tatars (Zertsalov, 1900; nos. 7, 8, 11, 12). Non-Russians also constituted an important element among the settlers at Insar (Kalachov, 1855). The government seems to have resorted to compulsory colonization among many sections of the new line, a policy it returned to once more in the construction of the Kama Line on the opposite bank of the Volga during the 1650s (Peretyatkovich, 1882:251 ff.; Gritsenko, 1948:26ff.).

The frontier on the Volga was thus characterized by a much wider variety of settlers than those who colonized the regions to the west. Servitors of differing races and statuses, peasants, monastic dependents, cossacks, and others were involved. Unlike the Belgorod Line, the incidence of middle-ranking servitors losing all their serfs through flight seems to have been less common in this region. The reason for this may have been the larger pool of potential settlers, including the non-Russian peoples, available to the government. This reduced the opportunities available to peasants contemplating fleeing from their masters in order to enrol as servitors in new towns and districts.

THE FRONTIER IN THE SECOND HALF OF THE SEVENTEENTH CENTURY

The completion of the Belgorod and Simbirsk Lines greatly enhanced the security of the lands lying to their north. Henceforth, the incidence of Tatar raiding into the heart of Muscovy was greatly diminished (but see Vtorov and Aleksandrov-Dol'nik, 1952:146; De-Pule, 1861; Bagaley, 1886:84–93, 157–163; 1890:91–101; Zagorovskiy, 1969a:278–281). Moreover, the large territories lying to the north of the lines which still awaited settlement now appeared particularly attractive, especially to the wealthier lords with large numbers of serfs. Thus, after the completion of the Simbirsk Line, lands along the now disused Tetyushi *zaseka* were distributed among wealthier servitors from Tetyushi, Kazan' and even Moscow (Peretyatkovich, 1882:187–189). North of the Belgorod Line a decree of 1672 opened areas such as Dankov district to settlement by higher-ranking servitors and their serfs (Zagorovskiy, 1969b:600 ff.). As already noted, such servitors had been forbidden to acquire southern estates since the 1630s, but colonization by higher-ranking servitors now became more common. An added feature of the latter half of the seventeenth century was the settlement of other areas north of the Belgorod Line by the lower-class servitors who had formerly inhabited only the towns. In view of the fact that the garrisons of many towns along the line had now reached their full complement, such servitors were now granted lands further from the frontier towns, and frequently settled such lands in groups. Thus, such districts as Zemlyansk, Nizhnedevitsk, and Zadonsk, to the north and north-west of Voronezh, were settled from the 1650s by lower-class servitors from Voronezh, Yelets, Dankov, and other towns. (See Germanov, 1857; Tserkvi, 1886). In this way the former sharp social distinctions between the lower servitor class and the middle-ranking junior boyars became less marked in this region.

South of the lines settlement continued to be a risky venture until the very end of the seventeenth century. Mention has already been made of the difficulties of settling the Slobodskaya Ukraina, but there at least the *Cherkasy* were protected by forested land. Further to the east, where the open steppe lands swept far to the north, the southward drift of settlement was hindered until much later. In the Voronezh region, for example, occasional settlements appearing south of the Belgorod Line in the 1660s and 1670s seem to have had a short life (Zagorovskiy, 1969b:526 ff.). And although the government pondered the building of a further defensive line along the Bityug in the 1680s, it seems to have had second thoughts because of security problems and possibly also because of the hostile attitude of the local cossacks (Bagaley, 1890:107–8, 116; Zagorovskiy, 1969b:39–40). This conservative policy continued in force until the 1690s. By this period the further weakening of the Tatars, promoted by Peter the Great's campaign on the lower Don in 1696, and the beginnings of an influx of *Cherkasy* from Slobodskaya Ukraina heralded the commencement of official settlement south of the line. Under Peter, a network of fortified towns and forts soon appeared and settlement began to take a variety of forms, including the establishment of larger estates. At the beginning of the eighteenth century the cossacks of the upper Don were forced to evacuate their lands in favour of the newer settlers (*Akty*, 1891: no. 123).

Along the Simbirsk Line the settlement process accelerated in the latter half of the seventeenth century. The cadastre of Podgorodnyy *stan* (subdivision of the district) in Karsun district (1672) described Mordva settlers in villages and hamlets paying tribute (*yasak*) and quitrent (*obrok*) from fishing and hunting rights and also arable lands at this period (Vereshchalin, 1968; no. 12, 31–33). A fuller description of payments from arable and other properties made by Russian, Tatar, Mordva and Chuvash settlers is to be found in the income and expenditure books for Simbirsk and its district in 1667 (Zertsalov, 1896:44 ff.). Official documents also describe the crown holdings and the significant monastic estates which appeared in this period (Zertsalov, 1890: nos. 13–1683, 14–1647, 21–1690, 23–1688, 26–1697). Simbirsk, which was the major town of the region, had a mixed population including traders, state craftsmen and dependent people (*Opis*, 1902). Like the servitors, these people paid taxes and were obliged to undertake various duties for the state.

Settlement south of the Simbirsk Line seems to have begun at an earlier period than in the case of the central and eastern parts of the Belgorod Line, possibly because relief and forests provided greater protection in some parts of this region. Servitors appear to have been occupying suitable lands, especially those along the rivers, from the 1650s. Eventually, the government resorted to further defensive measures in this region, constructing Penza in 1670 and linking it by *zaseki* to the older line to the north. In the 1680s a new defensive line was constructed to join Penza with the town of Syzran' on the right bank of the Volga (Kalachov, 1855:69; Peretyatkovich, 1882:233–4, 237–40; Osipov, 1976:64–70; Fig. 6.5). Settlers came from the Simbirsk Line, from northern towns such as Shatsk, and also from the Voronezh region. Even further south settlement was simultaneously encouraged by the presence of the fortified towns along the Volga. Samara, for example, provided protection for the Samara bend region which was colonized from an early period. In 1647, this area and adjacent lands included estates belonging to the Moscow patriarch, the crown, and several lords (Peretyatkovich, 1882:228–231). There were also many non-Russian landholders, and the non-Russians were among the first to colonize the western portions of Samara district in the 1650s (Peretyatkovich, 1882:228–231, 233–240).

Further south, in the Saratov district, gradual settlement occurred from the middle of the seventeenth century, in spite of continuing Tatar and Kalmyk raids and the disruption caused by cossack disturbances. Here again, initial settlement was by non-Russian elements, some of whom obtained servitor status, and by cossacks and runaway serfs. Towards the end of the century, lands along the Sura, Medveditsa, and other rivers were being taken up by these peoples (*Akty istoricheskiye*, 1841–12: no. 32, 110; *Materialy dlya istorii*, 1890:259–269, 270–274; *Materialy po istorii*, 1883: no. 3; 1889–90: nos. 1, 2; 1890: nos. 1, 2; Osipov, 1976:60 ff.) In the course of time, wealthier serf-holders, soldiers, monasteries, and Old Believers were also granted lands here, and there were many instances of compulsory colonization by servitors from lines to the north (Osipov, 1976:70 ff.) Protection was provided by such fortified points as Petrovsk on the Medveditsa and Kamyshin on the Volga (*Izvestiya*, 1883: nos. 4, 5). In the early years of the following century the government began to construct yet a further defensive line in the area of Tsaritsyn.

CONCLUSIONS

During the century and a half which forms the focus of this paper, the tide of Russian settlement flowed over extensive regions of the European forest-steppe and steppe, regions which had previously known only the wanderings of nomadic Tatars and cossacks. By the end of the seventeenth century, many new towns and villages had been established, a series of defensive lines had been constructed, tillage had expanded southwards on to hitherto virgin soil, and important modifications had been made to the natural flora. Historians have pondered the origins of this successful conquest of the frontier lands. To the pre-revolutionary scholar, the natural assertiveness and hardiness of the frontier settler, and the defensive organization of the state, were major sources of success (Bagaley, 1887:131–132; Platonov, 1898). Soviet historians, on the other hand, with their broader economic and social perspective, have pointed to the internal dynamics of Russian feudalism, to the enserfment of the peasantry and its consequent propensity to flee to the freedom of the frontier, and to the pretensions of Russian lords, with their extensive agricultural economies, to the fertile soils of the new lands (Vazhinskiy, 1974:45 ff.; see also, Hellie, 1971:174, 352 n. 57). While the latter viewpoint has much to commend it, a judicious assessment would also underline other factors operating to ensure the success of Russian settlement. The declining military effectiveness of the Tatars, for example, was a major contributing process. This military decline was in part the product of the growing organization and superior equipment of Russia's own military forces, but in part also of internal squabbling in the Crimean khanate and the Nogay hordes. It is also necessary to modify the Marxist interpretation of frontier settlement in certain respects. Thus flight by peasants to the southern frontier, at least in the sixteenth century, was encouraged as much by Russia's internal, economic and social upheavals as by the heavy hand of the serf-owner. And although lordly pretensions to fertile southern lands certainly shared some part in the settlement of the forest-steppe and steppe, over large parts of the frontier this factor did not play a significant role until the eighteenth century. For many decades, it was the cossacks, the refugees and the minor servitors who constituted the "outer edge of the wave" (Turner, 1966:2). In pursuit of its defensive policy along the Belgorod Line, the Tsarist Government was even prepared to deny the frontier lands to the wealthier lords and servitors.

Over the long period from the middle of the sixteenth century until the dawn of the eighteenth, the attitude of the Tsarist Government towards the frontier underwent many fluctuations. There seems, however, to have been a number of fairly constant priorities in the minds of the authorities. Alarmed by the incidence of peasant desertion from central estates, the government felt the need to attempt to regulate migration and settlement, lest depopulation in the centre should lead to impoverishment. By administering and defending the southern frontier, the government's control over such forces would be enhanced. Flight to the frontier also provided the authorities with an excellent opportunity to seize the forest-steppe and steppe-lands with their promise of revenue, and to defend the state against the depredations of the nomads. There is no doubt at all that in the late sixteenth century, and again in the 1630s and 1640s, defence was an overriding consideration in the official mind. In the 1640s especially, the government showed itself ready to go to great lengths to settle and defend its new frontier lines.

The instrument which the Tsarist authorities utilized to control the settlement process lay in the monopoly over land. Land was vested in the Tsar, title to land could only be granted in his name, and the granting of that title almost always carried with it the condition of service to the sovereign, as well as the obligation to pay dues and to render other duties. The most common type of service on the southern frontier was military service, but service of a broader type was such an integral feature of the society that it was also demanded of non-servitors—of merchants and town dwellers, monastic and court peasants, and others. In this way the state attempted to ensure the greatest possible control over the frontier region. That control was exercised by way of the towns, the most obvious visual expression of Tsarist authority in the south. The frontier towns were, to use McGee's (1964:172) term, "replica towns". That is to say, both in their morphology and institutional structure, they imitated older towns in the centre of the country. They therefore sought, on the frontier, to recreate the image of Tsarist power and authority which central towns appeared to proclaim. The frontier towns were defensive nodes for the southern settlers, and were the points from which much of the economic and social life of the frontier radiated (Shaw, 1977:109–114).

While the authorities thus sought to administer the frontier, their control was at best incomplete. The frontier's tendency, in Turner's words (1966:14), "is anti-social. It produces antipathy to control, and particularly to any direct control." Such antipathy characterized the Russian frontier, as it did the American. The southern frontier was marked by a turbulence which sometimes affected even the towns and their servitors (see, for example, Zagorovskiy, 1969a:253–276). Away from the towns the control of the state quickly diminished. Tatars, cossacks, religious heretics, political exiles, foreigners, outlaws, refugees, all contributed to an unsettled state. The defensive line was a physical expression of the desire of the authorities to minimize this problem. That desire was never completely satisfied.

The settlement of the southern frontier was therefore a complex procedure, involving many different elements and processes. Sometimes the government played a leading role, more often it was itself led. Everywhere it sought to imprint its authority and control. Nowhere, as long as frontier conditions prevailed, was it completely successful. Nevertheless, in the long run, the settlement of the south worked to Moscow's advantage. That success is testimony to the flexibility and opportunism of successive Tsarist governments over this period.

REFERENCES

Akty istoricheskiye, Vol. 4, St. Petersburg (1841–42).
Akty otnosyashchiyesya k istorii Voyska Donskogo, Vol. 1, Novocherkassk (1891).
Anpilogov, G. N., (1967). "Novyye dokumenty o Rossii kontsa XVI—nachala XVII veka", Moscow.
Apanovich, Ye. M., (1954). Pereseleniye ukraintsev v Rossiyu nakanunye osvoboditel'noy voyny, *In* "Vossoyedineniye Ukrainy s Rossiyey", pp. 78–104, Moscow.
Bagaley, D. I., (1886). "Materialy dlya istorii kolonizatsii i byta stepnoy okrainy Moskovskogo gosudarstva v XVI–XVII stoletiy", Vol. I. Khar'kov, Vol. II Khar'kov (1890).

Bagaley, D. I., (1887). "Ocherki iz istorii kolonizatsii i byta stepnoy okrainy Moskovskogo gosudarstva", Moscow.

Bakay, N., (1892). "K istorii kolonizatsii Levoberezhnoy Ukrainy v XV–XVI vv.", Khar'kov.

Belyayev, I. D., (1846). "O storozhevoy, stanichnoy i polevoy sluzhbe na pol'skoy ukrayne Moskovskogo gosudarstva do tsarya Alekseya Mikhaylovicha", Moscow.

Chechulin, N. D., (1889). "Goroda Moskovskogo gosudarstva v XVI veke", St. Petersburg.

Chermenskiy, P., (1911). Ocherki po istorii kolonizatsii Tambovskogo kraya, *Izvestiya Tambovskoy uchenoy arkhivnoy komissii* 54, 187–281.

Chermenskiy, P. N., (1917). Donskiye votchiny boyar Romanovykh, *Izvestiya Tambovskoy uchenoy arkhivnoy komissii* 57, 43–81.

De-Pule, M., (1861). "Orlovskiye akty XVII–XVIII stol.", Nos. 8, 22, 23, 26, 42, 45, 54, 64, 67, 69, 70, 71, 72, 75, 77, 80, 83, 88, 97, 98, 102, 103, 118, 119, 152, 209, 232, Voronezh.

Deystviya Uchenoy Nizhegorodskoy komissii. Sbornik statey, soobshcheniy, opisey i dokumentov, Vol. VI. Nizhniy Novgorod (1905).

Dokuchayev, V. V. (1949). Nashi stepi prezhde i teper'. *In* 'Izbrannyye sochineniya", pp. 163–228, Moscow.

Germanov, G., (1857). Postepennoye raspredeleniye odnodvortsev v Voronezhskoy gubernii, *Zapiski Imperatorskogo Geograficheskogo obshchestva*, 12.

Gritsenko, N. P., (1948). "Ocherki po istorii goroda Simbirska-Ul'yanovska i Ul'yanovskoy oblasti", Ul'yanovsk.

Hellie, Richard, (1971). "Enserfment and Military Change in Muscovy", Chicago.

Izvestiya Saratovskoy uchenoy arkhivnoy komissii (1888), 1.

Kalachov, N., (1855). Zametki (statisticheskiye i arkheologicheskiye) ob Insare i yego uyezde, *Arkhiv istoriko-yuridicheskikh svedeniy*, 2 part 1, Section 1, 35–96.

Kargalov, V. V., (1974). "Na stepnoy granitse", Moscow.

Kirikov, S. V., (1979). "Chelovek i priroda vostochno-yevropeyskoy lesostepi v X—nachale XIX vv.", Moscow.

McGee T. G., (1964). The rural-urban continuum debate; the pre-industrial city and rural-urban migration, *Pacific Viewpoint* 5, No. 2, 159–181.

Margolin, S. L., (1948). Oborona russkogo gosudarstva ot tatarskikh nabegov v kontse XVI veka, *Trudy Gosudarstvennogo istoricheskogo muzeya* 20, 5–28.

Materialy dlya istorii Saratovskogo kraya, *Izvestiya Saratovskoy uchenoy arkhivnoy komissii,* (1890), Vol. 2, No. 2.

Materialy po istorii Saratovskogo kraya, *Izvestiya Saratovskoy uchenoy arkhivnoy komissii,* (1888) Vol. 1; (1889–90) Vol. 2 ; (1890) Vol. 3.

Miklashevskiy, I. N., (1894). K istorii khozyaystvennogo byta Moskovskogo gosudarstva. Zaseleniye i sel'skoye khozyaystvo yuzhnoy okrainy v XVII veke. Vol. 1. Moscow.

Nikitin, A. V., (1965). Oboronitel'nyye sooruzheniya zasechnoy cherty XVI–XVII vv., *Materialy i issledovaniya po arkheologii SSSR* 144, 116–213.

Nizhegorodskiye gubernskiye vedomosti No. 7, (1848).

Novosel'skiy, A. A., (1948). "Bor'ba Moskovskogo gosudarstva s tatarami v pervoy polovine XVII veke", Moscow–Leningrad.

Opis' gorodu Simbirsku i yego uyezdu v 1678g., (1902), Simbirsk.

Osipov, V. A., (1976). "Ocherki po istorii Saratovskogo kraya konets XVI i XVII vv.", Saratov.

O vladeniyakh Velikoy staritsy inoku Marfy Ivanovny v Verkhotsenskoy volosti, *Izvestiya Tambovskoy uchenoy arkhivnoy komissii* 37, 73–147, (1893).

Pamyatniki diplomaticheskikh snosheniy Moskovskogo gosudarstva s Krymom, Nogayami i Turtsiyey, Vol. 2, St. Petersburg (1895).

Peretyatkovich, G., (1882). "Povol'zhe v XVII i nachale XVIII veke (Ocherki iz istorii kolonizatsii kraya)", Odessa.

Pistsovaya kniga novykh sel Verkhotsenskoy volosti, *Izvestiya Tambovskoy uchenoy arkhivnoy komissii* 30, 89–130 (1890).

Platonov, S. F., (1898). K istorii gorodov i putey na yuzhnoy okrainy Moskovskogo gosudarstva v XVIV. *Zhurnal Ministerstva Narodnogo Prosveshcheniya* CCCVI, March, 81–104.

Pronshteyn, A. P., (1967). K istorii vozniknoveniya kazachikh poseleniy i obrazovaniya sosloviya kazakov na Donu, *In* "Novoye o proshlom nashey strany", pp. 158–173, Moscow.

Razin, E. A., (1955–61). "Istoriya voyennogo iskusstva", Moscow.

Razryadnaya kniga Moskovskogo gosudarstve, 1485–1598 gg., Moscow (1966).

Russkaya Mysl' (1887), vol. 2, 405–408. Review of Bagaley (1887).

Shaw, D. J. B., (1973). "Settlement, Urbanism and Economic Change in a Frontier Context: The Voronezh Province of Russia, 1615–1800", unpublished Ph.D. Thesis, University of London.

Shaw, D. J. B., (1977). Urbanism and economic development in a pre-industrial context: the case of southern Russia, *J. Hist. Geog.* 3, 107 –122.

Shvetsova, E. A., (1966). Kolonizatsiya Tambovskogo kraya vo vtoroy polovine XVIIv., *Yezhegodnik po agrarnoy istorii Vostochnoy Yevropy*, 208–216.

Skazaniya knyazya Kurbskogo, St. Petersburg (1868).

Smith, R. E. F., (1977). "Peasant Farming in Muscovy", Cambridge.

Sokolova, I. I., (1975). "Sluzhiloye zemlevladeniye i khozyaystvennoye sostoyaniye priokskikh uyezdov russkogo gosudarstva v kontse XVI-pervoy treti XVII vv", Moscow.

Stroyel'naya kniga goroda Korotoyaka (1647). *In* Veynberg (1885–90), Vol. 16, No. 778.

Tikhomirov, M. N., (1962). "Rossiya v XVI veke", Moscow.

Tserkvi v Voronezhskoy yeparkhii za isteksheye trekhsotletiye 1586–1886, *Voronezhskiye yeparkhial'nyye vedomosti*, Nos. 6, 12, 13, 14, 16, 19–24, (1886).

Turner, F. J., (1966). The significance of the frontier in American history, Reprinted in G. R. Taylor, (ed.) "The Turner Thesis—Concerning the Role of the Frontier in American History", pp. 1–18, Heath.

Ukaznaya kniga Pomestnogo prikaza. Istoriko-yuridicheskiye materialy izd. Moskovskim arkhivom ministerstva yustitsii, pp. 121–122, Moscow (1889).

Vazhinskiy, V. I., (1974). "Zemlevladeniye i skladyvaniye obshchiny odnodvortsev v XVII veke (po materialam yuzhnykh uyezdov Rossii)", Moscow.

Vereshchalin, P. D., (1968). "Proshloye nashego kraya", Ul'yanovsk.

Veynberg, L. B., (1885–90). "Materialy po istorii Voronezhskoy i sosednikh guberniy. Drevniye akty XVII stoletiya", Vols. 1–16, Voronezh.

Veynberg, L. B. and Poltoratskaya, A. A., (1887). "Materialy dlya istorii Voronezhskoy i sosednikh guberniy", Vol. 1, Voronezh.

Veynberg, L. B. and Poltoratskaya, A. A., (1891). "Materialy dlya istorii Voronezhskoy i sosednikh guberniy", Vol. 2, "Voronezhskiye pistsovyye knigi", Voronezh.

Vtorov, N. and Aleksandrov-Dol'nik, K., (1851). *Drevniye gramoty i drugiye pis'-mennyye pamyatniki kasayushchiyesya Voronezhskoy gubernii*, Vol. 1, Voronezh, Vol. 2 Voronezh (1852).

Yakovlev, A. E., (1916). "Zasechnaya cherta Moskovskogo gosudarstva", Moscow.

Zagorovskiy, V. P., (1969a). "Belgorodskaya cherta", Voronezh.

Zagorovskiy, V. P., (1969b). "Belgorodskaya cherta", unpublished doctoral dissertation, Voronezh State University.

Zagorovskiy, V. P., (1980). "Izyumskaya cherta", Voronezh.

Zertsalov, A. N., (1896). "Materialy dlya istorii Sinbirska i yego uyezda (Prikhodno-raskhodnaya kniga Sinbirskoy Prikaznoy Izby), 1665–7 gg.," Simbirsk.

Zertsalov, A. N., (1900). "Materialy po istorii Simbirskogo kraya XVII–XVIII vv.," Simbirsk.

7 The Frontier in Central Asia

I. Stebelsky

Russian Central Asia is a vast and varied land. From the Ural mountains and the Caspian Sea it extends eastward to the Altay and the Tyan' Shan' mountains on the Russo-Chinese border. Its natural zones pass from the arctic tundra in the north through the broad taiga of the vast Ob' plain, across the wooded steppe of Western Siberia, to the steppe and semi-desert of Kazakhstan, and thence to the desert, oases, and mountains of Turkestan (Fig. 7.1).

Different environments supported different native cultures. For centuries hunters and gatherers inhabited the boreal forest, while primitive farmers and livestock herders claimed the wooded steppe of Western Siberia. Nomadic tribesmen ranged widely over the steppes and semi-deserts of Kazakhstan and into the deserts and mountain pastures of Turkestan. But in Turkestan the population was highly nucleated and mostly settled, consisting of urban dwellers and irrigation farmers.

Russian acquisition and colonization of Central Asia was incremental, progressing from one environment to another from north to south. It spanned vast distances and proceeded in stages over a period of four centuries. The Russian frontier advanced in keeping with changing geographical configurations of political power and military technology. The Russian officials perceived greater economic opportunities for colonization as political and economic circumstances changed at home and abroad. The pioneers who advanced the Russian frontier came from different homelands with different environments and brought with them different traditions and perceptions of the environment. They either possessed or were willing to adopt new technology to cope with the challenges of the frontier.

Russian advances into Central Asia opened up, in turn, three different frontiers: Western Siberia, Kazakhstan, and Turkestan. Each frontier, acquired at a different time, involved a different set of natural environments and represented Russian confrontation with a different set of cultures. The

RUSSIAN HISTORICAL GEOGRAPHY VOL. 1
ISBN 0 12 081201 0

Fig. 7.1. Russian frontiers in Central Asia.

frontiersmen produced settlement patterns and generated land uses that reflected their own preferences, the goals of the government officials, and the constraints of the physical and cultural realities.

WESTERN SIBERIA

Long before the conquest of Siberia, Russia acquired the north-western corner of the Ob' river basin (Fig. 7.2). This subarctic woodland, inhabited by the Finnic-speaking Khanty and Mansi—then known collectively as the Yugry—was visited by the men of Novgorod as early as the eleventh century, and became the easternmost extent of Novgorod's northern fur frontier (Lantzeff and Pierce, 1973).

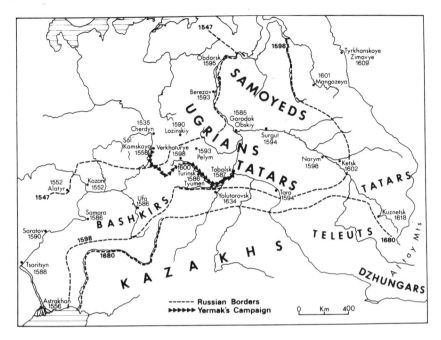

Fig. 7.2. The conquest of western Siberia.

The prince of Muscovy, having annexed Novgordo (1478), subdued the Yugry (1483–88) to collect his tribute in furs. To reach the Ob', however, Muscovite servitors had to follow the same northern rivers (Vychegda, Pechora, and the Severnaya Sosva) and to carry provisions with them over the rugged northern Urals, for the direct route up the Kama river and thence through the low middle Urals remained blocked by the Tatar principality of Kazan'. Only after Kazan' fell (1552) and the entire length of the Volga came under Muscovite control (1556), did the Russians strengthen their position in the Urals.

First the Bashkirs of the south-western Urals, former vassals of Kazan', were persuaded to submit to Moscow. Then the West Siberian Tatar leaders, seeking protection against Prince Kuchum, a Genghinid pretender, swore allegiance to Ivan IV (1555). Under such favourable political climate the Tsar granted the salt merchant, Stroganov, permission to extend his mining from Solvychegodsk (on the Vychegda river) southward to Sol Kamskaya (established in 1558, later called Solikamsk) on the Kama river.

New political instability, however, prompted military confrontation. Prince Kuchum seized power from the local Tatar princes of Western

Siberia. Encouraged by a successful Crimean Tatar campaign against Moscow, Kuchum negated his allegiance to the Tsar (1573), and initiated raids upon the Stroganov holdings and levied tribute on the Yugry of the Ob'. The Tsar retaliated by granting Stroganov the land beyond the Urals to the Tobol' river, and ordered the construction of Russian forts along the Ob' and Irtysh. The call was answered by Yermak and his force of cossacks (see Armstrong, 1975) who, in the service of the Tsar and Stroganov and with superior weapons, drove out Prince Kuchum and his followers (1581–84)

The first Russian forts, built to retain the conquest, were located at major river confluences amidst the Tatar population. Indeed, Tyumen' (1586) replaced the Tatar Chimga-Tura, and Tobol'sk (1587), located strategically at the confluence of the Irtysh and the Tobol', replaced the Tatar capital. Sibir'. Even the Tatar elite that did not side with Prince Kuchum was retained in local administration and was offered privileged positions in the Russian service.

The forts built later, notably Lozvinskiy (1590), Pelym (1593), Verkhotur'ye (1598), and Turinsk (1600), served as links with the Russian homeland while the first two also functioned as bases for controlling the Yugry and collecting tribute from them. Early fur-collecting bases on the Ob' included, Gorodok Obskiy (1585), Berezov (1593), and Obdorsk (1595). To the east and south, however, outposts such as Surgut (1594) and Narym (1598) on the Ob' and Tara (1594) on the Irtysh guarded against Kuchum and his followers who staged a number of raids to drive out the Russians. After Kuchum's ultimate defeat (1598) near the present-day Novosibirsk, the Siberian Tatars lost their will to resist the Russians. Having secured the remaining Tatar lands with Tomsk (1604) and Kuznetsk (1618) on the Tom river, the Russians avoided any conflict with the hostile steppe nomads to the south as they set about the task of developing their fur empire.

Following the conquest of Western Siberia the Russians swiftly expanded their fur frontier to the east. Since the best fur-bearing animals inhabited the tundra and northern tayga, the Russian fur trappers followed the northern rivers in search of "soft gold" (Fisher, 1943; Pavlov, 1973). Mangazeya, established (1601) by an expedition from Tobol'sk, became the sable capital of north-western Siberia and a gateway to the lower Yenisey. Ketsk (1602) became a launching place for fur-collecting expeditions to the middle Yenisey and beyond. Older forts along the middle and lower Ob' grew as tribute collecting centres and trans-shipment points (Vodarskiy, 1973). All these garrisons had to be supplied with provisions shipped over vast distances (Vilkov, 1968). To obviate distant shipping an effort was made to develop local farming.

The northern forts obtained meat from native fishermen, hunters, and reindeer herders, but attempts to grow crops there proved unsuccessful.

Even the southern forts of Western Siberia could not be locally supplied with bread. Only the Tatars near Tobol'sk produced some grain, and the Yugry along the Tavda river practiced rudimentary cultivation. The remaining Tatars kept livestock, whilst most Yugry depended on the chase. North and east of the Ob' river, the Nentsy and Selkupy—then known collectively as the Samoyedy—herded the reindeer, but raised no crops (Fig. 7.2). In order to feed the northern fur frontier the Russians had to open up the southern farming frontier.

The Russian administration tried a number of methods to induce grain production in Siberia (Drew, 1959). Garrison servitors, in addition to their military duty, were required to grow crops. Natives in the vicinity of southern forts who knew farming were levied with a grain tax, but attempts to impose farming on the other natives failed. Only the Russian peasantry was capable of increasing grain production.

Early records reveal that the Muscovite Government encouraged Russian peasant settlement in Western Siberia. When Pelym was founded, peasants were drawn from across the Urals to sharecrop the land for the garrison (Koretskiy, 1973:37–38). Voluntary peasant colonization, condoned by the government, contributed to the settlement of Verkhotur'ye, Turinsk, Tyumen', Tobol'sk and even Tomsk (Aleksandrov, 1964:269–270; Aleksandrov, 1973:12). The codification of serfdom in Muscovy (1649) and active retrieval of runaway serfs did not reduce spontaneous migration to Siberia, for it originated in areas where serfdom was not extensive (Preobrazhenskiy, 1972:56–164). The frontiersmen—descendants of the Novgorodians and the neighbouring Finnic tribes—migrated to avoid serfdom, military draft, and higher population pressure. They sold their old property and moved on to pursue slash and burn cultivation on land claimed individually by prior appropriation (Vlasova, 1973:249–260). By the end of the seventeenth century Russians and Russified Finns from Vychegda, Vyatka, and upper Kama, not only outnumbered the natives in the area, but the peasants outnumbered both the servitors and the merchants and craftsmen put together (Okladnikov and Shunkov, 1968:39).

In the course of the seventeenth century, as new settlements dispersed from the main forts, two agricultural regions emerged (Fig. 7.3). The larger of the two, located just east of the Urals and centered on Tyumen', extended eastward in a narrowing wedge to Tara on the Irtysh (Shunkov, 1956:44, 253). A smaller one emerged around Tomsk and other forts on the Tom' river. North of Tomsk and Tobol'sk farming was restricted by swampy terrain, podzolic soils, and a short (less than 105 days) frost-free season. Repeated crop failures north of this line convinced the servitors that they had to import food supplies from the south, or rely on their own fishing, hunting, and reindeer (Minenko, 1973:343–344). Thus, the Tyumen' agri-

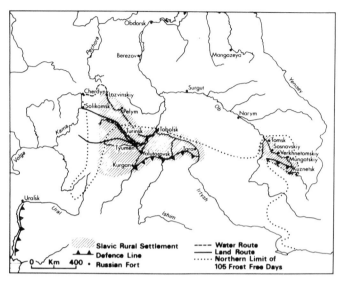

Fig. 7.3. The farming frontier in seventeenth-century western Siberia.

cultural region supplied Obdorsk, Berezov, and Surgut, whereas the Tomsk region shipped grain to Narym and even to the distant Mangazeya.

The southward advance of rural settlement was an internal Siberian migration. Lush glades in broadleaf woodlands and fertile soils only beckoned farmers to the south. The government encouraged the advancing frontier by granting the pioneers exemptions from taxes for several years. Enterprising *slobodchiki* organized peasants into pioneer parties that established new villages, or *slobody*, in the south (Kondrashenkov, 1973:296–297). The vacated farmsteads were in turn occupied by new migrants from the west, who would assume their former occupants' tax obligations (Preobrazhenskiy, 1972:57–68).

The southward displacement of rural settlement was spurred, initially, by the relocation of the main route through the Urals. In 1598, the water route along Vyshera, Lozva, and Tavda was replaced by a shorter road blazed from Solikamsk to the new fort and customs house at Verkhotur'ye (Pokshishevskiy, 1951:34). This road attracted peasantry away from Lozvinskiy and Pelym to settle along the Tura river, and gave rise to Turinsk (1600).

Although Verkhotur'ye remained the official entry to Siberia until 1763, rural settlements continued to leapfrog southward, through the woodland, as far as Irbit (*c.* 1630) on the Nitsa. Beyond the Nitsa, frequent nomad raids discouraged further settlement (Aleksandrov, 1973:11). Meanwhile, the construction of Kungur (1648) on the western side of the Urals led to the development of the Kungur trail that, in its unofficial capacity, attracted merchants who preferred to bypass the customs at Verkhotur'ye (Preobrazhenskiy, 1956:194). As a result Irbit, located at the eastern terminus of the trail, grew into a major Siberian market that hosted the silk trade merchants from Bukhara. This growing market, combined with the security that the forts of Yalutorovsk (1639) and Kurgan (1670) offered, encouraged further spread of rural communities as far as the Iset' and its southern tributary, the Miass (Okladnikov and Shunkov, 1968:39).

East of the Tobol' river the growth of Russian population was slow. Along Irtysh between Tobol'sk and Tara, the Tatar population still predominated, for Russian settlers felt safe only near the Russian forts (Kabo, 1949, foldout map in back of book). Settlements along the Ishim and the Irtysh could be reached with ease by hostile Bashkir, Kalmyk or Kazakh horsemen from the south who destroyed crops, dispersed cattle, and took captives. Obviously, defensive measures were needed. By the end of the seventeenth century a line of forts, linked to each other by sentinel service, was completed from Kurgan to Ishim and thence to Irtysh, to become known as the Ishim Line (Fig. 7.3).

South of Tomsk, Russian farming communities developed around forts that followed the Tom' river up to Kuznetsk (1608). From here settlers advanced towards the south-west and, in the seventeenth century, their gains were reinforced by a defence line that extended to the north-west of Kuznetsk along the Inya river (Fig. 7.3). By the turn of the century settlements were spilling over to the minor tributaries of the Ob' immediately north of the present-day Novosibirsk. Some settlers even braved the overland crossing from Tara through the wooded Baraba Steppe to claim free land on the west side of the Ob'. However, Russian advance into the upper reaches of the Ob', where Biysk (1709) was constructed, angered the Dzhungar prince who, with his nomadic horsemen, controlled Altay from the south. In retaliation, he claimed the entire Tomsk region, destroyed Biysk, and laid siege to Kuznetsk. The Russians, however, countered with determined military advances, culminating in the establishment of a continuous defence line that would protect Western Siberia from the south.

As the Russian frontier advanced southward, confrontation between the pioneer farmers and the steppe nomads became more frequent and intense. By the eighteenth century the advancing southern margin of Slavic rural settlement became a military frontier defined by the Siberian defence line. This line, begun with the construction of several forts on the Irtysh, grew immensely. By the second half of the eighteenth century a chain of forts extended from the Caspian, along the Ural river, across the West Siberian plain, along the Irtysh and thence along the foothills of the Altay to Kuznetsk—over 4000 kilometres in length (Fig. 7.4).

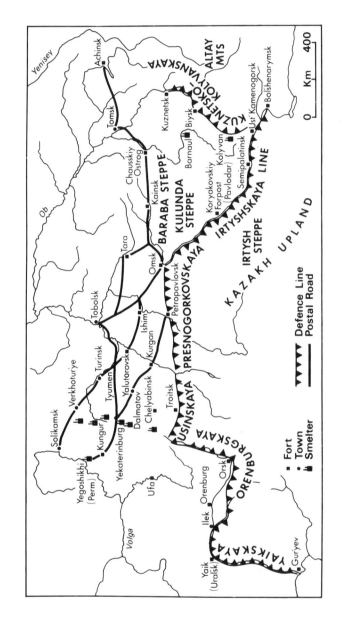

Fig. 7.4. The Siberian defence line.

The first forts on the Irtysh—Omsk (1716), Semipalatinsk (1718), Ust'-Kamenogorsk (1719), and Koryakovskiy Forpost (1720, now Pavlodar)—were built in a retaliatory campaign against the Dzhungar incursion. However, successful Chinese advances against the Dzhungars, who in turn drove the Kazakhs into the Irtysh and the Ishim steppes, caused the Russians even more concern. Although most Kazakhs and Dzhungars came to terms with the Russians, the Chinese claim to the Kazakhs and their threat to invade the steppe led the Russians to complete the Siberian defence line.

The chain of Russian forts had many new investments to protect. While the fabulous Siberian fur trade declined, other resources gained prominence by this time. The most strategic were the iron smelters of the Urals, that gave Russia the edge in her northern war with Sweden. Equally valuable were the new mines and smelters of copper and precious metals in the Altay. Workers of both industrial regions had to be fed and supplied by overland post roads. More rural population was needed to feed those engaged in mining, processing, commerce, and transportation, and all had to be defended.

At first the Urals metallurgical complex was sheltered from the south. A line of forts to the west and north of Orsk (1735) was raised to guard the approaches along the Ural river, and Orenburg (1743) was constructed to serve as the administrative centre of that military district (Semenov-Tyan-Shanskiy, 1914:5, 140). Beyond the Urals the agricultural district was protected by the Usinskaya Line with its headquarters at Troitsk (1743) on the Uy river. Further east, the Ishim Line became obsolete as Russian settlements pressed beyond its confines in the 1730s (Semenov, 1907:16,165). It was replaced by Petropavlovsk (1752) and its Presnogor'kovskaya Line (1755), named after the many fresh and saline lakes along its alignment, that spanned the entire Ishim Steppe from the Tobol' to the Irtysh (Fig. 7.4). The Irtysh Line was strengthened with five regular military regiments (1745).

In the foothills of the Altay mountains, Demidov's copper smelters at Kolyvan' (1725) and Barnaul (1739) were fortified from the start, but after their transfer to the Tsar's private (Cabinet) possession, a line of forts was built to protect the entire area. Starting from a site north-east of Ust'-Kamenogorsk, where deposits of lead and tin were discovered, the line proceeded to Kolyvan', Biysk, and Kuznetsk, and thus became known as the Kuznetsk–Kolyvan' Line. Meanwhile, the Irtysh Line was extended to Bol'-shenarymsk (Fig. 7.4).

Along these lines the forts were manned by Siberian cossacks. Initially, they were recruited from Siberian servitors and peasants of northern Russian, Finnic, and Siberian Tatar origins. Later they were joined by servitors from similar defence lines—by then no longer needed—west of the Urals, that included Mordvinians and Bashkirs. In the 1760s they were supplemented by banished serfs, a sect of Old Believers (settled principally near

Altay), Don Cossacks, and remnants of the Ukrainian Zaporozhian cossacks. This motley group, known after 1808 as the Siberian Line Army, was granted land allotments and tax exemptions. Because military duty allowed them little time to farm, the Siberian Line garrisons relied on supplemental grain from the peasants. Moreover, the garrisons emerged as trading posts where grain was sold to the Kazakh nomads in exchange for sheep, horses, hides, and wool.

The Siberian Line, by securing land and offering a grain market, enticed Siberian peasants to migrate from densely peopled districts (west of Yalutorovsk) to the south and east. The pioneers, however, avoided the line itself, for officers often drafted peasants to settle near forts for sharecropping or military service (Gromyko, 1965:98; Kondrashenkov, 1973:300). As Siberian rural population shifted to the south, the main Siberian tract also shifted southward to Omsk. In effect, the Siberian Line, from the Urals to Irtysh, coincided with the southern margin of the wooded steppe and defined the southern frontier of Russian settlement throughout the second half of the eighteenth and into the first quarter of the nineteenth century.

East of the Irtysh, behind the Irtysh Line, the grassy Kulunda Steppe and the parkland Baraba Steppe remained devoid of Slavic rural settlement. The only exception, the new Siberian tract, supported a string of posts across the Baraba Steppe. Since the local Tatars were not trusted, Russians were settled (1762–1780) along the trail that joined Tara or Omsk with Kainsk and thence Chausskiy Ostrog on the Ob'. These settlers, drawn from the trails further to the west, supported transit traffic and supplemented their livelihood with farming (Pokshishevskiy, 1951:106–109).

To the south, the Kulunda Steppe served as traditional summer pasture for the nomads. However, the Irtysh Line cut off the Kazakhs of the Irtysh Steppe from access to Kulunda. It forced them either to leave Kulunda or to adopt the storage of hay for winter and thus assume a more settled way of life (Apollova, 1976:240–253).

East of Kulunda, the upper Ob' river basin, evacuated by the Dzhungarled Teleuts, underwent the most active settlement (Bulygin, 1968). Warmer, milder climate, richer wooded steppe, and more fertile soil attracted Russian peasantry (including Russified Tatars) from the Tom' river basin and beyond. Already in the first decade of the eighteenth century several Russian forts claimed the rich Altay foothills. Following the discovery of copper ores, Demidov recruited craftsmen from his Ural smelters. Subsequently, the Tsar's Cabinet acquired the Altay smelters and recruited local peasants, prisoners, and exiled Old Believers. Meanwhile, the Kuznetsk-Kolyvan' Line, designed to stop the Kalmyk raids, was manned by Siberian cossacks drawn from servitors of various Siberian towns, exiled cossacks from the west, local peasants, and indentured natives, including Kazakhs, Kirgiz and

Altays (Lipinskaya, 1969:11–14).

South-east of Biysk, beyond the defence line, the wooded Altay mountains were inhabited by native tribesmen and, increasingly, by small groups of Russian fugitives. The latter were mostly Old Believers, a persecuted sect that, in a biblical fashion, searched for its promised land (Shkunov, 1911:93).

KAZAKHSTAN

Russians in Siberia perceived the grasslands of Kazakhstan as a hostile environment. When the Russian fur-seeking explorers crossed the tayga to the Pacific they avoided the nomads of the steppe. After the fur trade declined and interest shifted to mining and farming, the encroachment onto the steppes was slow and cautious. Changes in the geopolitical situation, however, allowed Russia to re-evaluate the steppe environment and make significant advances into Central Asia.

Since the seventeenth century the Russian Empire had gained considerable power. It harnessed the sabre-wielding Ural cossacks whose horsemanship rivalled that of the steppe nomads (Semenov, 1903:154). With their help and the servitors in Siberia it built forts from the Caspian to the Altay that daunted the mounted horsemen. What encouraged the Russian advance, however, was the Kazakh request for Russian protection.

The Kazakhs, who grazed the steppes beyond the Russian realm, were divided into three hordes (Demko, 1969:24). In the west, the Younger Horde ranged from the Ustyurt Plateau to the middle reaches of the Ural river. The Middle Horde grazed its flocks from the Ishim Steppe to the Syr Dar'ya. The Elder Horde controlled the pastures south and east of Lake Balkhash. Within each horde numerous clans competed against one another.

Faced with a Dzhungar invasion from the east (1726–29), the Kazakh hordes joined forces and repelled the foe. Their leader, however, feared inadequate support to drive off the Dzhungars again, and turned to Russia for military alliance (1731).

The Russians immediately accepted the Younger Horde as their vassal and prepared for advances to the south (Abdykalykov and Pankratova, 1943:156). They dispatched an expedition to build a fort at Orsk (constructed in 1735), to survey Kazakhstan for precious metals, and to assess it as a stepping-stone to Turkestan. The Bashkir rebellion prevented the accomplishment of the last two objectives, however. Only after suppressing the Bashkirs did the Russians regain the loyalty of the Younger Horde and obtain allegiance of the Middle Horde (1740). The latter, defeated by the Dzhungars and threatened with a Chinese invasion, assumed dual vassalage to both Russia and China (1757). Playing off one power against another, the Middle Horde managed to retain independence virtually until the end of the century. Meanwhile, the Elder Horde remained under control of China, while the Younger Horde, divided among several khans, fell under the sway of Russia.

The Russian border fortifications increasingly influenced the lifestyle of the neighbouring Kazakh clans. Sometimes the fortified lines shielded retreating Kazakhs from the Dzhungars or aggressive Kazakh leaders. More frequently they blocked free Kazakh movement to grove-sheltered pastures on the Russian side that traditionally protected livestock from the winter storms. Kazakhs who remained behind the Russian lines, as did the Bukeyev Horde west of the Ural river, came under complete control of Russia and began to assume sedentary living (Abdykalykov and Pankratova, 1943:193–194). By contrast, the Kazakhs who valued their traditional nomadic life viewed the construction of fortified lines an affront that had to be challenged with raids. The forts also served as markets. They provided the enterprising Kazakhs with an opportunity to gain wealth and an inclination to come to terms with the Russian rule.

By the nineteenth century conditions favoured Russian annexation of Kazakhstan. Chinese power declined. The Elder Horde was confronted with advancing garrisons of Kokand; the Younger and Middle Hordes, weakened by internal conflicts, had their khans appointed by the Tsar. Russia only needed an opportune moment to annex Kazakhstan.

When both khans of the Middle Horde died (1822), Russia annexed its territory to Omsk oblast and subdivided it according to the Russian pattern: *okruga*, *volosti*, and *auly*. The new statute, a brainchild of Speranskiy, provided the Russian-approved Kazakh candidates with elected posts at all three levels. However, each *okrug* was to be administered by a team consisting of an elected Kazakh *sultan*, two elected Kazakh officers, and two appointed Russian officers who in fact conducted the affairs. The highest level of Kazakh authority, the khan, was replaced by a council of sultans responsible directly to the Russian commanding officer of the Siberian Line Army at Omsk. Russian law supplanted traditional Kazakh law in all cases of crime against the state, robbery, and murder.

Russian territorial re-structuring of the Middle Horde ignored nomadism. The boundaries of each *volost*, named after a clan it included, were rigidly delineated and the clan's range of movement accordingly restricted. Each *okrug* was to be administered from a permanent site which, in effect, became a Russian garrison.

The enforcement of the new laws required Russian military presence among the Kazakhs. Siberian cossacks were dispatched to build the forts that would accommodate the sultans' *okrug* offices. Sites were selected with freshwater springs and trees for building material. The cossacks assigned to garrison duty were granted land for livelihood.

Within six years an arc of forts traversed the Kazakh Upland from south of Petropavlovsk to Lake Zaysan in the east (Fig. 7.5): Kokchetav (1824), Karakaralinsk (1824), Bayan-Aul (1826), Kokpekty (1826), Shchuchinsk (1828), Akmolinsk (1830), and Sergiopol' (1831). Near the forts were located cossack settlements (*stanitsy*), usually along steppe stream or lakes.

Unrest in the Younger Horde prevented the Russians from implementing identical reforms. Nevertheless, the Younger Horde was divided into three sultanates (1824), and each sultan, responsible directly to the Governor-General at Orenburg, was accompanied by a retinue of Russian military. The grasslands near the defence line were subdivided into thirty-two *distantsii*, each for the exclusive use of one group (1831).

The imposition of regulations was accomplished by means of a strong military presence. New fortified lines—the Ilek (1822) that enclosed a valuable salt quarry south of Orenburg, and the so-called New Line (mid 1830s) that crossed the steppe between Orsk and Troitsk—displaced many Kazakhs from the best pastures. They also served as foreposts that controlled the *distantsii*. Moreover, the Russians levied a household tax on members of both hordes (1837), instituted special taxes on cutting timber, gathering salt, or fishing, and even sanctioned cossack raids on Kazakh camps, allegedly in retaliation for raids on Russian caravans.

In response to this encroachment on freedom, the Kazakhs revolted. Led by Kasymov, the rebel forces took Akmolinsk (1838), but soon turned southward to help the Elder Horde fight off the Khanate of Kokand. Meanwhile, the Russians planted forts at Irgiz (1845) and Turgay (1845), strengthened their position on the Ishim River with Atbasar (1846) and shielded it with Ulutavskiy (1846). They increased their manpower and local food supply by recruiting experienced farmers, mostly Ukrainians, for cossack service at Atbasar (Ochevidets, 1891:130). The latter became very successful. They ploughed the virgin steppe, sowed unprecedented quantities of wheat, and kept many horses, oxen, and sheep (Ostafyev, 1897:56–57).

As Kasymov tried to persuade the Kirgiz to join him against Russia and Kokand, the Russian forces proceeded to isolate the rebels. The Russians gained allegiance of the Elder Horde (1846), built fort Kopal (1847) in the wooded slopes of Dzhungar Alatau, and temporarily came to terms with Kokand. Meanwhile, the Kirgiz loyal to Kokand destroyed Kasymov and his followers in the foothills of Tyan' Shan'.

Russians gained undisputed control over Kazakhstan after securing their border with China (Treaty of Peking, 1860) and establishing a line of fortresses against Turkestan (1864–65). Surrounded by Russian garrisons

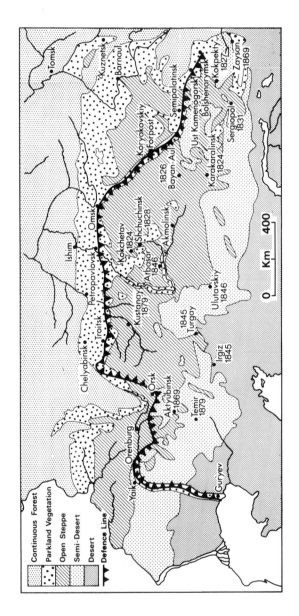

Fig. 7.5. Russian military penetration of the Kazakh steppes.

and isolated from outside influences, the Kazakhs were powerless to resist Russian colonization of the steppe with Slavic peasantry.

To ease the absorption of Kazakhstan into the Russian Empire a commission was established (1865) that devised a new code of administration (1868). The Kazakh steppes, governed from Orenburg and Omsk, were divided into four oblasts (Ural, Turgay, Akmolinsk, and Semipalatinsk) and subdivided, in descending order, into *uyezdy*, *volosti*, and *auly*. Elected Kazakh leaders became assistants to Russian officers administering each *uyezd*. Russian language ruled in official correspondence, schools, medical and postal service. Islam came under stringent controls. Taxation of the Kazakhs was increased, Kazakhs who grazed their herds on the Ural and Siberian cossack lands had to pay rent (Abdykalykov and Pankratova, 1943:268–270).

At the same time the new code provided a legal basis for expropriating the Kazakhs and accommodating Russian colonists. Land was decreed a state property that government would allocate for the use of Kazakhs and others. Private property was recognized only where charters were granted to Cossack officers or to descendants of the khans. The remaining land was considered common, although plots with structures belonged to individual households. Kazakhs could thus rent land to Russian settlers, but they could not sell it.

The code allowed peasants and townfolk to settle in the *uyezd* centres of Kazakhstan without becoming cossacks. Peasant settlers were granted free land to farm and free timber for housing. Similar privileges were extended to the Kazakhs who would become Christian and join a farming community (Auezov *et al.*, 1957:391–392).

For the clans of the Middle Horde inhabiting the Akmolinsk and Semipalatinsk oblasts the code of 1868 made little change. However, in the newly subdivided Ural and Turgay oblasts it precipitated a revolt (1869) of the Younger Horde. Russians retaliated by building fort Ak-Tyube (1869). Soldiers were followed by aggressive merchants, townfolk (1877), and peasants (1881), and the settlement became the town of Aktyubinsk (1882). The proposal to establish Kustanay (1870) also attracted many potential settlers to the border towns of Orsk and Troitsk, but the site for Kustanay was not selected until 1881. Immediately the settlement was inundated with unruly elements that seized Kazakh lands, destroyed scarce timber stands, and lynched Kazakhs for suspected horse thievery (Kaufman, 1897:2–17).

Peasant settlement in Akmolinsk oblast proceeded in a more orderly fashion. Prospective settlers from Western Siberia, often relatives of the Siberian cossacks, dispatched scouts who located suitable lands to rent from the Kazakhs. First they leased, ploughed and sowed small plots of land to test for conflicting claims or soil quality; then they contracted the good lands for several years. Often they stayed with their relatives at a nearby cossack *stanitsa*; later they would build a cabin in the vicinity of the land they rented. Within a few years a veritable Siberian village appeared. As increasing numbers of peasants encroached on Kazakh winter pastures, conflicts emerged. Russian officials usually ordered the peasants to vacate Kazakh lands, but the colonists kept coming back. When official permission for Russian peasant colonization was granted (1879) already some 300 peasant households resided in Akmolinsk oblast (Semenov 1903: 155–156).

Government-sponsored peasant colonization did not fare as well. Settlements were planted along postal trails to help transport and enhance local grain supply. Ukrainian peasants, who knew how to build houses of clay, were directed onto bare grasslands. Of the thirty plots surveyed (1879–1884), twelve remained unsettled because of unsuitable conditions. Even the occupied plots often had poor soils, inadequate meadows and forests, or lacked good drinking water. Despite generous subsidies, the settlers lacked knowledge of local climate and could not cope with drought, frost, or locust. Three consecutively poor years (1880–84) ruined many peasants and caused the government to close, temporarily, Kazakhstan to colonization (S.F., 1894:194–197).

Meanwhile, illegal settlement advanced successfully. Peasants from Western Siberia searched out the best ploughlands, meadows, woods, and lakes in the Ishim Steppe or near the Altay mountains along the Chinese border. Simultaneously, another group of peasants began to arrive from Saratov, Samara, and Orenburg provinces. Possessing effective tools for breaking the sod, they advanced from west to east, transforming the steppe with a cropping frontier.

The "sod busters" thrived on the vast grasslands they could rent cheaply from the Kazakhs for a short period. They built temporary shelters and used heavy iron (Ukrainian) ploughs pulled by four to five pair of oxen to break the sod. The wealthier frontiersmen employed factory-built iron ploughs. Settlers from the Urals or Western Siberia brought with them the Permian or Siberian *sokha* which was less effective for breaking the sod. The light wooden Russian *sokha* could be used only for loosening ploughed soil (Kaufman, 1897:188–189). After gathering three or four harvests of wheat the "sod busters" were ready to move on. Tense relations with the Kazakhs sometimes led to early termination of their contracts, but usually it was soil exhaustion. The "sod busters," not interested in proper crop rotations or fallowing, merely complained of poor soil, inadequate water, hay or woodland, and departed to "skim the cream" elsewhere (Kaufman, 1897:192–195).

A massive surge of settlers in 1890 signalled the beginning of "the great

Siberian migration". Deepening agrarian crisis in European Russia (especially in the Black Earth provinces) compelled emigration, but government administration favouring estate owners prevented the flight of cheap labour. In 1889 a bold migration law gave the peasantry sufficient legal and economic support to open the floodgates (Treadgold, 1957:78). The remaining restrictions collapsed following the 1905 peasant revolts. Between 1906 and 1915 more than one million peasants, mainly from the Ukrainian and Russian Black Earth provinces, migrated to the Kazakh steppes—a four-fold increase over the previous decade (Diyarov, 1967:30).

Increased accessibility to Siberia was an important contributing factor for the sudden influx of peasantry to Kazakhstan. Since 1894, the lands east of the Urals could be reached by the new Trans-Siberian railroad. Government bodies set low rates for legal migrants and promoted settlement in the east with publications and information offices.

Land availability was an essential requirement for colonization. Surveys indicated that good land along the Trans-Siberian already had been occupied (Komitet . . . , 1900:207–226). North of the railway, the tayga proved to be inhospitable to farmers and, except for several lightly wooded areas to the east of Tara, to the west of Tomsk and in the Baraba Steppe, where drainage was required, new lands for colonization had to be secured in the south. These were the Kulunda Steppe—now quickly being settled—and the vast Kazakh Steppes, where water supply often posed a problem.

The government expedition that surveyed the Kazakh Steppes in 1895 reported immense possibilities for peasant colonization. Out of thirty-six million *desyatiny* (one *desyatina* = 1.09 hectares) surveyed, seventeen million were considered necessary for the Kazakhs, and the remaining eighteen million could be disbursed for farming (Glinka, 1914b:542–3). Yet until 1905 colonization proceeded slowly, for the Kazakhs protested the alienation of their lands, whilst some Russian spokesman on the agrarian question doubted that more land could be withdrawn for settlement. Following the peasant revolts, however, another expedition (dispatched in 1905) proclaimed that the Kazakhs were beginning to settle, that less land would be needed to maintain the same number of livestock, and that more land would be available for settlement. Within a decade an additional ten million *desyatiny* were allocated to Slavic peasantry in northern Kazakhstan, and another three million to Kazakhs who were willing to take up farming (Demko, 1969:107, 109; Pokshishevskiy, 1951:151).

The advance of the farming frontier may be judged by the spread of settlement plots (Fig. 7.6). In 1905 the settlement plots were grouped in the most accessible and secure places: just beyond the Siberian Cossack Line, along the Ishim river, and between Kokchetav and Atbasar. By 1915 the plots extended over a much larger area, nearly coalescing in the north and

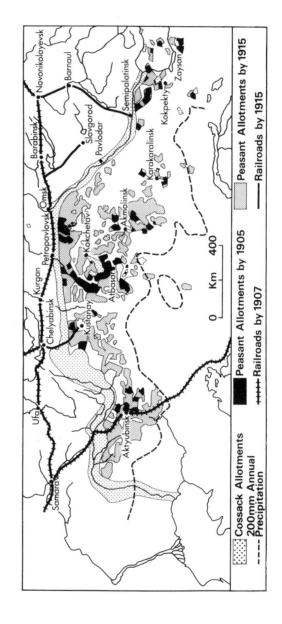

Cossack Allotments
200mm Annual
--- Precipitation

Peasant Allotments by 1905
+++++ Railroads by 1907

Peasant Allotments by 1915
——— Railroads by 1915

Samara

Ufa

Chelyabinsk

Kurgan

Petropavlovsk

Omsk

Barabinsk

Slavgorod

Pavlodar

Novonikolayevsk

Barnaul

Semipalatinsk

Kokpekty

Zaysan

Karakaralinsk

Akmolinsk

Kokchetav

Atbasar

Kustanay

Aktyubinsk

0   Km   400

Fig. 7.6. Slavic rural settlement of northern Kazakhstan by 1905 and 1915.

forming large clusters in the Kazakh Upland and the upper reaches of the Tobol river near Kustanay. Although conditions were drier in the vicinity of Aktyubinsk, the construction of the Turkestan railroad (1905–7) encouraged the spread of allotments as far as the Mugodzhar Hills that overlook the semi-desert. In the eastern flank, a smaller cluster emerged south of Semipalatinsk and near Kokpekty, but fewer plots were allocated in the remote steppes near Bayan Aul, Karakaralinsk, and Sergiopol'. In general, the Slavic farming frontier advanced to the limits of moisture availability, represented approximately by the mean annual precipitation of 200 millimetres.

TURKESTAN

Turkestan, the silk route to China and stepping-stone to India was long perceived as a rich prize. Rumours of gold deposits enticed Peter I to send an expedition (1717) that ended in disaster (Kostenko, 1871:90–96). In the end it was cotton that emerged as the most valuable attraction for Russia.

The first Russian plunge into Turkestan was vengeful: to punish the Khanate of Khiva for robbing Russian caravans and enslaving the captives. General Perovskiy's unsuccessful desert campaign (1839) gave way to methodical advances. First Fort Aleksandrovskiy (now Fort Shevchenko) was secured (1840) on Mangyshlak Peninsula. Then Irgiz was placed (1845) as a stepping stone to the mouth of Syr Dar'ya, where Perovskiy's troops built Raimskoye Ukrepleniye (1847). Advancing up the Syr Dar'ya, they raised two more forts and thus secured the entire caravan route from Orenburg to the outposts of Kokand (Fig. 7.7).

Outflanking Khiva, the Russians challenged the strife-torn Khanate of Kokand. A grower of cotton, Kokand became viewed as an alternative to the American fibre supply disrupted by the American Civil War (1861–65). The Russians took Kokand's Ak-Mechet (1858) and re-built it as Fort Perovskiy (now Kzyl-Orda). Meanwhile, the Siberian cossacks from Kopal crossed the Ili river and, seeking Kirgiz support, established Vernyy (1854, now Alma Ata) that blocked Kokand's route to China.

After a brief pause (the Crimean War, 1854–56), the Russians negotiated a new boundary with a weakened China (Treaty of Peking, 1860) and resumed their advance. The force from Vernyy took Pishpek (1862), Tokmak (1862), and Auliye-Ata (1864), thus establishing the so-called Kokand Line. Meanwhile, the force from Perovskiy took Suzak (1863), Turkestan (1864), and Chimkent (1864). With the capture of Tashkent (1865), Russia threatened the Khanates of Kokand, Khiva, and Bukhara. Concerned about possible British retaliation to further annexation, the Russian Government decided to consolidate its gains.

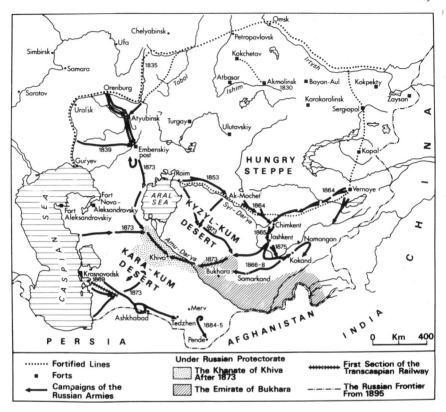

Fig. 7.7. The conquest of Turkestan.

The administrative structure imposed on the military frontier became known as Turkestan (1865). Its Governor General, Von Kaufman, was given (1867) not only military and administrative powers but also some latitude to conduct foreign affairs. He could wage wars on Central Asian states, conduct negotiations and conclude agreements with their rulers (Pierce, 1960:49). His two subordinate Governor Generals commanded forces and administered the constituent oblasts: Syr-Dar'ya and Semi-rech'ye. The former, facing south, consisted of the Syr-Dar'ya Line and most of the Kokand Line, and contained the sedentary Uzbeks as well as the Kazakhs formerly subordinated to Kokand. The latter, facing China, controlled the Kazakhs of the Elder Horde and the Kirgiz of the Tyan' Shan'.

   Conflicts with Kokand, Bukhara, and Khiva led to further Russian acquisition. First Russia defeated Kokand (1866) and absorbed its tributary Kirgiz-inhabited mountain region into Semirech'ye, securing it with forts on the Naryn' river (Naryn'skoye Ukrepleniye, 1868) and the eastern shore of Issyk-Kul (Karakol, now Przheval'sk, 1869). Then Bukhara was defeated. Its strategic upland territory, including Samarkand, was annexed to Turkestan (1868), but the remaining part of it remained a nominally independent protectorate of Russia. Finally, Khiva was overwhelmed in a massive campaign (1873). As in the case of Bukhara, Russia annexed the right bank of the Amu Dar'ya to control Khiva, and converted the populous oasis into a subservient protectorate that would bear its own costs of administration. Only Kokand was absorbed into Turkestan as Fergana oblast (1876) following a holy war and its bloody suppression (Pierce, 1960:29--37).

Russia's final advances secured her border with Persia and Afghanistan. First Russian forces from the Caucasus, in their campaign against Khiva, crossed the Caspian and established Krasnovodsk (1869) in what became known as Transcaspia. Subsequent skirmishes with the Turkmen resulted in the taking of Kyzyl-Arvat (1877). Advancing along the foothills of the Kopet Dag, the Russians took Geok-Tepe (1881), Askhabad (now Ashkhabad), Koakhka, and Tedzhen. Later they annexed the Merv oasis (1884) and upstream to the Afghan border town of Kushka (1885). Russia's last move almost provoked war with Britain. The Anglo-Russian agreement defined the Afghan boundary, ceded the Pamir to Russia and Bukhara (1895), and ended Russian annexations in Middle Asia. Transcaspia was joined to Turkestan (1899), but the intervening protectorates of Bukhara and Khiva remained.

The Russian military, advancing into Turkestan, secured their supply lines with garrisons. Cossack settlements were planted to provide military self-sufficiency and security for subsequent peasant colonization. In Turkestan, however, cossack settlement was not needed. Native farmers produced abundant crops on irrigated land that could feed the garrisons. Moreover, there was no vacant farmland that could be colonized.

The exception to this pattern was the cossack settlement of Semirech'ye. These sparsely-settled foothills of Tyan' Shan', offered good farming potential. The Russian Government attracted Siberian cossacks with generous land and cash grants to secure the Chinese border. Since cossacks usually neglected crop production, the government allowed diligent peasant volunteers from Altay to join the military colonists (Abdykalykov and Pankratova, 1943:245).

Settlement of Semirech'ye proceeded quickly. In twenty years, from the construction of Kopal (1847) to the establishment of the separate Semirech'ye Cossack Army (1867), it grew to fourteen cossack settlements with 15 000 persons (Semenov-Tyan-Shanskiy, 1913:32). Their prosperity, however, was due less to their farming efforts than to the rich lands and privileged position bestowed upon them. Von Kaufman, the Governor

General of Turkestan, complained that the cossacks neglected cultivation, destroyed scarce forests, impeded Kazakh trans-humance, and infringed on Kazakh water rights (Pierce, 1960:109–110). Von Kaufman believed that cossack colonization had outlived its usefulness and that subsequent colonization should depend on Slavic peasantry.

Attempts to feed the Syr Dar'ya line with cossack settlements proved unsuccessful. Flanked by semi-desert and desert on either side, the narrow strip watered by the Syr Dar'ya was either farmed by Uzbek irrigators or grazed by Kazakh herdsmen. The Ural cossacks, by contrast, preferred fishing to farming (Semenov-Tyan-Shanskiy, 1913:364).

Similarly, Russian garrisons on the Kokand line had to depend on native food producers. Watered sites were already settled by Uzbeks or indentured Kazakhs. In the foothills land suitable for dry farming was grazed and partly cropped by the Uzbeks. Moreover, Von Kaufman, viewing the cossacks as wasteful farmers, prohibited the expansion of cossack settlement west of Semirech'ye and encouraged Russian peasant settlement instead (Pierce, 1960:110). The meagre spillover from Semirech'ye towards Tashkent consisted mainly of vagabonds. The settlement of Slavic farmers increased only after the Russian peasantry were granted legal status in Turkestan (1886) and offered financial assistance (Yashnov, 1915:103–104).

Meanwhile, military colonization consisted of Russian garrisons placed in forts and modern quarters alongside the cities of Turkestan. Tashkent boasted, in 1873, a native population of some 100 000, a Russian garrison of 6000 troops and a Russian quarter of 3000 civilians and officers. Even when the city's Russian population (1914) approached 50 000, about one-fifth of the total, the military atmosphere prevailed (Pierce, 1960:96-103). Except for Semirech'ye, the towns in Turkestan had proportionately smaller Russian garrisons and settlements. Samarkand, with a population of about 80 000 in 1908, had a Russian component of some 12 000. In Semirech'ye, Vernyy (1911) was predominantly (26 000 of 35 000) Russian. Askhabad, the capital of Transcaspia, had 44 000 inhabitants in 1911, of whom 9000 were Russians (Bartol'd, 1927:161-169). Lonely Russian military outposts guarded the frontiers. Altogether, Russian garrisons in Turkestan seldom fell below 50 000 in order to control eight million natives (Wheeler, 1974:366).

Slavic colonization depended on the availability of farmland. In Turkestan the Russian conquerors, hoping to undermine the economic base of native aristocracy and gain support of the masses, recognized all lands with buildings and plantations as hereditary possessions of the tillers (Pierce, 1960:148; Semenov-Tyan-Shanskiy, 1913:418). Russians could purchase land from native farmers, but massive expropriation for the purpose of Russian colonization was risky. The only lands Russian colonists could legally acquire were the state pastures declared surplus to the nomadic Kazakhs and Kirgiz. The other alternative, necessitating huge capital investments, would involve new irrigation projects.

The influx of Slavic peasantry was negligible until "the great Siberian migration". The first wave consisted of some 3000 households that suffered the poor harvest of 1891. More than one-half were settled in Semirech'ye (Shkapskiy, 1907:20–21), and most of the remaining in the adjoining Syr Dar'ya oblast (Semenov-Tyan-Shanskiy, 1913:326). Over 90 per cent of the Slavic settlers came during and after the Stolypin reforms, about one-half of them originating from the Ukrainian provinces (Turchaninov, 1912:234–237). They settled mainly in Semirech'ye, somewhat less in Syr Dar'ya, and still less in the foothills of Fergana and along the Persian border (Fig. 7.8).

Semirech'ye offered abundant state-owned pastures for colonization. Eight-tenths of the land surveyed for settlers in Turkestan was prepared in Semirech'ye (Glinka, 1914a: Atlas, Map 35). The plots, selected for good soil moisture and streams, were prominent on the southern slopes of Tarbagatay (at 600–1000 metres elevation), the western slopes of Dzhungar Alatau (up to 1500 metres), along the well-watered northern slopes of Zailinskiy Alatau and the Kirgizskiy Khrebet (up to 1500 metres), in the eastern end of the Issyk-Kul basin (1600 to 2000 metres) and the equally high terraces of the Naryn river (Fig. 7.8).

The high terraces enabled Slavic settlers to maintain their traditional grain growing without irrigation. At first many settlers occupied the drier, more accessible piedmont steppes. Accepting Kazakh belief that the high terraces were too cool for grains to mature, they attempted irrigation. However, experiments after 1881 on humus-rich chestnut and chernozem soils at higher elevations (1700 to 2150 metres) revealed good yields of spring grains that sometimes surpassed those on irrigated fields, where inexperienced farmers overwatered their crops (Vorotnikov, 1910:301–305). Government surveyors thus began to seek high terraces as desirable sites for Slavic rural settlement.

Slavic peasants in Semirech'ye had abundant good farmland, worked hard and prospered. This impressed officials, who advocated the elimination of undue privileges for the cossacks and urged peasant colonization as the only effective way of securing the Russian frontier (Shkapskiy, 1907:33–49). The government promoted peasant colonization with propaganda and (following 1911) with a programme of generous monetary subsidies (Demko, 1969:118–120). Consequently Semirech'ye experienced a massive growth of Slavic rural population.

At first peasant settlements in Semirech'ye grew slowly: twenty-nine in 1882 and forty-one in 1908. By 1911 peasant settlements jumped to 123, while the cossack *stanitsy* and *vyselki* hardly increased from thirty in 1908

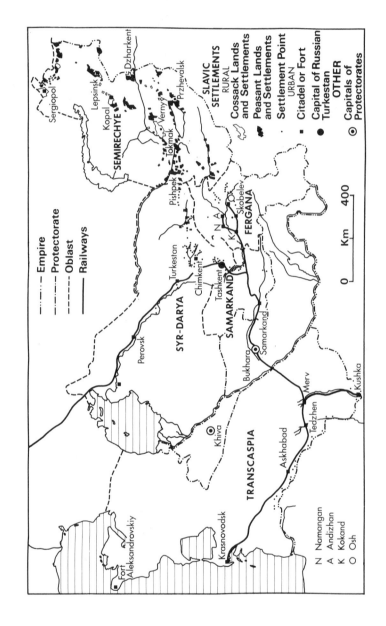

Fig. 7.8. Slavic settlement in Turkestan.

to thirty-two in 1911 (Semenov-Tyan-Shanskiy, 1913:322–34). Between 1897 and 1911 the Slavic rural population of Semirech'ye doubled (66 735 to 154 439). In both years it accounted for about two-thirds of Turkestan's Slavic rural population (Turchaninov, 1914:87). Semirech'ye contained all the cossack lands in Turkestan, one-half of the sown area of the old settlers (*starozhily*), and nine-tenths of the sown area of the new settlers (*pereselentsy*), or seven-tenths of all the Slavic sown area in Turkestan (Tsvetkov, 1914:274).

The Slavic farming frontier also penetrated into the Syr Dar'ya oblast. Until 1891 there were nineteen Slavic peasant settlements established mainly along the Kokand Line. The first influx (1891–92) produced twenty-three settlements, but shortage of land caused local administration to close Turkestan to immigration. Settlements increased slowly (fifty-five settlements in 1897, sixty in 1906), until the Stolypin reforms (ninety-two in 1909, and 108 by 1911).

Conditions for Slavic rural settlement in the Syr Dar'ya oblast were less attractive than in Semirech'ye. Widespread deserts thwarted dry farming. Southward, near Tashkent, the natives fully used their farmland. The Sarts, with their millenial irrigation, held the best land. Even the Uzbeks, who irrigated small plots of grain, feed crops and orchards, also dry-farmed wheat and barley and pastured livestock in the uplands (Rassudova, 1969:50–60) Moreover, the colonists faced stringent procedures for acquiring land. They had to negotiate directly with the natives, for the law sanctioning the government to designate nomads' pastures for colonization was not applied to Turkestan until 1910 (Semenov-Tyan-Shanskiy, 1913:328).

The emerging Slavic settlement pattern reflected accessibility, availability and environmental suitability (Fig. 7.8). Most settlements followed the Chimkent-Vernyy trail, the stream-fed western foothills of Tyan' Shan' (600 to 1500 metres) and terraces along the Talas river south of Auliye Ata. Some irrigated from the Arys' river north of Chimkent. To the south, availability of land declined. Only eighteen small settlements, some housing Russian veterans, were clustered near Tashkent.

Since land for colonization could not be secured in large blocks, new settlements in Syr Dar'ya were smaller than those in Semirech'ye. Despite the increase of Slavic rural population (19 045 in 1897, 36 518 in 1911), the natives prevailed (98.5 and 97.6 per cent, respectively) in Syr Dar'ya.

Elsewhere in Turkestan peasant colonists provided a token Russian presence. Following the Andizhan revolt (1898), Slavic peasantry (mainly from Ukraine) were settled in Fergana on high terraces (1000 to 1500 metres) overlooking Kara Dar'ya, where they would grow grain, raise livestock, and guard approaches from the Chinese border (Gavrilov, 1911:122–123).

Only Russkoye Selo represented a large lowland (600 metres) settlement from which the natives were evicted and Slavic peasants settled to irrigate cotton (d'Encausse, 1967:167–169).

The Transcaspian presented a hostile environment to Slavic peasant settlement. The desert coast offered no basis for sustenance other than fishing. Turkmen used the available water for irrigation along the foothills of Kopet Dag and in the Tedzhen and the Merv oases, and raised camels in the Kara Kum desert. Summer heat, poor water, lack of wood, and rampant malaria discouraged colonists (Semenov-Tyan-Shanskiy, 1913:641). Nevertheless, in order to facilitate troop movement along the Persian border a railroad was laid and worker settlements established (Il'yenko, 1902:57–58). Border settlements were planted in mountain passes and at river crossings near military outposts (Dranitsyn, 1910:117).

The Slavic and German colonists responded to the new environment in different ways. Russian peasants, settled near mountain passes in Kopet Dag on sites abandoned by the Persians, often grew grain without irrigation, sold their water downstream to Turkmen irrigators, and used the proceeds for drinking bouts (Dranitsyn, 1913:134, 144). The Molokane, a Russian sect from Saratov, raised angora goats (Semenov-Tyan-Shanskiy, 1913:628). German colonists from Saratov, settled at a border crossing on the Tedzhen river, succeeded in dairy farming. Ukrainian peasants, settled near Kushka on the Afghan border, established dry farming of wheat and millet (Dranitsyn, 1910:136).

The most valuable resources of Turkestan were irrigable lowlands for growing cotton. Since natives already occupied the existing oases and additional reclamation was expensive, the Russian Government exploited native labour to grow cotton. Nevertheless, Russian workers were needed for building and running the railroads (Taaffe, 1962:82–84), establishing and operating experimental stations to replace the inferior native cotton with American Upland cotton (Knize and Yuferev, 1914:275), purchasing cotton and providing the financial, marketing and communications services (Semenov-Tyan-Shanskiy, 1913:456–457).

As development proceeded, a "cotton fever" struck Turkestan. To meet the rising demand for cotton modern technology was applied, for the first time, to dam large rivers (Skornyakov, 1914:230–232, 245–246). More Russian workers, engineers and administrators were needed. Moreover, the Stolypin reforms unleashed a flood of colonists that needed accommodation.

Two irrigation projects were undertaken by Russians in Turkestan: the Hungry Steppe and the Murgab. The former tapped the Syr Dar'ya for irrigating a dry, rolling plain south of Tashkent (Matley, 1970:331). The latter expanded irrigation of the Murgab oasis by damming the Murgab river (Matley, 1975:421–423).

The Hungry Steppe development produced, by 1915, eighteen Russian settlements (Kasymov, 1968:53–67). Some of them originally housed canal construction workers and their families (Semenov-Tyan-Shanskiy, 1913:689–690). Even later settlements, like Spasskiy, were not purely agricultural, inasmuch as more than half of the households also derived income from services, trades, the railways, or industry. The Slavic peasants reluctantly adopted cotton growing after three to five years of learning how to cope with poor water supplies, locust, and saline soils (Skryplev, 1913:209–223). Development of the Murgab created only three Russian settlements (Skornyakov, 1914:251), and most of the cotton grown there was by native renters (Dranitsyn, 1910:126).

Slavic farming frontier in Turkestan was restricted to available lands in Semirech'ye and, to a lesser extent, the north-western foothills of Tyan' Shan'. Token Russian presence was provided by Slavic rural settlements in the foothills of Fergana leading to the border with China and along the frontier with Persia. Russian colonization of irrigation projects was minimal. The protectorates of Bukhara and Khiva enjoyed nominal independence and, for the time being, remained closed to Russian colonization. Only the cities of Turkestan were saddled with Russian garrisons, administration, and commercial control.

CONCLUSION

Russia advanced into Central Asia in stages of acquisition, military control, and assimilation. In different environments each of these stages assumed different forms. In the forest environment political acquisition and military control were easiest, for the superior Russian forces encountered poorly organized hunters, trappers, herdsmen, and primitive farmers. Moreover, the assimilation of the forest environment coincided with the eastward-moving Russian frontier of trappers, farmers, and miners who displaced the sparse native population (or assimilated it), assumed a similar ecological niche, and raised the carrying capacity with higher levels of technology. Open steppe, where military control could not be established, was screened off with a line of forts to protect the peasants from Kazakh raids and allow them to assimilate the land.

Changes in geopolitical configuration permitted Russia to lay claim in Kazakhstan. The establishment of Russian control, however, had to wait until the Kazakh tribes were politically fragmented, strategically isolated with surrounding lines of forts, and militarily overwhelmed by garrisons in their midst. Colonization of Kazakhstan proceeded according to the levels of migration generated by socio-economic factors within the Russian Empire. Legislation permitted the displacement of Kazakhs to accommodate colonists on the best lands for agriculture; Kazakh traditional mobility facilitated their relocation. Russian peasants from Siberia preferred the wooded, well-watered sites and avoided open steppe. Russian frontiersmen from Saratov and Ukrainian peasants, however, knew how to use the steppe. With their ploughs and oxen they broke the virgin sod, avoiding alkaline depressions and dry margins, and adjusted to the continental climate as they migrated eastward. Later peasant colonists were directed to the remaining vacant plots; many were ruined by frost, drought, and locust, and had to return home. Meanwhile, some Kazakhs began to take up farming in the adjoining areas. The farming frontier of Kazakhstan was thus predominantly, though not exclusively, Slavic.

The more advanced and better organized Khanates of Turkestan succumbed to Russian modern military might, some accepting indirect "protectorate" rule of what remained. Russian garrisons controlled the large native population, and Russians in the cities assumed command of Turkestan's economy. Slavic peasants, except in Semirech'ye, found little opportunity to colonize the land. They had no experience in irrigation or mountain farming, and the few that settled required considerable adjustment to the new environment. Nevertheless, a military frontier was established to enclose Russia's cotton colony.

REFERENCES

Abdykalykov, M. and Pankratova, A. (eds), (1943). "Istoriya Kazakhskoy SSR s drevneyshikh vremen do nashikh dney", Alma-Ata.

Aleksandrov, V. A., (1964). "Russkoye naseleniye Sibiri XVII—nachala XVIII v. (Yeniseyskiy kray)", Moscow.

Aleksandrov, V. A., (1973). Zaseleniye Sibiri russkimi v kontse XVI–XVIII v. *In* "Russkiye starozhily Sibiri. Istoriko-antropologicheskiy ocherk", (V. V. Bunak and I. M. Zolotareva, eds), pp. 7–49, Moscow.

Apollova, N. G., (1976). "Khozyaystvennoye osvoyeniye Priirtysh'ya v kontse XVI pervoy polovine XIX v.", Moscow.

Armstrong, T., (1975). "Yermak's Campaign in Siberia", London.

Auezov, M. O. *et al.* (eds), (1957). "Istoriya Kazakhskoy SSR", Vol. 1, Alma-Ata.

Bartol'd, V. V., (1927). "Istoriya kul'turnoy zhizni Turkestana", Leningrad.

Becker, S., (1968). "Russia's Protectorates in Central Asia: Bukhara and Khiva, 1865–1924", Cambridge, Mass.

Bulygin, Yu. S., (1968). Zaseleniye Verkhnego Priob'ya russkimi krest'yanami v XVIII veke po dokumentam Gosarkhiva Altayskogo Kraya, *In* "Iz istorii Sibiri i Altaya", (A. P. Okladnikov, ed.), pp. 26–34, Barnaul.

d'Encausse, H. C., (1967). Organizing and colonizing the conquered territories, *In*

"Central Asia. A Century of Russian Rule", (E. Allworth, ed.), pp. 151–171, New York.

Demko, G. J., (1969). "The Russian Colonization of Kazakhstan 1896–1916", Bloomington.

Diyarov, K. D., (1967). Sel'skoye khozyaystvo dorevolyutsionnogo Kazakhstana, *In* "Preobrazhennaya step", (N. L. Bereshchuk *et al.*, eds), pp. 25–80, Alma-Ata.

Dranitsyn, D., (1910). Kolonizatsionnyye zadachi v Zakaspiyskoy oblasti, *Voprosy kolonizatsii* 7, 117–139.

Dranitsyn, D., (1913). Zametki po kolonizatsii Russkoy Turkmenii, *Voprosy kolo-nizatsii* 12, 133–179.

Drew, R. F., (1959). The Emergence of an Agricultural Policy for Siberia in the XVII and XVIII Centuries, *Agricultural History* 33, 29–39.

Fisher, R. H., (1943). "The Russian Fur Trade, 1550–1700", Berkeley.

Gavrilov, N., (1911). "Pereselencheskoye delo v Turkestanskom kraye (oblasti Syr-Dar'inskaya, Samarkandskaya i Ferganskaya)", St. Petersburg.

Glinka, G. V. (ed.), (1914a). "Aziatskaya Rossiya. Lyudi i poryadki za Uralom", 3 vols. and atlas, St. Petersburg.

Glinka, G. V., (1914b). Zemel'nyye poryadki za Uralom, *In* "Aziatskaya Rossiya. Lyudi i poryadki za Uralom", Vol. 1, pp. 532–576, (G. V. Glinka, ed.), St. Petersburg.

Gromyko, M. M., (1965). "Zapadnaya Sibir' v XVIII veke; Russkoye naseleniye i zemledel'cheskoye osvoyeniye", Novosibirsk.

Il'yenko, I., (1902). "Zakaspiyskaya oblast'. Ocherk", Moscow.

Kabo, R. M., (1949). "Goroda Zapadnoy Sibiri. Ocherki istoriko-ekonomicheskoy geografii (XVII–pervaya polovina XIX vv.)", Moscow.

Kasymov, N., (1968). "Progressivnoye znacheniye obrazovaniya russkikh poselkov v khodzhentskom uyezde", Dushanbe.

Kaufman, A. A., (1897). "Pereselentsy-arendatory Turgayskoy Oblasti", St. Petersburg.

Knize, A. I. and Yuferev, V. I., (1914). Khlopkovodstvo, *In* "Aziatskaya Rossiya. Lyudi i poryadki za Uralom", Vol. 2, (G. V. Glinka, ed.), pp. 275–298, St. Petersburg.

Komitet Sibirskoy Zheleznoy Dorogi, (1900). "Kolonizatsiya Sibiri v svyazi s obshchim pereselencheskim voprosom", St. Petersburg.

Kondrashenkov, A. A., (1973). Krest'yanskaya kolonizatsiya Srednego Pritobol'ya vo vtoroy polovine XVII–nachale XVIII v., *In* "Russkoye naseleniye Pomor'ya i Sibiri (Period feodalizma)", (A. P. Okladnikov, *et al.* eds), pp. 295–304 Moscow.

Koretskiy, V. I., (1973). Iz istorii zaseleniya Sibiri nakanune i vo vremya "smuty" (konets XVI–nachalo XVII v.), *In* "Russkoye naseleniye Pomor'ya i Sibiri (Period feodalizma)", (A. P. Okladnikov, *et al.*, eds), pp. 37–59, Moscow.

Kostenko, L. F., (1871). "Srednyaya Aziya i vodvoreniye v ney russkoy grazhdanstvennosti", St. Petersburg.

Lantzeff, G. V. and Pierce, R. A., (1973). "Eastward to Empire. Exploration and Conquest on the Russian Open Frontier to 1750", Montreal.

Lipinskaya, V. A., (1969). Poseleniya, zhilishche i odezhda russkogo naseleniya

Altayskogo Kraya, *In* "Etnografiya russkogo naseleniya Sibiri i Sredney Azii", (G. S. Maslova and L. M. Saburova, eds), pp. 9–76, Moscow.

Matley, I. M., (1970). The Golodnaya Steppe: A Russian irrigation venture in Central Asia, *Geographical Review* 60, 328–346.

Matley, I. M., (1975). The Murgab Oasis: The modernization of an ancient irrigation system, *Canadian Slavonic Papers* 17, 417–435.

Minenko, N. A., (1973). Gorodovyye kazaki Obskogo Severa v XVIII v., *In* "Russkoye naseleniye Pomor'ya i Sibiri", (A. P. Okladnikov *et al.*, eds), pp. 336–349, Moscow.

Nazarevskiy, O. R. (ed.), (1957). "Kazakhskaya SSR. Ekonomiko-geograficheskaya kharakteristika", Moscow.

Ochevidets', (1891). Pereselencheskiy vopros v Zapadnoy Sibiri, *Nablyudatel'* 8, 121–141.

Okladnikov, A. P. and Shunkov, V. I. (eds), (1968). "Istoriya Sibiri s drevneyshikh vremen do nashikh dney. V 5-ti tomakh", Vol. 2, Leningrad.

Ostafyev, V. A., (1897). Zemlevladeniye i zemledeliye Sibirskogo kazach'yego voyska, *Trudy vol'nogo ekonomicheskogo obshchestva* 4, 29–72.

Pavlov, P. N., (1973). Kharakter peredvizheniya russkikh promyshlennikov v Sibiri vo vremya razvitogo sobolinogo promysla (20–80–ye gody XVII v.), *In* "Voprosy istorii Sibiri dosovetskogo perioda (Bakhrushinskiye chteniya, 1969)", (A. P. Okladnikov *et al.*, eds), pp. 99–111, Novosibirsk.

Pierce, R. A., (1960). "Russian Central Asia 1867–1917: A study in Colonial Rule", Berkeley.

Pokshishevskiy, V. V., (1951). "Zaseleniye Sibiri: istoriko-geograficheskiye ocherki", Irkutsk.

Preobrazhenskiy, A. A., (1956). "Ocherki kolonizatsii zapadnogo Urala v XVII–nachale XVIII v.", Moscow.

Preobrazhenskiy, A., (1972). "Ural i Zapadnaya Sibir' v kontse XVI–nachale XVIII veka", Moscow.

Rassudova, R. Ya., (1969). Zanyatiya naseleniya, *In* "Etnograficheskiye ocherki uzbekskogo sel'skogo naseleniya", (G. P. Vasil'yeva and B. Kh. Karmysheva, eds), pp. 50–113, Moscow.

Ryabinin, A., (1866). "Ural'skoye kazachye voysko", Vol. 1, St. Petersburg.

S. F., (1894). Ocherk kolonizatsionnogo dvizheniya v Akmolinskuyu oblast, *Russkoye Bogatstvo* 2, 190–217.

Semenov, V. P. (ed.), (1903). "Rossiya. Polnoye geograficheskoye opisaniye nashego otechestva", Vol. 18: "Kirgizskiy Kray", St. Petersburg.

Semenov-Tyan-Shanskiy, V. P. (ed.), (1907). "Rossiya. Polnoye geograficheskoye opisaniye nashego otechestva", Vol. 16: "Zapadnaya Sibir'", St. Petersburg.

Semenov-Tyan-Shanskiy, V. P., (ed.), (1913). "Rossiya. Polnoye geograficheskoye opisaniye nashego otechestva," Vol. 19: "Turkestanskiy Kray", St. Petersburg.

Semenov-Tyan-Shanskiy, V. P., (ed.), (1914). "Rossiya. Polnoye geograficheskoye opisaniye nashego otechestva", Vol. 5: "Ural i Priural'ye", St. Petersburg.

Shkapskiy, O. A., (1907). Pereselentsy i agrarnyy vopros v Semirechenskoy oblasti, *Voprosy kolonizatsii* 1, 19–52.

Shkunov, M., (1911). Zaseleniye Altayskogo okruga, *Voprosy kolonizatsii* 9, 91–127.

Shunkov, V. I., (1956). "Ocherki po istorii zemledeliya Sibiri (XVII vek)", Moscow.

Skornyakov, Ye. Ye., (1914). Iskusstvennoye orosheniye v Aziatskoy Rossii, *In* "Aziatskaya Rossiya. Lyudi i poryadki za Uralom", Vol. 2, (G. V. Glinka, ed.), pp. 219–255, St. Petersburg.

Skryplev, P., (1913). Khlopkovodstvo i russkiye pereselentsy, *Voprosy kolonizatsii* 12, 203–224.

Taaffe, R., (1962). Transportation and regional specialization: the example of Soviet Central Asia, *Annals of the Association of American Geographers* 52, 80–98.

Treadgold, D. W., (1957). "The Great Siberian Migration: Government and Peasant in Resettlement from Emancipation to the First World War", Princeton.

Tsvetkov, M. A., (1914). Zemledeliye, *In* "Aziatskaya Rossiya. Lyudi i poryadki za Uralom", Vol. 2, (G. V. Glinka, ed.), pp. 256–274, St. Petersburg.

Turchaninov, N. V., (1912). Kharakternyye cherty russkogo pereseleniya do vodvoreniya Sibirskoy zheleznoy dorogi i v posleduyushchiy za yeye sooruzheniyem period, *Voprosy kolonizatsii* 11, 208–240.

Turchaninov, N. V., (1914). Naseleniye Aziatskoy Rossii. Statisticheskiy ocherk, *In* "Aziatskaya Rossiya. Lyudi i poryadki za Uralom", Vol. 1, (G. V. Glinka, ed.), pp. 64–92, St. Petersburg.

Vilkov, O. N., (1968). Torgovyye puti i dinamika torgovo-promyshlennogo dvizheniya v Sibiri XVII v., *In* "Sibir perioda feodalizma", Vol. 3: "Osvoyeniye Sibiri v epokhy feodalizma (XVII–XIX vv.)", pp. 59–81, Novosibirsk.

Vlasova, I. V., (1973). Migratsii ustyuzhskikh krest'yan v XVIII–pervoy polovine XIX v., *In* "Russkoye naseleniye Pomor'ya i Sibiri", (A. P. Okladnikov *et al.*, eds), pp. 249–260, Moscow.

Vodarskiy, Ya. Ye., (1973). Chislennost' russkogo naseleniya Sibiri v XVII–XVIII vv., *In* "Russkoye naseleniye Pomor'ya i Sibiri (Period feodalizma)", (A. P. Okladnikov *et al.* eds.), pp. 194–213, Moscow.

Vorotnikov, V., (1910). Bogara v Semirechenskoy oblasti, *Voprosy kolonizatsii* 6, 301–309.

Wheeler, G., (1974). Russian conquest and colonization of Central Asia, *In* "Russian Imperialism from Ivan the Great to the Revolution", (T. Hunczak, ed.), pp. 264–298, New Brunswick.

Whitman, J., (1956). Turkestan cotton in Imperial Russia, *American Slavic and East European Review* 15, 190–205.

Yashnov, Ye., (1915). Kolonizatsiya Turkestana za posledniye gody, *Voprosy kolonizatsii* 18, 102–157.

8 Bering's Expeditions

T. Armstrong

This essay seeks to present a coherent account of a significant and extremely wide-ranging piece of exploration, on which a large amount of research has recently been done in Soviet archives. The enterprises with which Bering's name is associated spanned nearly two decades (1725–43). At that time, they had no special name, but they later came to be known as the first and second Kamchatka expeditions, since Bering's advanced base in each case was Kamchatka. The second expedition, however, was a much larger enterprise than the first, and incorporated much activity in inland and coastal Siberia, remote from Kamchatka and the North Pacific; parts of it have also been called the great northern expedition and the American expedition.

Most of what has appeared in English on all this—and there is not a great deal—has concerned the North Pacific voyages. F. A. Golder's two volumes, *Bering's voyages* (1922–25), are invaluable for the Pacific voyages of 1740–42 and helpful for the first expedition, but are not concerned at all with the Siberian explorations. R. H. Fisher's stimulating *Bering's voyages: whither and why* (1977) makes a notable and argumentative contribution to all the Pacific voyages (incidentally, correcting Golder on a number of points), but also is not concerned with Siberia. That aspect of Bering's expeditions tends to be dismissed by the histories of exploration in a paragraph or two. The fullest English account, albeit somewhat fragmented, is found in A. E. Nordenskiöld's narrative of his own voyage of 1878–79 in this region, *The voyage of the Vega* (1881). There is a useful short chapter in Jeannette Mirsky's *Northern conquest* (1934). Our aim here is to view the scope and effectiveness of the whole huge undertaking, placing major emphasis on the Siberian exploration, but outlining also the Pacific voyages, both for the sake of balance and in order to draw attention to new material. The basic source will be V. I. Grekov's *Ocherki iz istorii morskikh geograficheskikh issledovaniy v 1725–1765 gg.* (1960), which takes account of all preceding Soviet research, including the other major contributions, L. S.

Berg's *Otkrytiye Kamchatki i ekspeditsii Beringa* (1924) with its two revised and augmented editions, and the first volume of M. I. Belov's *Istoriya otkrytiya i osvoyeniya Severnogo morskogo puti* (1956).

BACKGROUND TO THE EXPEDITIONS

The ball was set rolling by Peter the Great's famous instruction signed on 6 January 1725 (all dates are Old Style), a few weeks before he died:

> 1. Build in Kamchatka or some other place thereabouts one or two decked boats.
> 2. [Sail] in these boats along the land which trends to the north in the expectation (since its limit is unknown) that this land is America.
> 3. And to find out where it joins with America, go to some town under European control, or if you see a European ship, learn from it what they call this coast, and write it down and go on shore yourself and get reliable information, and, having put it on a map, return here. (Grekov, 1960:20).

This instruction was given to Captain Vitus Bering, who spent the next sixteen years—the rest of his life—trying to carry it out. Its loose wording and lack of precision has caused argument among scholars. Bering himself seemed not to have been so puzzled, but he may have had other instructions, now lost, or perhaps oral. Fisher (1977:22–107) has discussed all this in detail.

There was, of course, a background to this action of Peter's. He had had his interest kindled in geographical matters of this kind by his contact with Leibniz and with the French Academy of Sciences which he had visited in 1717. In 1719 he had despatched two geodesists, I. M. Yevreinov and F. F. Luzhin, to proceed "to Kamchatka and beyond" and describe what they found there, particularly "whether America and Asia were joined". These two returned in 1722, and although they had made a useful voyage, it was to the southwards of Kamchatka and not to the north, so that their map was helpful chiefly in locating the Kuril chain. Peter, who may well have thought that America was just east of Kamchatka and perhaps even connected to it (some contemporary maps would have have led him to that conclusion) does not seem to have been displeased with their achievement. But he no doubt felt that his question remained unanswered.

Vitus Bering was a Dane in the Russian service who was well known to Peter, but who had been selected not by the Tsar himself but by the Admiralty College. He was known in Russia either as Vitez', a corruption of the Danish Vitus which sounds like the Russian word for a legendary hero (*vityaz'*), or simply as Ivan Ivanovich. He was born in Horsens, Denmark, in

1681, and took his mother's family name, apparently because it was more distinguished than his father's, Svendsen (Petersen, 1941:11). He entered the Russian service by joining the Baltic fleet as a sub-lieutenant in 1703, and over the next twenty years got to know many important figures in the Russian navy, including the Tsar. He was competent, painstaking, intelligent, and courageous, and it seems that he was liked by his subordinates. But he sometimes lacked resolution, vacillated, and was over-cautious; and, most importantly, he lacked the burning enthusiasm of the true scientist-explorer. The choice could have been very much worse, but it could also have been a little better. In the opinion of N. N. Zubov (1954:56), a Soviet admiral and scientist, it was the wrong appointment.

THE FIRST KAMCHATKA EXPEDITION

On 5 February 1725 Bering received his instructions from the Empress (Peter having died on 28 January) and set off within a few days. According to Grekov (1960:20), the key question now was to find out where, not whether, Asia and America joined; Peter had evidently concluded that they did. If that is so, he must have based his conclusion on something more indicative than Yevreinov and Luzhin's results. But Fisher (1977:23–24) questions this interpretation.

Most of Bering's party of thirty-three men had left the capital before he did, and he caught them up at Vologda on 14 February. His officers were Martin Spanberg (Shpanberg in transliteration from the Russian), another Dane and by all accounts a coarse and cruel man; A. I. Chirikov, a promising young Russian naval officer; and P. A. Chaplin, a naval cadet. Luzhin, the geodesist of the earlier expedition, was also of the party, but he died on the journey across Siberia.

The first task was to reach Kamchatka. There were no roads to speak of east of the Urals, and travel was by water in the traditional Russian manner. After awaiting break-up of the river ice in Tobol'sk, the party continued along the Irtysh, Ob', Ket', Yenisey, Angara, and Ilim, and overwintered at Ilimsk and Ust'-Kut. During this leg of the journey the expedition was joined by thirty-three soldiers, a monk, and fifty-two carpenters, blacksmiths, and coopers. In the spring of 1726 they descended the Lena to Yakutsk, reaching it on 16 June. Bering took some men on horseback to Okhotsk on the Pacific coast, while the rest of the party struggled across the mountains in the following winter and spring. The effort expended in this trek, where extensive portage was unavoidable, involved the Yakutsk administration in providing 250 men and 650 horses. By the summer of 1727 the expedition was assembled at Okhotsk. They set sail in the small ship they built there, named *Fortuna*, and another unnamed vessel. Leaving

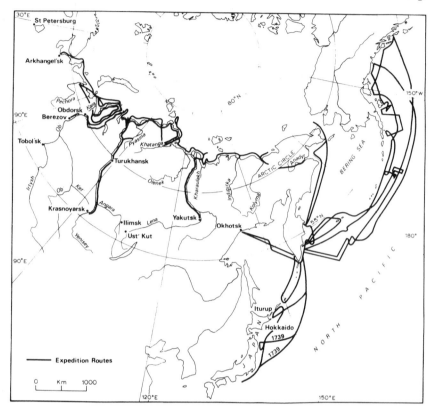

Fig. 8.1. The voyages of Bering's expeditions

Okhotsk on 22 August, they reached Bol'sheretsk on the west coast of Kamchatka on 4 September. The starting-point of the actual voyage of discovery was planned to be Nizhnekamchatsk, near the mouth of the Kamchatka river on the east coast of the peninsula. Bering would not attempt to sail round, apparently because of the prevalent idea that the waters round the southern tip were very dangerous, so they crossed the peninsula during the winter by dog sledge, reaching Nizhnekamchatsk in March 1728. At all these stopping points along the route, it should be explained, there were small settlements—a few houses—of immigrant Russians. The whole route traversed up to now, while hard, was not new. Ilimsk and Yakutsk were Russian villages nearly a century old, and Okhotsk not much less. The Kamchatka settlements were newer, but the territory had been indisputably in Russian hands for a generation, and Bol'sheretsk, Verkhnekamchatsk, and Nizhnekamchatsk had been Russian outposts since the first decade of the eighteenth century (Armstrong, 1965:55). It had taken the expedition just over three years to reach the end of Russian territory and the place from which it was to venture into the unknown.

A ship eighteen metres long, the *Svyatoy Gavriil* (or St. Gabriel), was built between April and June, and on 14 July it set sail from the Kamchatka river carrying forty-four members of the expedition with Bering in command. They followed the coast north-eastwards. Peter might not have expected them to go in this direction, because his idea that America might lie close to Kamchatka may not have been totally dispelled by Yevreinov and Luzhin; for it is thought that he might have had before him, in writing his instructions, a map by J. B. Homann of 1722 which shows land (unnamed, but called by others on later maps 'Company Land') close to and due east of Kamchatka (Polevoy, 1964). But one may suppose that locals in eastern Siberia and on the Pacific coast knew better, and turned Bering northwards, so that in due course he traversed what we now call Bering Strait. Keeping close to the Siberian shore, and indeed landing on it to seek water and to speak to the native Chukchi, he reached 67° 24' N lat. on 15 August (Sopotsko, 1978:166). On the way St. Lawrence Island was sighted, landed on, and named.

It was for long thought that poor visibility prevented their identifying at the time the most easterly tip of Asia (today's Mys Dezhneva) and therefore the trend of the coast north-westwards from that point; but this view seems to be mistaken and to have arisen from the failure of earlier scholars to consult the original logbook (Sopotsko, 1978:166). Before turning back, Bering invited Spanberg and Chirikov to record their views in writing. Spanberg was for turning, Chirikov for continuing westwards, towards the Kolyma, correctly pointing out that unless they did so they could not rule out a link between Asia and America further to the north. But Bering's own view was close to Spanberg's, and since continuing westwards would have involved accepting the risk of wintering in the Arctic, among probably unfriendly Chukchi, he decided for the sake of safety to turn. Had they sailed west for a day or two they would have eliminated the idea of the great northern promontory that was to appear on many later maps; and had they sailed east they would have found Alaska. With hindsight, one can see that failure to do either of these things was Bering's major error.

On their return they sighted and named Diomede Island (they did not see there were two), but caught no sight of land further to the east; bad luck indeed, for the American coast is often clearly visible from their position. Fast time was made back to Kamchatka, which they reached on 2 September. After wintering again at Nizhnekamchatsk, Bering decided the next summer to investigate a story he had heard from the locals, that on clear days land was visible to the east. This could only have been what came to be called Bering Island (Bering died there twelve years later). Perhaps Bering also had in his head the idea of Homann's unnamed land. But he sailed 200 *versty* to the east and found nothing (he must have failed by a narrow margin once again). Returning, he doubled the southern tip of Kamchatka and sailed to Okhotsk. From there he travelled overland to Yakutsk and was back in St. Petersburg on 1 March 1730. He had travelled for five years to get one week in the area he wanted to investigate. But even if he left part of his assignment unfulfilled (he never found out where America was), he did at least come back with a view as to where Asia ended, and there was satisfaction in the capital at his achievement. A report on the voyage was published in the *Sanktpeterburgskiye Vedomosti* of 16 March 1730.

DISCOVERY OF NORTH-WEST AMERICA

This is perhaps the place to describe how and when the American north-west was first seen by Europeans. Another party left St. Petersburg in 1727 with the task of pacifying the natives of the Pacific coast and the far north-east and collecting fur tribute from them—a quite separate undertaking from Bering's. A. F. Shestakov, a cossack leader from Yakutsk, had proposed the idea and was sent to carry it out, and he was joined at Tobol'sk by Captain D. I. Pavlutskiy, who took command of what was seen as a primarily military foray. The two men quarrelled incessantly. Shestakov was killed by the Chukchi in 1730. Pavlutskiy continued the campaign, and in its course in 1732 sent a boat to explore the islands and the mainland (*bol'shaya zemlya*) believed to lie beyond them. The *Svyatoy Gavriil*, which was the boat they had come in from Kamchatka, was to have been commanded by Ya. Gens, her captain, but he was ill. The next in line was I. Fedorov, who went along, but he also was ill, so effective leadership fell on M. S. Gvozdev, the geodesist of the expedition. The party of thirty-nine examined the two Diomede Islands and landed on one of them. They then crossed to the mainland, and on 21 August 1732 sailed along the shore which seems to have been that between modern Wales and Teller on the Seward Peninsula. They did not land, and on the following day approached a "fourth island", which is likely to have been King Island, before leaving for Kamchatka. The mention of a fourth island, but no third, had caused some to think, Golder (1922:24) among them, that the mainland was the third island, and that consequently Gvozdev thought he had only discovered several islands. But Grekov (1960:51–52) argues persuasively that this was not so. The third island, shown on a map of 1743 based on Gvozdev's log, was probably Fairway Rock, and in any case the frequent use of the phrase *bol'shaya zemlya* can only imply that local people thought of the land as mainland.

  The reports of Gvozdev's voyage, however, made no impact for ten years.

Two were written in 1732–33 (neither has survived), but the officials who read them cannot have seen their significance. Gvozdev himself was arrested in 1735 following denunciation by one of the sailors, and remained in prison until 1738. On his release he apparently judged it best to say nothing more about the voyage, but renewed interest caused officialdom to require it of him in 1741. When the importance of the voyage was finally realized, word went out (1743) that Bering must be informed—for had not Bering been asked to find out just this? But by then Bering had been dead for more than a year, and he had failed to make the discovery Gvozdev made.

THE SECOND KAMCHATKA EXPEDITION

Let us now return to Bering. His limited success in 1725–30 made a less bad impression on his contemporaries than on later commentators, who had the benefit of hindsight. At the end of 1730, before he had been back a year, the question of another expedition had come up. The Senate asked him to consider what there was in the eastern territories which might be useful to the state. One of his proposals was to send out ships from Kamchatka to "learn about" America. Other proposals touched on the economy of the mainland, social conditions of the local people, and the possibility of trade with Japan. The Senate discussed the proposals in 1732 and approved them. I. K. Kirilov, one of the most important of the new class of administrators thrown up by the reforms of Peter the Great, played an important role in planning the expedition. It was he who involved the Academy of Sciences and the Admiralty College and as a result the expedition became much more wide-ranging than was originally envisaged. Kirilov himself had keen geographical interests, and was one of the prime movers of the Russian atlases of 1734 and 1745. The Pacific exploration was to consist of following a great triangle, Kamchatka to the vicinity of Bering's farthest north, thence to 50° N lat. on the American coast, and back to Kamchatka. Joseph Delisle prepared a map of what was known up to that time (in which he unfortunately included much misleading information), and this was to be checked and added to where possible.

To the North Pacific explorations there were added many new commitments. The Academy was to send a team to study the natural history, ethnography, and history not only of any new territories discovered but of already known regions of the north Asian mainland. The Admiralty College, probably influenced by its President Admiral N. F. Golovin, enormously enlarged the project by proposing a survey of the whole north and east coast, from Arkhangel'sk to Kamchatka—an undertaking which would of course demonstrate the existence or otherwise of a north-east passage.

The Admiralty College also introduced into the programme a reconnaissance of the southern parts of the Sea of Okhotsk and of Japan. All this caused the expedition to grow to a considerable size. The permanent strength, as it were, was 440—a figure which excluded many members of family who came along too. Temporary help, especially in transporting stores across Siberia, greatly increased this number: for instance, 1046 men were called for in the Yakutsk region in 1740. Provisioning became a major problem, in view of the very small local food production in the regions to be traversed.

An interesting feature of the expedition's instructions was that the leader was obliged to consult his officers over important decisions, and where necessary to consult the academic members too. This may seem odd in an age of autocracy, but it was a Russian practice in certain areas of activity, and it was indeed carried out.

The expedition started its long travels in 1733. Parties left St. Petersburg in February, March, and August of that year, heading eastwards. Most wintered at Tobol'sk in western Siberia. The following summer Bering moved on to Yakutsk. The first of the north coast parties were sent off, as

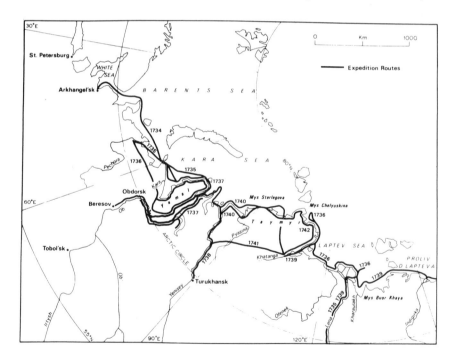

Fig. 8.2. The voyages of Bering's expeditions—western sector.

we shall shortly see. Bering remained at Yakutsk until 1737, nominally directing activities but frustrated by the enormous distances and unable in fact to exert very much influence. He was anxious to get on with his own assignment, the voyage to America. But severe delays beset the preparations, which were to be made at Okhotsk. Bering moved there in 1737 in order to stimulate construction work on the boats; but it was to require three more years of preparation before they were finally able to set sail. By that time, the activities of the coastal survey were approaching completion.

From Arkhangel'sk to the Ob'

This sector of the survey was subordinated directly to the Admiralty College, and was to some extent independent of Bering. Two sturdy sailing ships of the type known as *koch* (length 16.5 metres, beam 6.4 metres) were built in the Admiralty yard at Arkhangel'sk. Lieutenant S. V. Murav'yev commanded the detachment and the ship *Ekspeditsion*, and Lieutenant M. S. Pavlov commanded the *Ob'*. The two crews numbered fifty-one men. They set sail on 4 July 1734. Good time was made across the White Sea and the Barents Sea into the Kara Sea, and the west coast of Yamal was reached by 31 July. There was no ice about, but contrary winds delayed them, sickness set in among the crew, and Murav'yev was forced to turn back when almost at the northern tip of the peninsula and less than 150 kilometres from the Ob' estuary. They returned to the mouth of the Pechora, where they wintered. On 1 June 1735 they set forth again, and this time took six weeks battling against the winds as far as the entrance to the Kara Sea, a distance of under 400 kilometres. That sea was ice-filled, so progress remained slow. By mid-August they had penetrated further than the year before, and were actually north of the tip of the peninsula. They were sighted by a party sent down the Ob' to look for them—but nevertheless they failed to break through, and returned a second time to their old wintering place. The Admiralty College decided to persevere—but not with Murav'yev and Pavlov. These two had quarrelled and denounced each other, and were accused by others of various malpractices; as a result both were reduced to the ranks. Murav'yev was succeeded in the command by Lieutenant S. G. Malygin, the officer sent out to investigate the case.

Malygin left the Pechora on 25 May 1736. *Ekspeditsion* was crushed by the ice, and Malygin transferred to the *Ob'*. A short way out to sea he met Lieutenant A. Skuratov, who had sailed up from Arkhangel'sk with two new boats, *Pervyy* and *Vtoroy*. *Ob'*, leaking, limped back to Arkhangel'sk, while Malygin and Skuratov, still with fifty men, pressed on into the Kara Sea. Ice there was heavy, and although the boats penetrated half-way up the west coast of Yamal, they were obliged to turn back and winter on the Kara river further south. During the winter V. M. Selifontov, another member of the expedition (but not of Malygin's detachment) travelled overland and erected markers at key points along the coasts of Yamal. In July 1737 the boats set sail once again, and this time they finally rounded the tip of the peninsula and sailed up the Ob' estuary. On 2 October they reached Berezov, 300 kilometres upstream, and wintered there. Malygin journeyed overland to St. Petersburg, and reported to the Admiralty College on 12 February 1738. What might seem to be a relatively simple voyage—and one which Russian seamen had performed in the sixteenth century, but taking a short cut across the base of Yamal—had taken nearly four years and a great deal of tenacity. Skuratov took the two boats back to Arkhangel'sk by the same route, and again took two seasons to do it, arriving in 1739. It was on this voyage that the map of the coastline was chiefly compiled. The five-year period of exploration had yielded in the end a solid and worthwhile result.

From the Ob' to the Yenisey

While Malygin and his predecessor were battling their way to the Ob', another group of fifty-five men under Lieutenant D. L. Ovtsyn was trying to make the passage from the Ob' to the Yenisey. The distance is not great, and it is likely but not certain that others had made the voyage earlier, but nevertheless four seasons were necessary to complete the voyage. The two-masted double sloop *Tobol* (length 21 metres; beam 4.8 metres) left Tobol'sk on 14 May 1734, reached a point about half-way down the estuary (70° 04′ N lat.) on 5 August, and then turned back because of damage to the ship and wintered at Obdorsk (modern Salekhard), the village nearest the mouth of the river. The 1735 season was still less successful, and the ship was obliged by prevalent scurvy to turn back on 10 July at 68° 40′ N lat. regaining Tobol'sk on 5 October. Ovtsyn reported to St. Petersburg, and was told firmly that he must complete his assignment.

So in 1736 he set out once again. This time he nearly made it, being stopped by ice just short of the end of the estuary. The ship again wintered at Obdorsk, while Ovtsyn himself went on to Berezov. The following year, which witnessed the success of Malygin, was favourable also for Ovtsyn. The *Tobol* was joined by a new boat, the slightly smaller *Ob'-Pochtal'yon*, and each had a crew of thirty-five. The ships actually reached 74° 02′ N lat., or some 100 kilometres clear of the estuary entrance, before meeting ice. This was on 7 August. They turned, gained the mouth of the Yenisey on 31 August, and ascended the river to Turukhansk. The freeze-up caught them there, and they reached Yeniseysk, the regional centre 1,000 kilometres further upstream, on 21 July 1738. Ovtsyn set off for St. Petersburg, but he never arrived. At Tobol'sk he was arrested for having consorted, while at

Berezov two winters before, with the exiled Dolgorukiy family. For this he was reduced to the ranks and sent off to join Bering as an able seaman. But even in these circumstances his superior ability was apparent, and he played a distinguished part in Bering's own voyage.

The mapping done by this party was much helped, as in the case of the previous sector, by shore-based parties; and in these the geodesists F. S. Pryanishnikov and M. G. Vykhodtsev were prominent, covering much of the coastline off which the ships sailed.

From the Yenisey Eastwards

Ovtsyn, before his unfortunate undoing, wanted to extend his operating area and find out about the eastward continuation of the coast beyond the Yenisey. He therefore entrusted this task to a midshipman in his group, F. A. Minin. The idea was to go right round the peninsula of Taymyr to the Khatanga river. Minin took the *Ob'-Pochtal'yon* and twenty-seven men, leaving Turukhansk on 4 July 1738. He reached a point on the west coast of Taymyr at 73° 14′ N lat. (between Ostrov Diksona and the mouth of the Pyasina) before ice forced his return. He could not get back up the river to Turukhansk and had to winter near the mouth. This fact went far in ensuring that his next season would also be unsuccessful, since he had to go up to Turukhansk in the spring to obtain stores, and so lost valuable time. Thus in 1739 he barely reached the estuary before having to turn back. But he did return to Turukhansk this time. In the winter following, he did what each detachment before him had done and sent a party overland to survey the coast. D. V. Sterlegov, his helmsman, led the party and reached the cape now bearing his name at 75° 26′ N lat. This was the major achievement in this sector. Minin duly made another attempt in 1740, but failed (though not by far) to reach Sterlegov's farthest point. Although his results were decidely meagre, Minin was persistent and set off for a fourth attempt in June 1742. But this time he was stopped by human rather than natural agency, for Kh. P. Laptev, the commander of the next sector to the east, ordered Minin back and took command himself. Minin returned to St. Petersburg, where, in what was becoming a common pattern of events, he was denounced by his men, tried, and reduced to the ranks.

From the Lena Westwards

The parties working out of the Lena river and further east were close enough physically to the leader of the expedition, Bering, for him to have some real influence over what went on. He appointed Lieutenant V. M. Pronchishchev as leader of the group bound westwards, and gave him the double sloop *Yakutsk*. Pronchishchev had a crew of fifty, including the helmsman S. I. Chelyuskin and the geodesist N. Chekin; furthermore he took with him his wife Mariya. They set sail down the river from Yakutsk on 29 June 1735 and reached the open sea on 13 August. That summer, however, they only reached the Olenek river, immediately west of the Lena delta, and decided to winter there because of leaks in the ship.

They left the Olenek on 1 August 1736 and followed the coast westwards and then northwards. There was much ice, but they persevered, and on 18 August reached 77° 29′ N lat.—only fifteen nautical miles south of the latitude of the northern tip of the Taymyr peninsula, and of Asia—but they had been forced a long way from the shore. Scurvy was rampant, Pronchishchev himself was a victim of it, and they decided to return. On 29 August they were back at the Olenek, but Pronchishchev died that day, and his wife a fortnight later. They had indeed come very close to rounding the peninsula, and might well have found easier going down the west coast. But there was now an interval of three years, occasioned by the problems not only of this party but also of the party heading eastwards out of the Lena. Of this more later.

Pronchishchev was replaced by Lieutenant Kh. P. Laptev, already mentioned, who turned out to be one of the best of the detachment leaders. He sailed down the Lena with a crew of forty-five in the *Yakutsk* in June 1739 and wintered, after encountering ice, in the Khatanga river. He at once set about building here a base for future operations, and at the same time sent off land parties to explore the coast. He sailed north in 1740, but met heavy ice not far up the coast and in 75° 26′ N lat. was obliged to leave the ship, which was soon after carried off by the ice. The party walked back to the wintering place, and, undeterred by the loss of their ship, set about planning a land-based survey. Laptev organized three small parties, led by himself, Chelyuskin, and Chekin, and they all set out overland in the early spring of 1741. Each was to follow a separate course, but it was not possible to adhere exactly to the agreed plan. Laptev and Chelyuskin met on the west coast, rather close to the furthest north attained by Sterlegov—of whose journey the previous year, however, they knew nothing. Both went back to the Yenisey, where Chekin joined them. It was found that the central, northern, section of the coast remained unexplored. Laptev planned trips the following year, 1742, to fill in the gap. Chelyuskin was to follow the east coast of the peninsula from the Khatanga, while Laptev would descend the Nizhnyaya Taymyra river and meet him. Chelyuskin started first, left the Khatanga on 3 April, and on 8 May reached the most northerly point of the peninsula. He called it Vostochnyy Severnyy Mys (Cape North East), but today it bears his own name. On 14 May his party, continuing south-westwards along the coast, met a member of Laptev's party sent to meet him. The whole of the coastline had now been travelled, and all parties returned to the Yenisey and thence to St. Petersburg. Oddly, Chelyuskin's achievement was underemphasized and almost forgotten for a century. A. F. Middendorff, a Siberian traveller in the 1840s, re-established his reputation. Laptev's own diary of the expedition, which would have made things clear, was published only in 1851.

From the Lena Eastwards

The eastbound parties had the most fearsome assignment of all—to go along the coast to the Kolyma, thence round a cape thought to extend to 73° N lat. and on to the Anadyr' and Kamchatka. Bering Strait itself lay on this course. The party was put under the charge of Lieutenant P. Lassenius, a Swede in the Russian service. His boat, the *Irkutsk* (length 18.3 metres, beam 5.5 metres), carried a crew of fifty-two. He descended the Lena in company with Pronchishchev's *Yakutsk* in July 1735. Ice was met just outside the delta, and the ship was obliged to winter little more than 100 kilometres from the mouth of the Lena, on the Kharaulakh river. Scurvy quickly set in, and it killed Lassenius and thirty-nine of the crew. Bering made up the numbers again, and sent in as commander Lieutenant D. Ya. Laptev, a cousin of the other Laptev. He arrived at the boat on 17 July 1736, having travelled overland from the lower Lena. They set sail on 11 August, heading north-east, but at 73° 16′N lat. and north-west of Mys Buor-Khaya they encountered ice extending as far as they could see. Laptev, having heard that ice was always very bad in this area, returned to the Lena delta where he wintered.

Bering, having received the reports of Pronchishchev, Lassenius, and D. Laptev, clearly wondered if any progress were possible, and invited the academic members of his expedition to comment. Their opinion, and that of his council of officers, was negative. D. Laptev was then sent to St. Petersburg to explain. But the Admiralty College were not impressed, and urged further attempts. They emphasized that if ships could not get through, land-based surveys must be made. D. Laptev in particular was allowed, if necessary, to cut across the neck of the peninsula of Chukotka and go from the Kolyma to the Anadyr' overland—a distance of 800 kilometres as the crow flies. And having reached Kamchatka and met Bering there, he was to obtain a boat and provisions from him and sail back to the Kolyma. The assignment was not totally unrealistic, but it was certainly large.

So Laptev returned from St. Petersburg to Yakutsk and sailed down river once again in the *Irkutsk* in June 1739 with thirty-five men. In the open sea ice was met, but overcome, and on 14 August they rounded Mys Svyatoy Nos to enter the strait now bearing Laptev's name. After further adventures with wind and ice they reached the mouth of the Indigirka, where they

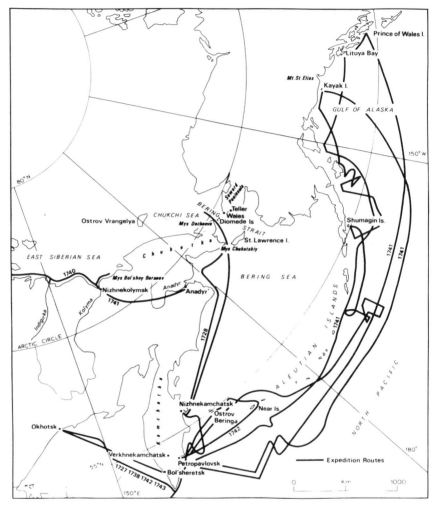

Fig. 8.3. The voyages of Bering's expedition—eastern sector.

wintered. Shore parties were active in surveying the coast during the winter. Next summer, after difficulty in freeing the ship from the ice, the party again headed eastwards on 31 July. The Kolyma was reached on 8 August, and an attempt was made to proceed further. But ice halted them at Mys Bol'shoy Baranov, about 100 kilometres further on, and they returned to winter at Nizhnekolymsk (where, it is worth noting, there had been a Russian settlement since 1643).

The following summer, 1741, Laptev tried once more to sail eastwards, but got no further than he had the previous autumn. He returned to Nizhnekolymsk on 10 August, and prepared to take the overland option he had been given. The journey to Anadyr was made in forty-nine sledges and took only twenty-two days (27 October–17 November, 1741). Local surveys were made in this area, and the following winter Laptev returned overland to Nizhnekolymsk and thence to Yakutsk, arriving on 8 March 1743. Chirikov, acting for Bering who had already died, sent him on to St. Petersburg which he reached on 1 December that year. His seven-year labour, though often frustrating, had yielded significant results.

Voyages to Japan

Martin Spanberg, Bering's companion of the first expedition, had the job of getting to Okhotsk and building the ships needed for the Pacific voyages. He was also to command the first expedition to leave—destined for Japan. His three ships were ready in 1738, and he set out on 13 July in his own brigantine *Arkhangel Mikhail* with a crew of sixty-three, together with the double-sloop *Nadezhda* (Lieutenant William Walton (V. Val'ton) from England) and *Gavriil* (Midshipman A. Schelting (Shel'ting) from Holland), each with a crew of forty-three. They went to Bol'sheretsk on the west coast of Kamchatka, whence they sailed southwards on 15 July. Within a fortnight the three ships had lost each other. None of them persevered very markedly thereafter. Spanberg reached Iturup, the most southerly but one of the Kurils, and Walton got 200 kilometres further south in the same area, but Schelting turned round almost at once. All three were back in Bol'-sheretsk by 24 August.

After wintering in Kamchatka, they all set out again in May 1739, joined by a fourth boat, the sloop *Bol'sheretsk*, built during the winter. *Gavriil* was separated early, but the other three sailed along much of the east coast of Japan between 37° 30'N lat. and the eastern tip of Hokkaido. The Russians did not land on the major islands, though they came close inshore and welcomed Japanese aboard their ships. Spanberg returned to Okhotsk on 29 August, with many ill or dead, while *Nadezhda* returned to Kamchatka, where she wintered. Walton in the *Gavriil* covered parts of the same coast but penetrated further to the south (33° 30'N lat.) and made landings. He, and the *Bol'sheretsk*, returned to Okhotsk on 22 August.

Two years, the time allowed in the plan, had now passed, so Bering did not permit a voyage in 1740. But there was reconsideration, followed by administrative delays, after which Spanberg set out again, in May 1742. He was himself aboard a newly built ship, *Svyatoy Ioann*; *Arkhangel Mikhail*, *Nadezhda*, and *Bol'sheretsk* came with him. The voyage was not a great success. Once again the ships got separated. *Svyatoy Ioann* sprang a leak before they sighted Japan and so had to return, and the others did likewise, it turned out, for similar reasons, and all were back at Okhotsk by 26 August.

All these voyages did achieve some results, however. A number of islands unknown to the western world were put on the map. In addition, members of the expedition made useful coast surveys of Kamchatka and round Okhotsk.

Voyages to North-west America

It is this part of the series of expeditions which is most fully written up in English, so the story may be told in the barest outline. The two ships *Svyatoy Petr* and *Svyatoy Pavel*, twenty-four metres long, twin-masted, and with fourteen small cannon each, were completed at Okhotsk in the summer of 1740. Bering commanded the first, Chirikov the second, and they set sail on 8 September with a total of 150 men. One of the ships was damaged on the way to Kamchatka, so they wintered in Avachinskaya Guba on the east coast, giving the name Petropavlovsk to the settlement they established on shore there. The main voyage started the next year, on 4 June. They headed south-east rather than north-east, because they still wanted to investigate the alleged Juan de Gama Land shown on Delisle's map (close to Company Land) which they thought might be part of America. After proving its non-existence, they turned north and shortly afterwards, on 20 June, the two ships were separated in a storm. At this point, not far south of the western end of the Aleutian chain, both ships turned south and east rather than north, which would have been the correct course for the Bering Strait region. The reason for the eastwards course seems to have been favourable winds, coupled perhaps with the thought that the great triangle they were to follow could as well be done one way round as the other. As it later turned out, both ships followed substantially similar courses, and both fulfilled the major objective of sighting America.

Bering sighted land on 16 July. It was a mountain which he called Mount St. Elias, standing at the present frontier of the USA and Canada at the head of the Gulf of Alaska. Four days later a party went ashore for a few hours on nearby Kayak Island, primarily for water, and the naturalist Steller accompanied them and made a collection of plants. But it was the only landing at this, the high point of the voyage, reached after sixteen years of endeavour. Bering, old, tired, and already ill, decided to head for home, and on the 21st they turned west. The voyage back was hard. Scurvy became rampant, storms and contrary winds abounded. Landfall was made at several of the Aleutian Islands and a landing on one (in the Shumagin group). Finally, on 4 November, they put into a coast they thought might be Kamchatka, but turned out to be an uninhabited island 200 kilometres to the east. As they came to shore, few of the crew were strong enough to work the ship, and disaster was narrowly averted by the action of seaman Ovtsyn. Forty-nine men on board were ill, there was no food and almost no water. The abundant wildlife on the island kept them alive, but *Svyatoy Petr* was wrecked as she lay offshore. Bering died on 8 December. The following summer the survivors, commanded by Lieutenant Sven Waxell (Vaksel'), originally from Sweden, built a new *Svyatoy Petr* out of the wreckage of the old, and succeeded in reaching Petropavlovsk on 27 August after a two-week voyage. They could not reach Okhotsk that season, so wintered again in Kamchatka and reached Okhotsk on 27 June 1743. They brought along with them some hundreds of sea otter pelts, taken on Bering Island (Berg, 1946:264), and this, curiously enough, brought about one of the most significant results of the voyages—the hunt for furbearers which took the Russians along the Aleutian Islands and into America.

The remarkable thing about the voyage of the other ship, *Svyatov Pavel*, was its similarity to Bering's. Chirikov sighted land one day earlier than Bering, on 15 July, and 700 kilometres further south, near modern Prince of Wales Island. A few days later, putting in for water at Litvya Bay, he lost fifteen men and both his ship's boats—possibly through action by Indians, or possibly through the boats being wrecked. This caused him to turn for home. His voyage back followed a course very similar to Bering's, but was more successful in that he reached Kamchatka on 11 October, although beset by scurvy. Six men died during the last three weeks of the voyage. The following summer on 2 June Chirikov set out again to investigate the last island group he had sighted the previous autumn (the Near Islands, Attu and Agattu), and after doing so passed close to another group which was probably that on which Bering's crew were at that very time building the ship that was to take them out. Chirikov returned to Petropavlovsk and thence to Okhotsk, where he arrived on 16 August 1742. He finally regained St. Petersburg in the spring of 1746.

The Academic Detachment

The attachment of a group of scientists to the second expedition was a highly interesting feature, and one which yielded successful results. The outstanding man in the group was G. F. Müller (Miller) of Herford, a German polymath who went to Russia in 1725, aged twenty, and was made an Academician in 1731. He covered the social science aspect—history, archaeology, ethnography, economics, geography. With him from the start were two other foreigners, covering the natural sciences: the German botanist J. G. Gmelin of Tübingen and the French astronomer Louis Delisle de la Croyère (half brother of the more famous Joseph-Nicolas Delisle, who was also an astronomer brought to Russia, and of the great Guillaume Delisle, the leading French cartographer of his time). These three were later joined by two more Germans, the historian J. Fischer and the naturalist G. Steller. The Russian contribution came in at a lower level, in the form of five, later six, "students", and four, later five, geodesists. There were also three artists.

The group was given much freedom of action, and travelled, severally or in pairs, over huge expanses of Siberia. Their work started in 1733, and several travelled more or less continually for ten years. Some of them accompanied the exploring parties: de la Croyère sailed with Chirikov (and died at the end of the voyage), Steller sailed with Bering, two of the geodesists, Chekin and Ushakov, accompanied north-coast parties. But mostly they were following their own interests.

Müller and Gmelin frequently travelled together and worked as a team. Müller's erudition and mastery of the task in hand is well exemplified by the instructions he gave Fischer, who took over part of his work: the ethnographic instructions alone comprised 923 points and occupies forty-six pages in the later printed version. He interested himself also in the history of Russian colonization of the area, and among his achievements was the discovery in Tobol'sk of the Remezov chronicle, a fascinating illustrated account of the first Russian advance into western Siberia, which he took back to Moscow (Armstrong, 1975:26). His other discoveries in Siberian archives included the report, found in Yakutsk in 1736, of Semen Dezhnev's voyage round the north-east tip of Asia in 1648. Müller's own major contribution was his *Opisaniye Sibirskago tsarstva* (1750). But he left a whole series of notes and papers which are preserved in the Academy's archives as "Müller's portfolios". These have been the source for much subsequent work, but are still by no means fully exploited or made available. Gmelin produced as his main work *Flora sibirica* (1747–69), and also, after his return to Germany, *Reise durch Sibirien* (1751–52). Steller made the most of his good fortune, if one can call it that, of accompanying Bering on the Pacific voyage. He died in 1746, while still in Siberia, but left several scientific records, some of which were later published. He is remembered particularly for his work on sea mammals, especially his description of the sea cow, observed in the Bering Sea, which became extinct soon afterwards. The outstanding Russian scientist on the expedition was S. P. Krasheninnikov, who travelled extensively in Kamchatka in 1737–41, and recorded his observations in his *Opisaniye zemli Kamchatki* (1755). Very valuable and extensive ethnographic collections were made, involving the participation of most of the members of the detachment, and as a result laid a firm foundation for this science in Russia (Kosven, 1961).

These were the highlights. Much more material was recorded and some of it has been published, piecemeal, during the two following centuries. It includes sixty-two maps, the publication of almost all of which was delayed owing to considerations of state security.

The End of the Expeditions

By the time all survivors of the North Pacific parties had returned to the mainland (1743), the expedition had been functioning for many years. Being set up more or less as a government department, it had accumulated a great deal of inertia, and proposals were made for its continuation on a long-term basis. But its demands on the local population in Siberia remained very considerable, and for this and other reasons the Senate decreed a stop to all exploratory work on 26 September 1743. Many more years passed, even so, before the expeditions' affairs were finally wound up.

THE RESULTS

The Russian Government gained greatly from the enterprise, in two main ways. First, the large increase in the amount of factual knowledge about the northern and eastern territories, as well as new information about their location and extent, helped to fill an obvious gap. Material was obtained which would permit a map to be made of the whole north coast from the White Sea to Mys Bol'shoy Baranov, east of the mouth of the Kolyma. The stretch of coast from there to Bering Strait was the one significant omission; it measures 1200 kilometres, compared to well over 5000 surveyed, but its omission allowed another lease of life to the idea of a large northeast-facing promontory on that coast. In Bering Strait and the North Pacific, the new discoveries took their place in the gradually forming picture. Achievement was great, but publication of this material was slow, uncoordinated, and hampered by security restrictions, so that the impact on the rest of the world was not what it might have been. The best of the maps to come out in the immediate aftermath was Müller's (1758). But even this did not use all the material obtained (and was criticized by Cook (1967:433) when he was in the area twenty years later), because, as we now know, the Admiralty College refused to allow the Academy of Sciences to have certain items of information.

The second advantage to Russia was that she began to exert political influence in the North Pacific at a crucial time, for within half a century Spain, Britain, France, and the United States were all actively pursuing imperialist aims in the region. Of these powers, Russia was potentially in the strongest position, with contiguous territory actually facing the Pacific. Kamchatka had been explored by cossacks at the end of the seventeenth century, but Bering's visits confirmed Russian sovereignty. Had Bering not made his expeditions then it is unlikely that Russian fur-hunters would have moved out along the line of the Aleutians into Alaska in the years immediately following, and it is very possible that some of the other contenders, who had more effective sea power, would have moved in the reverse direction and perhaps laid claim to Kamchatka and other parts of the long seaboard from Chukotka southwards. It is clear from the instructions issued by the Senate for the second expedition that there was thought to be a real danger of showing others the way to Kamchatka. Bering may be seen therefore to have played an important imperial role, although his instructions contained no specific reference to the claiming of territory. In Fisher's opinion, however, (1977:152–179) the imperial role was never far from the minds of the organizers.

The parties exploring the north coast did not need to fulfil this role, for the whole of the area they explored had already, in a loose and general way, been visited by Russians during the preceding century and more. Russians had descended the major rivers, leaving settlements, and had sailed along much of the coast. No maps of significance had been made, so the expeditions' work was in no way a duplication of earlier effort; it was always seen as complementary. There can have been no doubt in the minds of the members or the organizers of the expeditions that all this territory was already Russian; and in fact no other country, before or since that time, laid claim to it (the only exception was Vilhjalmur Stefansson's somewhat freakish claim to Ostrov Vrangelya in the twentieth century). Thus the work of the northern parties must be seen as a successful consolidation of Russian power in the area, rather than as an advancing of the frontier—except in the sense that it sometimes revealed that the country possessed more land than might have been thought earlier. Similarly, the beneficiaries of the mapping program were the Russians themselves; it would be more than a century before non-Russians ventured into these seas and coasts. Such a consolidation perhaps did have direct and practical usefulness as a deterrent to would-be claimants (if any existed), in that it showed Russia to be the indisputable master of the region and not just the absentee landlord.

One should also mention the status of the expeditions as a major undertaking in the geographical sciences. Whereas the Pacific voyages no doubt had a rather strong imperialist motivation, the Siberian explorations, and in particular the work of the academic detachment, had the character of a more scientific venture. That section of the enterprise may indeed be seen as the first of the great scientific quests of the eighteenth century, although its importance at the time was largely obscured by the slowness of publication.

It is impossible to contemplate the manifold activities of this great undertaking without being impressed by the truly Russian scale and character of it all: the deployment of hundreds of men over nearly two decades, the astonishing courage and dogged tenacity displayed by many of them, the amassing of great quantities of data of the most diverse kinds; and on the debit side, the inefficient and overcentralized control, the secrecy, the severe disciplinary measures, the apparent losing of the thread of what was to be done next, and, finally, the discovery by Müller of the report of Dezhnev's voyage of 1648 showing that Asia and America were indeed separated, and therefore evidence that a main geographical objective of the expedition had been known eight-eight years before, and forgotten.

REFERENCES

Armstrong, T. E., (1965). "Russian settlement in the north", Cambridge.

Armstrong, T. E. (ed.), (1975). "Yermak's campaign in Siberia", London.

Belov, M. I., (1956). "Istoriya otkrytiya i osvoyeniya Severnogo morskogo puti", Vol 1, Moscow.

Berg, L. S., (1946). "Otkrytiye Kamchatki i ekspeditsii Beringa", 3rd edition, Moscow and Leningrad. [First published 1924, second edition 1935.]

Cook, James, (1967). "The voyage of the *Resolution* and *Discovery*, 1776–1780", (J. Beaglehole, ed.), Cambridge.

Fisher, R. H., (1977). "Bering's voyages: whither and why", Seattle.

Gmelin, J. G., (1747–69). "Flora sibirica", 4 vols., St. Petersburg.

Gmelin, J. G., (1751–52). "Reise durch Sibirien", 4 vols., Göttingen.

Golder, F. A., (1922–25). "Bering's voyages", 2 vols., New York.

Grekov, V. I., (1960). "Ocherki iz istorii morskikh geograficheskikh issledovaniy v 1725–1765 gg.", Moscow.

Kosven, M. O., (1961). Etnograficheskiye rezul'taty Velikoy Severnoy ekspeditsii 1733–1743 gg., *Trudy Inst. Etnogr.* 64, 167–212.

Krasheninnikov, S. P., (1755). "Opisaniye zemli Kamchatki", St. Petersburg.

Mirsky, J., (1934). "Northern Conquest", London. [Reissued as "To the Arctic!", 1949, London and New York and 1970, Chicago.]

Müller, G. F., (1750). "Opisaniye Sibirskago tsarstva", St. Petersburg. [Fuller version, with annotation, issued in 1937 as "Istoriya Sibiri", Vol. 1, Moscow].

Müller, G. F., (1758). "Nachrichten von Seereisen, und zur See gemachten Entdeckungen . . .", St. Petersburg.

Nordenskiöld, A. E., (1881). "The voyage of the *Vega*", 2 vols., London.

Petersen, J., (1941). "Søfareren Vitus Bering", Copenhagen.

Polevoy, B. P., (1964). Glavnaya zadacha pervoy Kamchatskoy ekspeditsii po zamyslu Petra I, *Voprosy Geografii Kamchatki* 2, 88–94.

Sopotsko, A. A., (1978). Vakhtennyye zhurnaly korabley V. I. Beringa, *Izv. vses. geogr. Obshch.* 110, 164–70.

Zubov, N. N., (1954). "Otechestvennyye moreplavateli—issledovateli morey i okeanov", Moscow.

9 Diversification on the Frontier: Russian America in the Middle of the Nineteenth Century

J. R. Gibson

THE FUR TRADE

Russian America, the sole overseas holding of the Tsarist empire, was long synonymous with the colonial fur trade, as indeed was the rest of the boreal half of the North American continent. Since the return to Kamchatka of Vitus Bering's second expedition (1733–42) with sea otter pelts, Russian *promyshlenniki* had been drawn across the 'Aleutian land bridge to the North West Coast in pursuit of what they called the "sea beaver," the most valuable fur bearer on the world market. Sea otters and more numerous, but less precious, fur seals became the mainstay of the Russian-American Company, which was chartered in 1799 as the Empire's first joint-stock monopoly to regulate and stabilize Russian exploitation of Alaska.

By then, however, the maritime fur trade of the North West Coast was peaking. American and British traders had entered the competition a dozen years before, and the proficient "Bostonians" soon predominated. When the Russian-American Company's first twenty-year charter expired in 1821, the heyday of the coastal trade was already over. The sea otters had been relentlessly hunted year after year in the same places, and noisy rifles and numerous small hunting parties had frightened the animals and driven them far asea, where they could not be reached by deadly Aleut kayaks (which should not venture farther than fifty kilometres from shore). In 1796, 700, and in 1803, 880, kayaks hunted sea otters in the Kodiak District, but in 1860 only 300 were hunting in the whole of Russian America (and in 1861 a mere ninety-two in the Kodiak District). Similarly, the catch of fur seals on the Pribilof Islands fell from 127 000 in 1791 to 80 000 in 1811, 50 000 in 1821, and 18 000 in 1831. So under its second charter (1822–41) the

RUSSIAN HISTORICAL GEOGRAPHY VOL. 1
ISBN 0 12 081201 0

company turned inland and procured more land furs, particularly beaver, land otter, mink, and marten. In 1825 Semen Yanovskiy, onetime governor (1818–21) of Russian America, wrote to the company's Head Office in St. Petersburg to suggest that

> the annual decrease in the catch of sea otters, which constitute one of the main revenues of the R.-A. Co., must direct particular attention to the continental interior of northwestern America, which . . . is far from having been penetrated and heretofore has been almost untouched by the company's enterprise, although it is known from the inhabitants that plenty of land fur bearers, especially beaver, are found there. It can be said that this is the only reserve left for the R.-A. Co. to compensate strongly for the declining catch of sea otters.

And in 1828 the Head Office acknowledged that

> from the beginning sea otters have constituted the principal item of company business, and because of their value they have brought the company the bulk of its profits, so that more and more hunting of these animals was attempted, whereby this species has finally been almost completely exterminated, at least along our coast, and now the hunting of sea otters does not bring nearly—and henceforth cannot bring—the former profits. Although the decline of this hunting occurred some time ago, it was not felt by the company because of the high prices not only for sea otters but for all of our furs, but now prices for some animals—especially foxes—and circumstances have changed and have gone so far that the unprofitable state of our business [resulting] from the decline of its main source [of profit] has by itself harmed the company; in order to forestall this it remains for us to seek ways of replacing the losses from the hunting of sea otters with other items. After fur seals, beavers and land otters must take precedence . . .

The Head Office added that "it is known . . . that in the interior of America along the courses of the Nushagak, Kuskokwim, and Kvikhpak rivers there is a great abundance of beavers and land otters." To open the interior trade the company mounted the Northern Land Expedition in 1829 under Ivan Ya. Vasil'yev, the expedition of Andrey Glazunov and Ivan Chernov in 1835, and the crowning "pedestrian journey" of Laventriy Zagoskin in 1842—all to the basins of the Kvikhpak, Nushagak, and Kuskokwim rivers. The Glazunov–Chernov venture, for example, was undertaken "in order to gradually acquaint us more and more with the interior of the country along the Kvikhpak river and to open the richest beaver places". In 1853, Governor Ferdinand von Wrangel (1830–35) established a settlement on Stuart Island in Norton Sound to tap the fur trade of the Alaskan interior and the adjacent Asiatic coast. Meanwhile, the hunting of sea otters and fur seals was renewed around the Kurile and Commander Islands. Elsewhere conservation measures were implemented as early as 1822 in the form of *zapuski* or bans on hunting in certain places, at certain times, of certain species or with certain weapons. Thus, during the term of its second franchise the company exported twice as many land otters and thrice as many minks as it had during the period of its first franchise but only two-fifths as many sea otters and fur seals (Davydov, 1977:194–195; Golovin, 1862:99, 157; Khlebnikov, 1973:18; Tikhmenev, 1978:153, 207; USNA, roll 4, 417, roll 6, 101–101 v., roll 37, 258–258 v.).

When its charter was renewed in 1842, the company undertook a wide-ranging and far-reaching policy of retrenchment in order to reduce costs. That same year its exclave of Russian California, an economic and political failure, was sold. Fort Ross's fate had been sealed two years earlier, when the Hudson's Bay Company had agreed to supply Russian America reliably and economically for ten years, a task that neither Russian nor even Mexican California since the secularization of its missions had managed to accomplish. This agreement also meant the withdrawal of the Russian-American Company's Yankee rivals from the coast, for no longer were they able to realize profitable voyages by selling supplies at the colonial capital of New Archangel (Sitka) (Fig. 9.1). Thus, two of the colony's chronic weaknesses—inadequate supply and American competition—were overcome, at least for a while. Under the same agreement, the company leased the mainland panhandle (*lisière*) of Alaska (and abandoned St. Dionysius Redoubt) to the Hudson's Bay Company. The post of New Alexander was reduced from a redoubt to an *odinochka* (one-man outpost) in 1845, and the Atka and Unalaska Districts of the Aleutian Islands were abolished and subordinated to the New Archangel District in 1846 and 1847, respectively. Also in 1845 the Russian-American Company's factory at the exposed and shallow port of Okhotsk on the Siberian coast was moved to Ayan, and its traffic was shifted from the Yakutsk-Okhotsk to the longer but faster Yakutsk-Ayan route a year later. Even the advantageous 1839 accord with the Hudson's Bay Company was bettered. From 1846 until 1853 provisions and manufactures were shipped to New Archangel from Europe on chartered vessels at nearly half the cost of the British shipments, and from 1850 the Russian-American Company obtained goods directly from manufacturers in Hamburg rather than indirectly from retailers in London, at a saving of almost half the cost of hauling and loading. Additional money was saved by lessening the insurance on shipping between the colony and the motherland. From 1846 through 1853 the company spent 155 000 roublwa[1] on

---

[1] All rouble figures are silver rather than paper values. In the first half of the 1850s one silver rouble equalled 3–5½ paper roubles. This was equivalent to 75 cents American.

Fig. 9.1. View of New Archangel in the middle 1850s (courtesy of Yale University Library).

insurance for furs and teas sent from, and for ships and cargoes sent to, Russian America and received no payment for losses, so it decided in 1854 to insure fur and tea shipments only (although this decision could not be implemented until 1856 because the neutral ships that were used during the Crimean War, 1853–56, had to be insured). In 1843 the company began to market fur seal skins in London and New York, where they fetched "good" prices. Conservation measures, such as closed seasons and the reintroduction of breeding stock, were continued. Governor Mikhail Teben'kov (1845–50) was able to report in 1849 that owing to such measures on the Pribilofs, "where formerly only dozens or even no fur seals at all were to be seen, now there are thousands". By 1860 the company could club 60 000 fur seals annually on the archipelago without depleting the rookery; in 1862 80 000 were taken. The depletion of sea otters was also arrested. Consequently, just as many sea otter and almost as many fur seal pelts were exported from Russian America under the third as under the second charter (ORAK 1854–55:25–27; Tikhmenev, 1978:327–328, 330, 360; USNA, roll 55, 287, roll 63, pt. 1, 193, roll 64, pt. 1, 122).

Nevertheless, the company's maritime fur trade was still problematical. Although rival American "coasters" had abandoned the traffic by the early 1840s, they were succeeded by the Hudson's Bay Company, a more powerful and more efficient monopoly than the Russian-American Company. Moreover, Yankee whaling vessels were soon dotting Russian-American waters, and they did not hesitate to trade furs from any natives under Russian jurisdiction. More than 100 American whalers hunted off the North West Coast in 1843. By the middle 1850s an average of 453 whaling ships, mostly American, were plying Russian American waters, and in some years there were as many as 600. And when the whalers disappeared, they were replaced by fishermen. In 1866 Governor Dmitriy Maksutov (1863–67) complained that up to forty foreign schooners were fishing for cod in colonial waters, each vessel with a crew of eight catching in five months 3000–4000 cod, each weighing nearly three kilogrammes and bringing 14 to 33 cents per kilogramme. The pox of American and British competition harmed the company's "Kolosh [Tlingit] trade" in particular. The Russians had not been able to subdue the Tlingits, thanks to the Indians' phratic solidarity and American gunrunning, so every autumn from 1844 one or two company ships visited the Kolosh Straits (the numerous channels separating the islands of the Alexander Archipelago) to barter furs and provisions (potatoes and mountain goats) from the Tlingits for blankets and calicoes. From the 1850s more and more of this traffic was usurped by the Hudson's Bay Company and American whalers, who offered the Indians spirits and guns. Internecine warfare among the Tlingits also served to disrupt their trading activity during the 1850s. By the end of the decade all Tlingit furs were being traded to American (mainly) and British merchants for guns, gunpowder, lead, and liquor. In the fall of 1859 Governor Johan Furuhjelm (1859–63) asserted that the Tlingits obtained liquor from American and British traders "in such abundance that they not infrequently supply rum to our own workers". By 1860, he reported, that company's Kolosh trade had "completely ceased", and in order to revive it the company would have to offer firearms, ammunition, and rum. In 1861 Furuhjelm repeated that "our trade with the Koloshes has completely ceased ... partly because the Hudson's Bay Company and foreign whalers in the straits pay much more for furs than our price". The company's hopes of rejuvenating the fur trade via the Tlingits were thereby dashed (*Doklad*, 1863–64:I, 116, II, 157; Golovin, 1862:113, 158–159; HBCA, A. 11/62, 1843–49:1; USNA, roll 62, pt. 3, 38, roll 63, pt. 1, 77, pt. 2, 56 v., roll 65, pt. 2, 109 v.).

The furs the company did manage to acquire were not well dressed. In 1851 Governor Nikolay Rosenberg (1850–53) complained that, despite repeated instructions to his subordinates, "pelts are still sent to New Archangel in worse and worse condition from year to year" because of improper dressing. Consequently, Russian American furs did not fare as well as Canadian furs on the world market (USNA, roll 57, 286 v.).

Furthermore, the value of furs in general was declining in the wake of changing fashion. Furs were no longer in vogue from the middle of the century, hence the demand for, and the price of, pelts fell. In Europe silk hats replaced beaver (felt) hats. Sea otter was outsold by cheaper "German" beaver (that is, Canadian beaver imported from Great Britain and finished in Germany), and in Russia lambskin was substituted for sea otter on the collars of army uniforms. It is little wonder that the rouble value of fur exports from Russian America was halved between 1849 and 1859. By then the company's chief source of income was the traffic not in furs but in goods that were imported from Europe or America and sold to the colony's inhabitants—Russians, natives, and Creoles (crossbreeds). In the late 1840s the company made a net profit of 25 to 40 per cent on the sale of goods brought overland via Siberia or overseas on company ships; the mark-up amounted to 259 per cent on tea, 251 per cent on rum, 192 per cent on gin, and 100 per cent on cloth. During the 1850s the company's gross mark-up equalled 77 per cent and its net profit 35 per cent, which was guaranteed by its monopoly. By comparison, at the Oregon Country entrepôt of Fort Vancouver in the last half of the 1820s, Hudson's Bay Company goods were sold at 50 to 70 per cent above their "prime" cost (*Doklad*, 1863–64:I, 123, 133–135, II, 158, 211–213; Golovin, 1862:117, 186; Tikhmenev, 1978:366; USNA< roll 56, 118, roll 58, 5).

Thus, the decline of the fur trade, stemming from the depletion of fur bearers and the inconstancy of fur buyers, forced the Russian-American Company to find new sources of profit or go bankrupt. But two other significant events—the fall of China and the rise of the United States—also contributed to this decision to diversify. From the late 1830s the Manchu dynasty deteriorated under foreign pressure and domestic turmoil, and with it deteriorated the company's principal fur market. Eventually, China's infirmity was to prompt Russia to abandon Alaska in favour of more promising lands astride the Russo-Chinese frontier. The rise of the United States was meteoric during the 1840s when much of the Oregon Country was acquired and the Lone Star and Bear Flag republics were annexed. American settlers flocked to these new possessions and quickly established the United States as the dominant power and richest market on the eastern side of the Pacific (and indeed in all of the Americas). It was at this market, swollen by the California gold rush, that the Russian-American Company's new activities were largely aimed. And, of course, it was the seemingly irresistible juggernaut of the United States that was eventually to gain Russian America itself. Another event of some economic moment was the Russian financial crisis of 1857, but the Russian-American Company suffered almost no losses from it (ORAK 1857:39–40).

DIVERSIFICATION IN RUSSIAN AMERICA

Diversification was not totally new to the colony. From the very beginning of permanent Russian settlement in the first half of the 1770s on Unalaska Island, the fur trade had to be supported by a variety of ancillary activities— lumbering, fishing, farming—in order to minimize costly importation. Brickmaking, for example, was developed early. Many bricks were needed for stoves and chimneys. Kodiak Island produced 3000 to 6000 bricks annually around 1800, and could have made more if better clay, more lime, and competent masons had been available. From 1823 Kodiak's brickworks were located at Middle Bay; in 1831 it produced 10 000 bricks. Meanwhile, other brickworks were established at Fort Ross, New Alexander Redoubt, and St. Dionysius Redoubt. With the abandonment of St. Dionysius Redoubt in 1840 and the sale of Fort Ross in 1841, brickmaking was commenced at St. Nicholas Redoubt on the Kenai Peninsula in 1841 to compensate for the small quantity and low quality of bricks made at New Alexander Redoubt. With timber, clay, sand, and water at hand, the Kenai brickworks was rated the best in Russian America by Governor Teben'kov in 1847. It was expected to kiln 20 000 bricks per year; it made enough to send as many as 19 000 to New Archangel in 1847, and the same number again in 1848. Nevertheless, like most colonial ventures, brickmaking's product was high in price but not in quality, while bricks from Victoria on

Vancouver Island were superior and cost two-fifths as much. Moreover, sometimes not enough were made to meet colonial needs. In 1855, for instance, Governor Stepan Voyevodskiy (1854–59) bemoaned the "constant shortage" of bricks. The colony required 30 000 yearly in the middle 1860s; New Archangel alone needed 12 000–15 000 in the early 1850s (Tikhmenev, 1978:87; USNA, roll 34, 152, roll 46, 202v.–203, roll 54, 211, 249v., roll 55, 123–123v., roll 57, 527, roll 60, pt. 2, 165v., roll 65, pt. 1, 116–116v.). In the summer of 1864 New Archangel obtained 20 000 bricks from Victoria and San Francisco. The old kiln at St. Nicholas Redoubt had been disabled by a collapsed dome, and although 23 000 bricks had been made, 17 000 were needed to build a new kiln (USNA, roll 64, pt. 3, 59–59v., 61).

Retailing in Kamchatka

Diversification under the third charter, however, was designed to create alternative sources of revenue, not merely ancillary services, by supplementing the fur trade. The new ventures were aimed at the external, not the colonial, market. They were what Captain Pavel Golovin, who helped to inspect Russian America in 1860–61, was to term "productive" activities because they incurred income, as opposed to "unproductive" ones, which did not. The first of these commercial ventures was the retailing of goods in Kamchatka. The Russian-American Company had a long and close association with the peninsula. From 1803 until 1827 there had been a company agency at Petropavlovsk, and at the request of the government the company had periodically supplied Kamchatka with salt from the late 1820s (especially after the closing of the Okhotsk saltworks in 1837), and with grain from the early 1840s (after the signing of the 1839 agreement with the Hudson's Bay Company). It was not until the conclusion of the 1839 pact and the 1841 sale of Fort Ross (mainly for wheat) that the Russian-American Company felt that it possessed provisions (from the Oregon County) and manufactures (from Great Britain) in amounts and at prices that enabled it to compete against foreign (primarily American) traders in Kamchatka. Since 1828 foreign vessels had been permitted to import all goods (except liquor) into the peninsula duty free; they brought mostly textiles, paper, pottery, grain, fresh foodstuffs, and beverages (including illicit grog). Their success, plus the proximity of Kamchatka to Russian America, prompted the company's Head Office to send Governor Adolph Etholen (1840–45) to Petropavlovsk in 1843 to evaluate personally the peninsula's commercial prospects. He reported that in "many respects" it would be advantageous for the company to undertake trade there, asserting that it could sell goods in Petropavlovsk for 40 to 50 per cent more than in

New Archangel and that it could attain a trade turnover of 500 000 to 700 000 roubles annually in the peninsula. The company therefore decided to reopen the Kamchatka trade on a trial basis in order to "augment its resources." In 1844, 50 000 roubles' worth of company goods were shipped to Petropavlovsk for sale by local merchants on commission, although the latter were soon replaced by a company agent. Only 20 000 roubles' worth were sold, however, because American traders had arrived earlier with a wider assortment of goods at lower prices. Governor Teben'kov visited Petropavlovsk in 1846. His report persuaded the company's Head Office to continue the Kamchatka trade for three more years, even though it brought but "inconsiderable profit" because of opposition from local merchants and foreign traders and the general poverty of the peninsula. The company's trade in 1847, however, was "very profitable," for no foreign traders arrived that year. By 1847, in fact, the company was making "handsome profits" from the delivery of state goods to Petropavlovsk from St. Petersburg and Hamburg on its own ships. The government could not spare vessels from its fledgling navy, and overseas supply was cheaper than overland supply across Siberia. From 1851 to 1853 the company's own trade goods were also shipped directly to Kamchatka from Europe rather than via Russian America. This permitted a larger volume and a greater variety of articles to be sent and to be received earlier, with the result that trade brought "some profit". The company's flour was "much cheaper" (by two roubles per pood [16.5 kilogrammes]) than state flour from Okhotsk, despite the company's mark-up of 20 to 35 per cent. Nevertheless, as Governor Rosenberg acknowledged in 1852, the company's Kamchatka trade was conducted in a "very unsatisfactory manner." He reported that unsold goods were accumulating at the company's agency because: (i) they were subject to tariffs; (ii) they could not be bartered for local furs at the prices set by the company, as in Russian America; (iii) some of them were not in demand; (iv) they were priced too high (40 per cent higher than in Russian America); and (v) the company lacked "capable" agents. The depletion of Kamchatkan furs and the disruption of company shipping during the Crimean War were additional obstacles. The *coup de grâce* came in the spring of 1855, when Petropavlovsk lost its naval administration and personnel to Nikolayevsk at the mouth of the Amur river, which by then had become the focus of Russia's Far Eastern aspirations. The company's agent and goods were moved in the summer to Kodiak on the *Turku* and eventually to New Archangel (Doklad, 1863–64:I, 85–86, 311, II, 208; Golovin, 1862:116; ORAK 1843:34, 1844:48–49, 1846:47–48, 1847:45, 1853:31–32, 53–54; Tikhmenev: 1978:331; TsGIAL, f. 1,263, op. 1, d. 2,095, 135–136; USNA, roll 14, 410–410v., 412, roll 48, 636, roll 57, 349–349v., roll 58, 3, 5).

TRADE WITH CHINA

With the shift of Tsarist imperial interest from Kamchatka (and eventually from Alaska as well) to Amuria, the company tried to follow suit. It already had some experience in the region, having just helped the government to explore the river valley. In 1855 the company began retailing on the Amur. As in Kamchatka, however, it was outdone by local merchants (in this instance the Amur Company) and especially by foreign (again primarily American) traders, whose goods were admitted duty free (*Doklad*, 1863–64:II, 208; Golovin, 1862:116).

From the very beginning of Russian America its sea otter pelts had been marketed mostly in China, whose Manchu rulers prized the dark, lustrous fur as trim. In accordance with a treaty of 1727, private Russian-Chinese commerce was restricted to Kyakhta on the Mongolian frontier just south of Lake Bykal. Here Russian furs were exchanged for Chinese cottons, silks, and tea. More and more tea was traded from the late eighteenth century, when it became the favourite non-alcoholic beverage of Russians. Since its inception at the end of the century the Russian-American Company had participated "very profitably" in this trade, swapping mainly furs and broadcloth for teas, cottons, silks, and candied sugar. In the 1840s, however, the company's Kyakhta tea trade declined as the Chinese market began to falter in the wake of foreign intervention and internal discord.

Table 9.1. Imports of tea from Kyakhta by the Russian-American Company, 1842–1863.

Year	Boxes	Year	Boxes
1842	6660	1853	0
1843	6654	1854	69
1844	8173	1855	1157
1845	6150	1856	1043
1846	6453	1857	1633
1847	5740	1858	2198–2235
1848	4285	1859	2902
1849	3142	1860	2425
1850	3154	1861	85
1851	4436	1862	2344
1852	4250	1863	1005

Source: ORAK 1842:14, 1843:12, 1844:12, 1845:12, 1846:12, 1847:12, 1848:12, 1849:12, 1850:supp. 3, 1851:supp. 3, 1852:supp. 3, 1853:5, 1854–1855:supp. 4, 1856:supp. 3, 1857:10 and supp. 3, 1858:7 and supp. 3, 1859:6, 1860:8 and supp. 3, 1861:6 and supp. 3, 1862:7, 9, and supp. 3, 1863:41 and supp. 3.

Between the beginning and the end of the decade tea imports decreased by one-half at Kyakhta (Table 9.1). In addition, Russian manufacturers lobbied St. Petersburg to decree that a certain amount of the Kyakhta tea had to be exchanged for Russian manufactured goods; the government agreed because it wanted to promote domestic manufacturing. This measure, however, brought little benefit to the trade in manufactures and much damage to the trade in tea. On the one hand, while some manufacturers did profit at the expense of Russian tea drinkers others did not because, faced with a guaranteed market, they felt no need to spend money and effort on the improvement of their products. On the other hand, Russian tea traders likewise paid little attention to the quality of the manufactured goods. They were concerned only with obtaining them as cheaply as possible. The Chinese traders in any case were little interested in Russian manufactures and did not value them very highly. They could get cheaper and better British and French manufactures, which were now flooding the Celestial Empire. Russian broadcloth, for example, was undervalued so much that it cost half as much in Shanghai as in Moscow. The tea traders' losses were absorbed by their Russian customers, who paid five to six times as much for tea as its cost in China. Unable to exchange manufactures for tea, Russian traders turned to silver plate from 1854, so much so that it began to go out of circulation in Russia. The costs of the tea trade rose further when the charges for packing and hauling at Kyakhta were increased in 1842. The Russian-American Company's profits on tea declined accordingly, plummeting from fifty to eighty roubles per box in 1835–40 to only six roubles in 1845. Finally, in 1845 the Russian customs duty on tea was lowered from 1.32 roubles to 88 kopeks per kilogramme on ordinary tea but raised from 1.32 to 1.76 roubles per kilogramme on premium ("flower blossom [pekoe]") tea. Because two-thirds of the company's Kyakhta tea was premium, this change cost the shareholders up to 10 000 roubles annually. The company's tea trade to Kyakhta even ceased altogether in 1853 (*Doklad*, 1863–64:II, 214, 216–217; Golovin, 1862:121–122; Tikhmenev, 1078:331–332).

Thus it was that the company decided to try to rejuvenate its tea trade as part of its programme of adjustment through diversification. The old "Kyakhta system" was obviously failing, so the company sought new Chinese markets for furs and new Chinese sources of tea. This option materialized when the European powers forced the weakening Manchus to open China's ports to "foreign devils". In 1848 Captain Lindenberg succeeded in selling company pelts for tea at Shanghai, which had been opened to foreign trade in 1842 and which was to accommodate the International Settlement in 1863. Lindenberg repeated his success in 1850. For his efforts, Captain Lindenberg was awarded 1000 roubles by the Head Office in 1852 and promised 57 kopeks for every box of tea that he obtained thereafter.

The Shanghai trade was especially promising because the company's fur seal skins could be marketed there more readily than at Kyakhta and the tea could be conveyed to European Russia more cheaply by sea. The company also tested new markets on China's western frontier at Kuldja (Ningyuan) and Chuguchak, which were opened to barter trade by treaty in 1851. The Chinese merchants there, however, were not accustomed to furs and under-valued them, so trade was discontinued in 1855 (*Doklad*, 1863–1864:II, 215; ORAK 1853:6; Tikhmenev, 1978:332). The company had petitioned the Russian government in 1850 for permission to import tea from Shanghai by sea at the Kyakhta tariff. The government consented, allowing the company to import 2000 boxes annually for two years; subsequently this amount was increased to 4000 boxes until the expiration of the firm's third charter in consideration of its services to the state (in exploring the Amur Valley, for example) (Table 9.2). This "imperial favour" boosted the trade of the company "greatly" by giving it a monopoly on Russian importation of tea by sea until 1861. It also brought the company "enormous benefit", for while Shanghai tea cost less than Kyakhta tea and was transported to Russia more economically, the company was required to sell Shanghai tea at the same price as Kyakhta tea so as not to undermine the other Kyakhta traders (Golovin, 1862:122). So enormous was the benefit that during the 1850s tea was the principal source of company income, accounting for nearly one-half (*Doklad*, 1863–64:II, 215, supp. xxiii; Golovin, 1862:122; Tikhmenev, 1978:333).

Table 9.2. Imports of tea from Shanghai by the Russian-American Company, 1848–1862.

Year	Boxes	Year	Boxes
1848	71	1856	0*
1849	0	1857	4943
1850	489–492	1858	5096
1851	2052–2112	1859	5014–5017
1852	1930–3000	1860	5939
1853	2906–3000	1861	4977
1854	3514	1862	9837
1855	4536		

* None was imported in 1856 because of turmoil in South China and a blockade of Shanghai.

Sources: ORAK 1850:6 and supp. 3, 1851:7, 1852:7, 1854–1855:supp. 4, 1856:6 and supp. 3, 1857:10–11 and supp. 3, 1858:8 and supp. 3, 1859:7 and supp. 3, 1860:9 and supp. 3, 1861:5–6 and supp. 3, 1862:8 and supp. 3, 1863:8–9 and supp. 3; USNA, roll 54, 409v., roll 56, 323, roll 57, 516 and 578v., roll 58, 463, roll 59, 229v.

The 1860s brought an abrupt end to the company's tea trade and hence to much of its *raison d'être*. The Kyakhta traffic had rallied in 1855 under new regulations and amounted to nearly 2500 boxes in 1860, although the quality that year was "not high". In 1861 fewer than 100 boxes were traded; few Chinese merchants participated and they offered low prices for company furs. Finally, in 1863 they brought little tea to Kyakhta and in exchange demanded silver rather than furs or manufactures. Consequently, at the end of that year the company closed its Kyakhta agency and ordered its Irkutsk office to handle any future overland tea traffic. Meanwhile, the company's overseas tea trade also collapsed. In the spring of 1862 its monopoly was broken when the Russian government allowed all Russian merchants to import Chinese tea by sea or land. And, in the autumn, the tariff on tea imports was reduced by one-half. Competitors thus appeared, supply rose (particularly of contraband tea), and demand and prices fell. The company's profit on Shanghai tea was halved that year. These "significant losses" prompted the company to suspend its tea trade with China in 1863 (*Doklad*, 1863–64:I, 389; ORAK 1854–55:22–23; 1860:8; 1861:6–7, 10–11, supp. 3; 1863:9, 40, 42; 1865:9–10).

WHALING

From its very founding the Russian-American Company had been bedevilled by New England traders. As competitors in the maritime fur trade of the North West Coast, Yankee skippers had better ships and sailors, and better and cheaper trade goods. The 1839 agreement between the Russian-American and Hudson's Bay Companies was designed in part to rid the coastal trade of the Americans by depriving them of their New Archangel market for provisions and manufactures. But the pact did not stop American whalers, who were already combing the Gulf of Alaska for the Kodiak right whale and later the Bering Sea for the Kamchatka bowhead whale. They not infrequently trespassed on Russian territory, infringed the company's monopoly, and traded illicit goods (guns and spirits) to the natives. Russian protests were dismissed by Washington, which replied that it had neither the right nor the capacity to police Russian waters. The Russian navy could not afford to dispatch the number of cruisers that were necessary to patrol effectively the coasts of Russian America and the Russian Far East either. The company therefore decided to join, rather than fight, the foreign whalers. Traditionally, colonial whaling had been limited to local hunting by Kodiak natives for subsistence. In 1833, the company had hired an American whaler, Thomas Barton, for five years to demonstrate whaling to the Aleuts, but his efforts had proven "unsuccessful". Then in 1857 Governor Teben'kov proposed that the company undertake "coastal whaling" around Afognak Island and the Shumagin and Commander Islands, using four clippers or schooners and hiring American crews on shares and marketing the catch in the Sandwich (Hawaiian) Islands and Europe. The large profits to be made on whale oil and bone persuaded the Head Office that Teben'kov's proposal was too modest. In 1850 the company joined some Finnish businessmen to form the Russian-Finnish Whaling Company. It had a fixed capital of 200 000 roubles divided into 200 shares, half of which were owned by the Russian-American Company (*Doklad*, 1863–64:I, 96, II, 178; ORAK 1850:30; USNA, roll 53, 65v.–70).

The new company was an abject failure, lasting only thirteen years and outfitting a mere five vessels. The Russians were too lame and too late. Not only did they undertake whaling in conjunction with others, rather than on their own, but they also entered the business after the whaling grounds were depleted. The whalery had peaked in the middle 1840s, when some 200 whaling ships—most of them sailing from New Bedford and rendezvousing at Lahaina Roads—plied the North Pacific annually. By then the Gulf of Alaska had been overhunted, and so had the Bering Sea by 1850, when the Yankee "hellships" were concentrating on the Okhotsk Sea. Then it was not a *mare clausem*; during the 1850s an annual average of 100 foreign whalers hunted the sea, each taking 1000 barrels of whale oil. Foreign whalers already scoured its frigid waters in the 1840s and only their presence prompted the Russian-American Company to seriously consider whaling, the sea apparently being too close to home and too clearly Russian simply to be left at the mercy of foreign exploiters. The American whalers were "active and enterprising men, abounding in energy and means", according to State Councillor Sergey Kostlivtsov, who, with Captain Golovin, inspected Russian America in 1860–61. The Americans' rapacity left little for the listless Russians. The diminution of whales in Russian American waters was such that the amount of sperm oil that was sent to New Archangel from the rest of the colony fell from 435 vedros (5351 litres) in 1856 to 120 (1476 litres) in 1860, when the colonial capital required more than 500 vedros (literally, "buckets") annually (*Doklad*, 1863–64:II, 178–179; Tikhmenev, 1978:321; USNA, roll 53, 66, roll 63, pt. 1, 185).

The Russian-Finnish Whaling Company was not only lame and late, but unlucky as well. No sooner did it begin operations than the Crimean War erupted. On the eve of the conflict the Russian-American and Hudson's Bay Companies signed a neutrality pact that exempted their territories but not their shipping from the hostilities, even if their vessels sailed under the flag of a neutral nation. As Governor Voyevodskiy stated in the autumn of 1854, "although the colony is neutral during the war with England and France, ports are liable to blockade and ships to seizure on the open sea". The small Russian navy was no match for the Allied fleet. In 1855 an

Anglo-French squadron reconnoitred New Archangel, bombarded Petro-pavlovsk, and occupied Ayan. Two Russian-American Company ships, the *Okhotsk* and the *Sitka*, were lost to the enemy. Russian-Finnish Whaling Company vessels ran the same risk, so their activity and hence their catch were limited. During the war years of 1854, 1855, and 1856, when they had to lie low, 490, 436, and 350 American whalers, respectively, hunted the North Pacific out of Hawaiian ports (*Doklad*, 1863–64:II, 185; USNA, roll 60, 121).

Another obstacle to success was the high capitalization of whaling. As a result government subsidies were sizeable. Outlays for ships and crews were large but returns were small. For example, the Russian-American Company spent 100 000 roubles on the whaling venture, but had receipts amounting to only 7875. Losses therefore amounted to 92 125 roubles (ORAK 1863:46; Tikhmenev, 1978:322).

The Russian-Finnish Whaling Company's first ship was the 500-ton *Suomi*, built at Turku (Åbo) in 1851 and outfitted at Bremen. Foreign whaleboaters, harpooners, and coopers were hired. The *Suomi* hunted the Okhotsk Sea in 1853–54 and fared well, but upon its return to Europe barely escaped capture by the Allies and had to be sold at a loss for fear of seizure (Tikhmenev, 1978:323–324). The company's second ship was the *Turku*, likewise built at Turku in 1852. It began whaling in 1853, but in the spring of 1855 it took refuge at New Archangel, where it remained until the end of the war, having hunted only two seasons (1853 and 1854). At the height of the 1854 season the foreign crew members quit for fear of capture and detainment by Allied warships. Its cargo was sold at Bremen in 1857 for a meagre net profit of 3075 roubles (ORAK 1856:35–36; Tikhmenev, 1978:324–326). The 540-ton *Ayan*, built at Turku in 1853, was the company's third ship. It commenced whaling in 1854 but was captured and burned by the Allied fleet in the spring of 1855 (ORAK 1856:36; Tikhmenev, 1978:324). The 600-ton *Count Berg* was bought in 1857 and the 276-ton *Amur* in 1858. They were joined on the whaling grounds by the *Turku* in 1858. In the summer of that year the *Count Berg* and the *Turku* encountered 130 foreign whaling ships in Udsk Bay alone. Again in 1859 whaling did not yield "satisfactory results" because there were too many whalers and too few whales. The 1860 catch was no better and so at the end of that season the *Count Berg* and the *Turku* were sold. In 1863 the *Amur* was sold and the company liquidated. Nine years of whaling had produced only 2700 barrels of oil and 6136 kilogrammes of bone, as much as one or two American whalers would take in one year (ORAK 1858:61, 1859:42, 1861:65–66, 1862:52, 1863:46; Tikhmenev, 1978:325).

TRADE WITH HAWAII AND THE SANDWICH ISLANDS

The Russian-American Company's commercial diversification program was really aimed at two bourgeoning markets—Arcadian California and Elysian Hawaii. The Sandwich Islands had become the coaling station of the North Pacific, offering fresh food and water, timber, and crewmen (as well as relaxation and procreation) to ships halfway between Asia and America. Their salubrious climate and congenial people, plus resources like sandalwood and sugar cane, attracted thousands of Euro-Americans—drifters, traders, missionaries, deserters, whalers, plantationers. They represented a sizeable market by the middle of the nineteenth century, especially for Russian American fish and timber, the archipelago's waters not abounding in edible fish and its lands having by then been severely deforested. Furthermore, the islands had a surplus of tropical foodstuffs and salt, both of which were in short supply in Russian America. The latter was needed for salting fish and fur seal skins. In 1863 Governor Maksutov estimated that 350 tons[2] of salt were required every year for this purpose. Additional salt was needed by the company for Kamchatka. Hawaiian salt had the advantage of cheapness; in 1864 it was one-third the cost of California salt (USNA, roll 64, pt. 2, 88).

The company's Hawaiian initiative was launched in 1846, when it sent the *Baykal* under Captain Lindenberg to Honolulu to open a new market for fur seal pelts and to obtain economical provisions. He sold 125 barrels (these were "ten-bucket" barrels of 123 litres each) of salted fish, 20 000 board feet of timber (logs, spars, planks), and 5576 fur seal skins, plus some lavtaks (dressed sea lion hides), iron, rope, sailcloth, whalebone, and walrus teeth; and bought 226 tons of salt and some sugar, molasses, and coffee for a net profit of 15 000 roubles. This "trading experiment" demonstrated that there was "obvious benefit" to be gained from trade with the island kingdom, especially from the sale of fish, timber, and lavtaks. In 1847 *Alexander's Heir* took 125 barrels of salted fish, 20 000 feet of timber, 5600 fur seal skins, 30 lavtaks, 4104 kilogrammes of iron and steel, and 821 kilogrammes of walrus teeth to Honolulu and returned to New Archangel with 226 tons of salt and some sugar and molasses. The fish and timber found a "fairly ready sale" (495 feet were not sold) but the fur seal skins did not (2600 were not sold); they had been accepted in payment for goods as readily as money in all Pacific ports until 1830, but thereafter they went out of circulation with the depletion of the rookeries, and it was difficult for Hawaiian traders to put a definite value on them. The salt, however, was particularly cheap, certainly much cheaper than that from California. The

[2] All ton figures are long (2240-pound) rather than short (2000-pound) values.

voyage netted 4009 roubles in profit (ORAK 1845:47–49, 1846:45–46; USNA, roll 51, 305, roll 52, 124v.–125, 338, 483v., 485–485v., 487, roll 54, 18v.).

The advantages of company trade with the Sandwich Islands, to which the Hudson's Bay Company had begun exporting fish and timber in the 1820s, prompted Governor Teben'kov to recommend that it be expanded to an annual turnover of 200 000 roubles by acquiring two ships and establishing a commercial agent in Honolulu. The chief advantage of such expansion, he asserted, would be the reduction in the cost of upkeep of the colony by 25 per cent through the disposal of fur seal pelts on the islands. The Head Office supported Teben'kov's proposal. In 1848 it agreed to trade 200 to 500 barrels of salted fish and 15 000 to 300 000 feet of timber annually for three years for salt, sugar, and coffee. A commercial agent—Pëtr Kostromitinov, onetime manager of Fort Ross (1830–38)—was set up in Honolulu in 1848 as well. At the same time 209 barrels of salted fish, 19 000 feet of timber, 6000 fur seal skins, and some lavtaks, iron and steel, sailcloth, and linen were sent to Honolulu, where they were exchanged for a bark (the *Angola*, renamed the *Prince Menshikov*) and 169 tons of salt, 3283 kilogrammes of molasses, 2430 kilogrammes of sugar, 673 kilogrammes of coffee, and 378 kilogrammes of tea. The company made 13 000 roubles on this transaction. The *Prince Menshikov* returned in 1849 with 100 barrels of salted fish and 400 planks, which were traded for 41 tons of salt, 12.5 tons of sugar, 3283 kilogrammes of molasses, and some coffee, jam, sardines, and varnish (ORAK 1847:39–40, 43–44; USNA, roll 52, 486v.-499, roll 54, 277v.-278, 446, roll 55, 122, 283v.).

Traffic, however, was already faltering. The first blow was the California gold rush, whose irresistible lure reduced the archipelago's population. In the fall of 1848 George Pelly, the Hudson's Bay Company's agent in Honolulu, reported that "the foreign population are all leaving the Islands, and going to California". Fewer customers remained for Russian American fish and timber. At the same time, the native population was decimated by "contagion"—an outbreak of measles and whooping cough that took 12 000 lives. Consequently, the price of Hawaiian products soared. In 1848 also, the Russian-American Company's sawmill at New Archangel was temporarily disabled by a flood, so less timber could be cut for export. In the words of Governor Teben'kov, 1848 was "one of the most unfavourable years" of the company's Hawaiian trade (HBCA, A.11/62, 1843–49, 322, 326v.; ORAK 1850:28; USNA, roll 55, 283v.).

By 1851, following the "continual" exodus of islanders to California (including Kostromitinov, who was relocated to San Francisco), the Hawaiian market had become "overstocked" and business "very dull", according to a Hudson's Bay Company representative. In the summer of that year a "large portion" of Honolulu's populace left for Australia's gold fields. Demand was eroded still further in consequence. By 1852, commerce in California was recovering from the recession which followed the end of the gold rush, and this recovery took more and more company business away from the Sandwich Islands. In 1853 still another epidemic, smallpox, ravaged the islands. This "frightful disease" struck Oahu in the spring of that year with a mortality rate of 20 per cent. It caused a "stagnation" of trade. Likewise in 1853 the Crimean War began and soon terminated traffic from Russian America. All that the company was able to obtain during the first half of the 1850s was some salt for Alaska and Kamchatka—113 tons in 1850, 96.5 tons in 1851, 135.5 tons in 1852, 129 tons in 1853, and 193.5 tons in 1854 (*Doklad*, 1863–1864:I, 91; HBCA, A.11/62, 1849–52:628, 660, A.11/63, 11, 13; USNA, roll 56, 237v., roll 57, 262v., 312, roll 58, 208v., roll 59, 9, 94v., 326v., roll 60, 22, 32).

It was not until 1860 that the Hawaiian economy recovered from the setbacks of the late 1840s and early 1850s. At that date the Russian-American Company resumed the exportation of salted fish to Honolulu— 865 barrels in 1860, 1050 barrels in 1861, 830 barrels in 1863, 350 barrels in 1864, 859 barrels in 1865, and 1055 barrels in 1866. Governor Maksutov in particular increased fish exports to the islands, where "salmon was prized most of all" and where the company's agent contended that he could sell 2000 barrels annually. Brick-making at St. Nicholas Redoubt and coal mining at nearby English Bay were therefore supplanted by fish salting. This expansion was countered by better and cheaper salmon exports from British Columbia and Oregon, exports that reached the Hawaiian market earlier. No sooner had the company succeeded in selling more fish than its colony was ceded to the United States (ORAK 1860:44, 47; USNA, roll 63, pt. 1, 204v., pt. 2, 133, roll 64, pt. 2, 88, pt. 3, 64–64v., roll 65, pt. 1, 115v., 141, pt. 2, 67, 77, 90v.-91, 93v.-94).

CALIFORNIA AND THE ICE TRADE

California, not the Sandwich Islands, was the primary target of the company's diversification programme. Company trade with California had begun in 1806, when Count Nikolay Rezanov procured grain and beef for a starving New Archangel. From the late 1810s, when California's ports were opened to Russian ships, until the middle 1830s, when the bountiful missions were secularized and abandoned, traffic between Russian Alaska and Mexican California was heavy. The sale of Fort Ross further diminished this traffic, which did not revive until the gold rush. The thousands attracted by the gold, very pure and widespread, formed a large new market. Governor Teben'kov informed the Head Office in 1849 that everyone is making his way closer to the gold to find it by various means. With seductive announcements the government of the United States has promised the lucky ones untold wealth and has bestirred the entire East. Seekers of golden fortunes have come from China, India, Europe, and even New Zealand.

The company itself joined the scramble. Lieutenant Pëtr Doroshin, a mining engineer, with four Russian and six Tlingit workers panned 152 troy ounces of gold (worth 12 245 roubles) from 156.5 tons of sand from the Yuba River in fifty-five days during the winter of 1848–1849, despite rainy weather that swelled the river. The venture did not last longer for fear that the workers would desert (Golovin, 1862:123). The same ship that brought Doroshin's party also brought various goods of inferior quality and dilapidated condition that had been lying unsold in company warehouses for several years. All of this otherwise dead capital was sold for a net profit of 35 714 roubles. The company concluded that although prices fluctuated in California, it was a growing market for Russian goods and an economical source of European goods. The commercial agent in Honolulu, Pëtr Kostromitinov, was therefore transferred to San Francisco in 1851 for a three-year trial to monitor business and expedite transactions. He was not alone in trying to capitalize on the boom. In 1850 and 1851 a glut of foreign goods developed in San Francisco. Of the company wares sent there in 1850, only one-third sold. By 1852, however, business was recovering, the company's Head Office even asserting that "the possibility of the company gaining considerable benefit from trade in California was developing . . . in the following items: *ice, coal, wood products,* and *salted fish*" (*Doklad,* 1863–64:I, 91–92; Golovin, 1862:123; ORAK 1849:33–35, 1850:26, 28; USNA, roll 20, 639, roll 55, 311v.–312).

This trade opportunity was quickly taken up by the company. In September 1851, the American schooner *Exact* under Captain Folger tried, unsuccessfully, to get a cargo of glacial ice from the Taku river for sale in California. Folger, an agent for an ice company in Portland, then put in to New Archangel and proposed that the Russian-American Company sell him 1000 to 2000 tons of lake ice at $6 per loaded ton. Since Folger did not have the authority to grant the guarantees demanded by Governor Rosenberg, no contract was signed. But the prospect of an ice trade had been raised, and in San Francisco Kostromitinov was instructed to investigate the local market for ice. Rosenberg knew that some lakes near New Archangel were often covered with fifteen to thirty centimetres of ice, and he also knew that there was a profitable trade in ice on the West Coast of the United States. Ice from Boston sold for 44 to 88 cents per kilogramme in Panama and for $1.10 to $1.21 in Acapulco. Rosenberg figured that ice could be supplied more rapidly and more cheaply from New Archangel than from Boston (around the Horn) to satisfy California's growing population (Golovin, 1862:106; USNA, roll 57, 496v.–497, 501v.–504).[3]

In February 1952, a different Captain Folger docked at New Archangel on the *Flovius* to buy ice, but again no deal was struck. No sooner had he left than Captain Savage, likewise out of San Francisco, arrived on the *Bacchus* at the suggestion of Kostromitinov. Savage bought a full cargo (250 tons) of ice at $75 per ton for the San Francisco ice company of Hutton *et al.* This sale brought the Russian-American Company "much profit". The San Francisco company subsequently complained that at $75 per ton it could not compete with Boston ice prices. The Russians agreed to lower the price to $35 henceforth. In the autumn the Russian-American Company and the new American-Russian Commercial Company concluded a three-year contract whereby the latter agreed to take up to 1200 tons of ice annually on American ships at $20 to $25 per ton and to build an ice house at New Archangel and a log rollway from the ice lake (Kolosh [Swan] Lake) to the harbour. These terms were "very advantageous" to the Russian-American Company, for cutting, hauling, storing, and loading the ice cost the company only $2 to $3 per ton. In addition, the American ships could bring provisions (grain, beef, salt) and manufactures to New Archangel instead of ballast. Russian America's annual grain requirement equalled 403 tons in the middle 1850s and 484 in the late 1850s (*Doklad*, 1863–64:I, 117; USNA, roll 61, pt. 1, 10). New Archangel consumed more than one-half of this amount (USNA, roll 61, pt. 2, 112v.-113). By the early 1860s New Archangel was importing 290 tons of salt and 250 bales of hay annually from California (USNA, roll 63, pt. 1, 211v.). As Governor Voyevodskiy noted in 1857:

> in California it is sometimes possible to buy grain at very low prices, especially in the fall with a good harvest, and its delivery to the colony on ships that are used for the transport of ice can likewise be economical, so that grain imported by the colony in this way can cost less than that supplied by any other method.

The delivery of grain, salt, and textiles to New Archangel by American ice ships was crucial during the Allied naval blockade of the Crimean War. Furthermore, communication between New Archangel and St. Petersburg via San Francisco would be shortened to three months or less from the seven- to eight-month oceanic route and the five-month Siberian route. To facilitate this lucrative new commerce and Kostromitinov's relations with

---

[3] Until 1856 an ice ton contained 2240 pounds (one long ton) but 2120 pounds thereafter.

civic and state officials, a Russian vice-consulate was established in San Francisco (*Doklad*, 1863–64:I, 186, II, 192, supp. xviii; Golovin, 1862:123–124; ORAK 1852:23–25; Tikhmenev, 1978:335; USNA, roll 58, 37–37v., 40–41v., 409v.-411, roll 60, pt. 1, 30v., roll 61, pt. 2, 111v.).

It was not long before facilities were built and operations begun at New Archangel. In 1852–53 an ice house was constructed with a storage capacity of 1500 tons, as well as a rollway from the lake to the ice house and harbour. A second ice house with a capacity of 2000 tons, together with a rollway between it and the lake, was built in 1853–54. A third ice house was erected in 1855–56. At Kolosh Lake a horse was hitched to an iron sledge with one smooth and one serrated runner. The horse pulled at a steady pace, and the sawtoothed runner etched a groove across the ice surface to a depth of five centimetres; then the horse turned around and pulled steadily in the opposite direction with the smooth runner in the groove and the other runner cutting a new groove. This operation was repeated until the entire surface was cut into equal strips. Transverse strips were then cut in the same way, the surface being divided into squares like a chequer board. The grooves were deepened another fifteen centimetres with a ploughshare-like saw. The blocks of ice were loosened with a crowbar. Several Russian workers and Tlingit day labourers, the latter wearing only a blanket and going barefoot, removed the blocks, placed several of them in a row, and dragged them over the wooden rollers to the ice house or dock (*Doklad*, 1863–64:II, 196; Golovin, 1862:107; ORAK 1852:20, 1853:22–23, 1859:111; Rimskii-Korsakov, 1863:285; USNA, roll 59, 245, roll 60, 30, roll 61, pt. 1, 105v., pt. 2, 4v.).

New Archangel alone could not meet the demands of the ice contract. Winters were usually not cold enough to produce more than 1000 or 2000 tons of lake ice. "There was almost no winter at New Archangel" in 1855–56 Governor Voyevodskiy observed, and the American-Russian Commercial Company's ship *Zenobia* took on only 710 tons of ice instead of an expected 2000 tons. The *Zenobia* returned in early December of 1856 but had to wait a month because "winter began rather late, and ice was not yet found on the lake". In the winter of 1857–58 the stocking of ice cost 25 per cent more than in the previous winter on account of "the irregular weather and the unusual amount of snow". To ensure pure ice the frozen lake had to be broken up three times, and on the last occasion up to twenty centimetres of snow had to be scraped off. In the spring Governor Voyevodskiy reported that

in the course of last winter at New Archangel there were no more than 14 days of fairly favourable weather for stocking ice; until February the weather varied constantly from several degrees of frost to full-fledged thaws with an unusual abundance of snow, so that the lake froze for 2 or 3 inches and then was covered with up to 12 inches of snow, which alternately thawed and froze to form a crust of snow on the thin ice that impeded the freezing of the ice to a thickness which would be suitable for piling in the ice houses.

Snow-covered ice, even if it freezes after a thaw, is not suitable, so in order to obtain pure ice it was necessary twice—when several freezing days were expected—to break up and take out the unsuitable ice from the lake before it froze; this took a lot of labour; finally, at the end of January [beginning of February] several cold days ensued, so that the ice began to solidify and although it was soon covered with a layer of snow, it was already thick enough and could withstand the weight of horses, so the snow was cut off and then, having begun to put ice in the ice house on February 3 [14], they succeeded in stocking up to 2,500 tons by the 12th [23rd], when thaws again occurred and alternating snowy and rainy weather, making it impossible to stock any more.

In the winter of 1858–59 only a "very meagre" amount of ice (1200 tons) could be cut at New Archangel, again owing to "the irregular weather and the unusual abundance of snow". The winter weather of 1859–60 was the foulest in the memory of longtime residents of the colonial capital. Thanks to "incessant rains and wet snow" and "fogs and warm weather" in December and an outbreak of influenza in January that incapacitated as many as 300 men daily, no ice was stocked. The winters of 1862–63, 1863–64, and 1865–66 were so mild ("changeable") that it was "impossible" to stock any ice at New Archangel (USNA, roll 61, pt.1, 12v., 39, 232v.-233, roll 62, pt. 1, 29v., 34v.-35, roll 63, pt. 1, 5v.-6v., 18v.-19, roll 64, pt. 2, 41v., pt. 3, 29, roll 65, pt. 1, 57, pt. 2, 32v.).

Consequently, ice was also taken from lakes on Kodiak Island, primarily on Woody Island. There the climate was "more equable and winter more severe," the supply of "pure and hard" ice being more certain as a result. An exception was the winter of 1855–56, which was "no better" on Kodiak than at New Archangel (USNA, roll 61, pt. 1, 105v.). Both places experienced little frost, much rain, and frequent thaws, and altogether no more than 1000 tons of ice were cut (ORAK 1856, 31). Nonetheless, in comparison with 2500 tons cut at New Archangel in the winter of 1857–58, 1200 tons in 1858–59, and none in 1859–60, 4000, 5000 and 6000 tons respectively were cut on Kodiak. An ice house and a dock were built on Woody Island in 1854–55, prompting Governor Voyevodskiy to state confidently that

> henceforth it will be possible (without any danger from the weather) to virtually guarantee that neither the Boston company nor the recently organized company under contract to the Hudson's Bay Company will be in a position to compete with the colony in the supply of ice.

A second ice house was built in 1858–59, together with a rollway between the lakes and the two ice houses. A third ice house was constructed in 1859–60 after Fleet Lieutenant Matskevich had reconnoitred the Kodiak District and rated Woody Island the "most convenient" site for ice cutting. In 1858 a sawmill was established to produce sawdust, which served as chinking for the ice houses and as insulation for the ice blocks during storage in the houses and on the ships. A dam was also erected to raise the level of the lake; otherwise the sawmill could function only after rains or thaws had swollen the lake. Owing to the foul weather and the rather open site, the most difficult job was the construction of the dock. (ORAK 1852:24, 1857:35–36, 1858:55–57, 1859:35–36, 111–113, 1860:39; Tikhmenev, 1978:335; USNA, roll 60, 30, roll 61, pt. 1, 39v., roll 62, pt. 1, 32v., pt. 2, 71v., 87v.-88, roll 63, pt. 1, 5v., 6v., 119v.).

As at New Archangel, the ice was quickly marked and cut to the proper size by a special horse-drawn saw. The ice surface had to be at least twenty-five centimetres thick as thinner ice could not be sold. Such thick ice was seldom obtained at New Archangel, whereas on Woody Island the ice was usually thirty to thirty-three centimetres thick. When it snowed and then thawed and froze, the ice became veneered with a "snowy scum", which sometimes measured eight to ten centimetres in depth. This had to be removed, laboriously, with a special scraper pulled by three horses. Such impure ice was useless because of its friability. The winter of 1858–59 on Woody Island, for example, was cold but stormy and snowy. It was necessary to scrape a five-centimetre layer of frozen snow from the ice surface on five occasions, and once to clean the ice before stocking it. In the winter of 1862–63 a layer of impure ice twenty-three centimetres thick had to be removed. Blocks of ice taken from the lake were trundled on the rollway to the ice houses for storage. Subsequently they were moved on the same rollway to the dock for loading. This heavy work was done by Russian workers and Aleut and Creole day labourers. The former received a glass of vodka and the latter 29 kopeks daily, the same pay as at New Archangel. To minimize melting the ice was packed in sawdust. The normal loss from melting after leaving Russian America and before vending in California was 40 per cent. According to the America-Russian Commercial Company, ice shipped in vessels of less than 500 tons suffered "considerable melting." Full loads on large ships were therefore desirable. Thus, the Russian-American Company brig *Shelekhov* (270 tons) and bark *Prince Menshikov* (273 tons), which transported ice in the middle 1850s, were inefficient. Additional ice was lost when the corners of the blocks chipped during stacking in the ice houses and ship holds.[4] All told, probably more than half the ice was lost

---

[4] One of the Russian-American Company's annual reports stated that the loss from melting and chipping totalled one-third (ORAK 1859:116).

between the time of its extraction from Alaska's lakes and the time of its sale on San Francisco's streets. Most ice was marketed in California during summer, particularly in June (*Doklad*, 1863–64:II, 196; Golovin, 1862:107; ORAK:1860, 36, 1862: 47; USNA, roll 61, pt. 1, 153, roll 62, pt. 2, 88).

The terms of the 1852 contract were advantageous to the Russians but not to the Americans, who complained to Kostromitinov that their ice company was not making enough profit. In 1854 Kostromitinov obliged them by reducing the contracted price of ice by $15 to $25 per ton. However, this reduction was deemed "not only disadvantageous but even improper" by Governor Aleksandr Rudakov (1853–54), who contended that as a result the Russian-American Company stood to lose 28 500 to 43 000 roubles yearly. He warned the Head Office that "it is a well-known fact that an American, as primarily a practical man, will not contemplate venturing anything unless he sees material benefit in it for himself". He added that

> in my opinion any close acquaintance of the Americans with our colony or close ties between them and us would not seem to be of real benefit to us but in reality would always prove very unbeneficial to us . . . In my opinion on no account must the Americans be permitted to be their own boss in our colony, for there is no doubt whatever that in time they will fancy our sea otters and everything else just as now they fancy our ice, timber, and fish, and they will certainly come to reproach us for our inability to make use of the fur bearers here, just as they now reproach us for our inability to make use of the timber, fish, etc. (USNA, roll 59, 181–182).

Rudakov's fears were soon realized. In the spring of the same year the president of the American-Russian Commercial Company, Beverley Sanders, a "pushy and clever man", arrived in St. Petersburg with impressive letters of recommendation and succeeded in renewing the ice contract for twenty years (beginning October 21, 1855), even though the third charter of the Russian-American Company was due to expire in eight years. The latter agreed to sell all ice that was extracted in Russian America and the Russian Far East to the American-Russian Commercial Company at cost, with the ice company's profit being split between the two firms. The Russian-American Company also agreed to supply coal, timber, and fish on the same terms. It was additionally required to build ice houses at New Archangel, on Kodiak, and at San Francisco, with the two companies sharing the cost, and to transport the colonial products on its own ships (at 75 cents per ton of ice and $1.50 per ton of coal, timber, and fish). For its part, the American-Russian Commercial Company agreed to sell the products on the West Coast of the United States and in Australia. The terms were "disadvantageous" to the Russian-American Company, which may have acceded to them in the hope of facilitating renewal of its charter (*Doklad*, 1863–64:II, 193, supp. xviii; Golovin, 1862:124; ORAK 1854–55:16–18; Saul, 1972:156–170; Tikhmenev, 1978:335–336; USNA, roll 21, 109–110).

The Russian-American Company soon became dissatisfied with the 1855 contract, mainly because of overdue payments from the American-Russian Commercial Company. The latter's business suffered from a recession in California and competition from other ice companies. In 1859, for example, the American-Russian Commercial Company imported 2732 tons of Alaskan ice but sold only 1849 tons on account of the state's "commercial slowdown" (ORAK 1859:36). In 1858 the company imported 3585 tons (including 836 tons that were lost when the *Zenobia* was wrecked at the entrance to San Francisco Bay) but sold only 1167 tons (ORAK 1858:57–58). In 1853 a group of San Francisco businessmen formed the North West Ice Company to obtain glacial ice from the Alaska panhandle's *lisière*. This *lisière* had been leased since 1841 to the Hudson's Bay Company by the Russian-American Company for 1500 roubles ($7200) annually (from 1854). Glacial ice, being denser, lasted longer than lake ice, and it could be cut year round. But cutting such ice was not without problems. In the spring of 1856, for example, following the mild winter when little ice was cut either at New Archangel or on Kodiak, the American-Russian Commercial Company wanted its *Zenobia* to obtain a full load (800 tons) of ice from glaciers in Prince William Sound and the Kolosh Straits, but the Russian-American Company refused because the cutting of ice from steep, slippery, and crevassed glaciers far from an anchorage was too difficult and too dangerous. Moreover, the local natives were unfriendly and the waters were hazardous for large ships. Thanks to the resultant shortage of ice, the American-Russian Commercial Company lost out to an outfit which procured ice from the Sierra Nevada (USNA, roll 61, pt. 1, 157, 161–161v.). In the summer of 1853 the North West Ice Company signed a six-year contract with the Hudson's Bay Company whereby the former paid the latter $14 000 annually (nearly double its annual rent) for the exclusive right to cut ice in the *lisière*. The North West Ice Company operated half a dozen ships and even tried to market ice on the Asiatic coast of the Pacific. Increasing competition simply brought lower prices for ice in San Francisco. Thus, in 1855 the two ice companies decided to collude in order to raise prices. A year later the North West Ice Company was absorbed by the American-Russian Commercial Company, but the possibility of competition from *lisière* ice remained. Indeed, potential competition was cited by Governor Voyevodskiy in 1857 as one of the main obstacles to the stabilization of the ice trade. Competition notwithstanding, the ice trade brought the Russian-American Company "fairly large profits." In 1859 the Russians renewed the British lease to the *lisière* but under terms that permitted the Hudson's Bay Company to exploit furs not ice, coal, timber, or fish (ORAK 1854–55:18–21, 1859:34–35; Tikhmenev, 1978:336; USNA, roll 60, 84v.-85, 117v., roll 61, pt. 1, 218v; see also Ostenstad, 1977).

"Misunderstandings" and disagreements, as well as limited traffic, prompted discussions between the two companies in 1858 and 1859. On one occasion, the American-Russian Commercial Company complained that 75 cents per ton of ice and $1.50 per ton of coal, timber, and fish were excessive (ORAK 1856:32). Because of the seasonality of supply not much ice was traded. During especially mild winters, like that of 1855–56, trade was non-existent. Trade was also hampered because the American-Russian Commercial Company lacked the capital for acquiring the additional ships, warehouses, and agents that were necessary for tapping new markets. Governor Voyevodskiy felt that it would be "unprofitable" to market ice elsewhere on the Pacific as long as there was competition in California. Besides, he added, the Chinese and Indian markets were marred by "disorder", and the cutting of ice from Russian America's glaciers to satisfy these potential markets would be "very expensive" (USNA, roll 62, pt. 1, 35). At the end of 1859 Governor Furuhjelm visited San Francisco and finalized a new contract lasting from the beginning of 1860 until the end of 1862. The American-Russian Commercial Company agreed to buy at least 3000 tons of ice yearly at $7 per ton at the dock, paying for that amount even if it did not take it all. The Russian-American Company agreed to provide 20 per cent more than the minimum amount (that is, 3600 instead of 3000 tons) as an allowance for meltage. The ice could be shipped on the vessels of either company; for its vessels the Russian-American Company was to be paid $8 per ton. The contract covered ice only, the Russians being free to trade coal, timber, and fish wherever and whenever they wished. Their sale of ice was no longer restricted to California (*Doklad*, 1863–64:II, 194, supp. xviii; Golovin, 1862:125, 128; ORAK 1859:37–41, 1860:62–63; Tikhmenev, 1978:337). Indeed, the Russian-American Company contemplated shipping ice to the Sandwich Islands in 1860. In 1859 it built an ice house at Nikolayevsk on the Amur, although by 1861 no Amurian ice had yet been traded (ORAK 1860:63–64).

This third contract brought the Russian-American Company "much benefit", despite such setbacks as the sinking of the *Kodiak* off Woody Island in 1860 with 356 tons of ice, and the foundering of the *Tsaritsa* in Sitka Bay in 1861 with 928 tons of first-grade ice, whereby the company was deprived of $24 000 that summer from lost freightage on the shipment of 3000 tons to San Francisco. At a cost of $1 per ton to provide the ice, the company netted $6 per ton, or at least $18 000 annually. In addition, the company profited handsomely from freightage; in 1862, for instance, its ships carried 800 of the net export of 3500 tons for a return of $6,400 (*Doklad*, 1863–64:II, 194, 221; Golovin, 1862:126; ORAK 1860:54, 1864:47; USNA, roll 63, pt. 2, 37, 55, 63–63v).

The ice contract was renewed for the last time at the beginning of 1863.

Table 9.3. Exports of ice to California by the Russian-American Company, 1852–1866.

Year	Prepared	Exported	Value
1852	325 long tons	250 long tons	$18 750
1853	2000	1133	24 050
1854	3270	2869–3000	7 173
1855	5000	3315–4301	16 952
1856	900	830	3 237
1857	11 335	3445	13 475
1858	6800	3585–4027	15 745
1859	?	2732–3690	?
1860	?	2553–3189	?
1861	?	3271–3504	?
1862	?	4275–4555	?
1863	6930	3426–3568	?
1864	?	4785	?
1865	?	1305	?
1866	?	1440	?

Sources: *Doklad*, 1863–1864:II, 195, supp. xvi and xviii; Golovin, 1862:186 and 188; ORAK 1853:29, 1854–1855:52, 1858:58, 1859:36, 1860:63, 1861:37, 1862:27, 1863:37; USNA, roll 60, pt. 2, 158v., roll 63, pt. 1, 210, roll 64, pt. 1, 117v., roll 65, pt. 1, 32, pt. 2, 32 and 128.

This new two-year contract for the first time stipulated that the American-Russian Commercial Company pay the Russian-American Company the additional sum of $500 per month (for a two-year total of $12 000). This contract was even more lucrative than the previous one. In 1866 Governor Maksutov acknowledged that the company made "enormous profits" from the ice trade. It cost the company just $2 per ton to provide the ice; the ice sold at $10 per ton, a profit of 400 per cent. (In fact, the profit reached nearly 500 per cent if an error in addition in the original document is corrected). The company's profits would have been even larger if the Americans had taken all the ice that the Russians had provided. During the early

1860s, 5000 to 6000 tons were prepared every year, nearly enough for two years. Usually 25 to 50 per cent more ice was stocked than was exported; in 1863, for example, 6930 tons were cut but only 2855 net tons (excluding the meltage allowance of 20 per cent) were shipped. From the beginning of 1852 until the middle of 1862 18 185 tons of ice were prepared at New Archangel and 19 200 tons on Kodiak, and during the same period 27 500 tons (virtually three-quarters) were exported for a return of $250,000 (Table 9.3). The ice trade was unquestionably the most profitable of the company's new ventures (Golovin, 1862:107; ORAK 1863:37, 1864:47–49; Tikhmenev, 1978:337; USNA, roll 65, pt. 2, 80v).

COAL MINING

The 1855 contract between the Russian-American Company and the American-Russian Commercial Company also stipulated traffic in coal, timber, and fish. Coal mining was launched for two reasons. Firstly, colonial coal would be cheaper than imported coal as fuel for the company's steamships, which had been introduced in the 1840s in order to improve its fleet. Secondly, colonial coal would sell profitably in California, where monthly demand reached 20 000 tons in 1855. In 1848 Governor Teben'kov, who reported that "coal is found in abundance in many places in the Russian-American Company's colony" and that only miners and docks were needed, assured the Head Office that "now a demand for this item has arisen abroad: coal is needed in California and on the Sandwich Islands". It was especially in demand in San Francisco for steamships, according to Leidesdorf, Kostromitinov's predecessor, and Russian American coal was "very highly regarded" for this purpose. The booming city's homeowners also preferred coal to firewood, which cost $12–$15 per cord, with wood choppers charging $6–$8 per day to split it. By 1851 Australian coal fetched $7 per ton in California, English coal $12 per ton, and eastern American coal $17 per ton. Imported coal, however, was becoming more and more expensive because of the increasing cost of shipping insurance to cover the risk of spontaneous combustion in transit. Californian coal was difficult and costly to mine and low in quality. By the end of 1859 coal was bringing $20 to $30 per ton in San Francisco (Golovin, 1862:108; USNA, roll 54, 138, 262v.–263, roll 57, 505–505v., roll 63, pt. 1, 7).

All that remained was for the Russian-American Company to exploit its coal. In 1848 Governor Teben'kov ordered the managers of several localities, including Kodiak and Unga Island, to submit reports on any coal found within their jurisdictions. In the same year Lieutenant Doroshin of the Mining Corps arrived in the colony to prospect for minerals. He investigated the Kolosh Straits, Cook Inlet, both sides of the Alaska Peninsula, Unga Island, Bristol Bay, Iliamna Lake, and several rivers. He found coal in "very great abundance" and of "fairly good" quality on the Kenai Peninsula, with an anchorage "very suitable for loading". The same coal beds had been noted by Portlock and Dixon in 1786 (see Portlock, 1789, map facing 102 and view facing 108). But samples from the peninsula and Unga Island proved to be low-grade brown coal (lignite). This disappointment was soon forgotten in the excitement of gold fever, which distracted Doroshin until 1852. In fact Doroshin spent nearly half of his time looking for gold (USNA, roll 57, 319v.-320). As Governor Rosenberg said:

> if it pleases God to bless the Russian-American Company with success in finding gold, then in that case it will not have to begrudge money or other resources for the mining of this precious metal, for in selling it the company can almost always expect no less than 100 per cent net profit in its favour.

Besides, as Rosenberg admitted in 1851, there were not enough workers or facilities in the colony to mine both gold and coal; another 100 workers and four mining engineers at least would be needed. The company lacked skilled personnel in particular. The governor suggested that an American engineer be hired to demonstrate the "best and cheapest methods of mining, transporting, and embarking coal," for "among us in Russia the practical business of mining and transporting coal is still found almost in its infancy" (USNA, roll 55, 170–170v., roll 57, 318, 322–324v., 506v.).

Doroshin failed to strike gold, however. In 1852 he was ordered to test the coal deposits of the Alaska Peninsula near Katmai and on Unga Island and to commence coal mining on the Kenai Peninsula at English Bay. Early the following year Doroshin submitted his final report, which stated that in the colony "no true [i.e., anthracite or bituminous] coal has yet been found" but that there were many small Tertiary deposits of brown coal of "fairly good quality". These included: (1) English Bay, with a discontinuous bed up to 2.5 metres in thickness, free of sulphur and "suitable for steamships", with a "good anchorage" and "sufficient timber", as well as land suitable for gardening and a fishable stream; and (2) Kachetmak, or Kochekmak (Chuchamik) Bay, with less accessible beds of "very considerable" size that would likewise be "suitable for steamships" but more expensive to mine. Doroshin, his five-year contract having expired, then left Russian America without having adequately tested the quantity and quality of the coal deposits. A mechanical engineer named Petri, one of many Finnish employees of the company, was sent to the Kenai Peninsula in the spring of 1853 to do so. Apparently he was unsuccessful, for in 1854 the expert that Governor Rosenberg had requested three years previously arrived in the person of another Finn, Enoch Furuhjelm (whose brother Johan was to become governor in 1859), a mining engineer with a degree from Freiberg, one of Europe's best mining schools. In the spring of that year he prospected the Kolosh [Alexander] Archipelago for coal but found only coarse-grained brown coal at Keku. "It is not worth mining," he reported.[5] It was then decided to use the Kenai Peninsula deposits. In early 1855 Furuhjelm went to San Francisco and bought mining equipment, including steam engines and pumps, and hired some men at the joint expense of the two companies. With forty-six men (including twenty-five workers and fifteen soldiers) he finally began operations on the peninsula in the summer (Doroshin, 1868:45–57; ORAK 1859:116; Pierce, 1975:106; USNA, roll 59, 40v.–41v., roll 60, pt. 1, 84v.). Fraser, an American engineer, helped to open the mine.

Furuhjelm had intended to start mining at Kachetmak Bay, but upon inspection he found that English Bay was more suitable "in all respects". There was less coal than at Kachetmak Bay, where the deposit stretched eighty to one hundred kilometres along the coast and far inland, but it was more localized, being found in three small cauldron-shaped basins that extended 610 metres along the shore and five or six kilometres inland. (The actual extent of coal at English Bay, however, was never determined by the Russians [Doklad, 1863–64:II, 198]). The coal outcropped on Coal Cove on English Bay's northern side, which rose steeply from the sea for fifteen to eighteen metres. Ships could stand at anchor in the cove within several fathoms of the shore but were exposed to west and south-west winds; sailing vessels had to anchor farther out in the deeper water of the bay. Kachetmak Bay, by contrast, was completely sheltered, though it sometimes froze. English Bay rarely froze and was free of icebergs. In addition, there was more timber around English Bay. All in all, mining at English Bay promised to be more convenient, and more profitable. Furuhjelm hired some Creoles and Kenais as day labourers, and by the spring of 1856 some sixty men, including twenty Creoles and several Kenais, were working there. In 1859 the Kenai Coal Expedition, as it was officially designated, employed an average of thirty-eight Russians and eight natives, and in the spring of that year the settlement comprised twenty-seven buildings, including fourteen houses. In 1860, twenty-nine Russians, twenty-two Creoles, and one Kodiak were employed at the mine. By 1862, the settlement—Coal Village—was the third largest in Russian America having a population of eighty to ninety (Fig. 9.2) (Doklad, 1863–64:II, supp. ii; Golovin, 1862:108; ORAK 1858:49–51, 1859:117; Pierce, 1975:107; Tikhmenev, 1978:376; USNA, roll 61, pt. 1, 29v., 106v., roll 62, pt. 2, 88v.–89).

Mining began auspiciously. In the fall of 1855 four tons of coal of

---

[5] Coal that was suitable for steam generation had been discovered near New Archangel in the summer of 1851 (USNA, roll 57, 506).

Fig. 9.2. View of coal village in the late 1850s (courtesy of Yale University Library).

"excellent quality" were shipped to San Francisco on the American *Zenobia* and one ton was tested on the Russian steamship *Astoria*, whose engineer reported that "the quality of this coal is very good, and one could not wish for better for steam or gas [generation]". It was planned to supply 5000 tons to the American-Russian Commercial Company in 1856. By the spring of that year a dock and a road and all the necessary buildings had been constructed. A coal seam two and a half to nearly three metres thick was mined, and in the summer 500 tons were shipped to San Francisco on the *Lucas*. The American-Russian Commercial Company wanted more and urged the Russian-American Company to increase production. But Furuhjelm warned in the autumn that "premature and improper mining of the coal will spoil the seams and halt the course of preparatory work, without which the mining of the coal in large amounts will be quite impossible." He added that there was "sufficient" coal at English Bay and that it was "excellent for steam [generation] in particular"; however, despite already "fairly substantial outlays", more investment would "unavoidably" be required to hire the men and buy the machinery necessary to mine the 10 000–12 000 tons of coal needed to meet the demands of the American-Russian Commercial Company and to make a profit for the Russian-American Company. After Furuhjelm encountered difficulty opening shafts, and the American captains of the *Lucas* and the Russian-American Company ship *Nakhimov* found English Bay's harbour unsatisfactory in 1856, the American-Russian Commercial Company lost interest in the venture. In the summer of 1857 it formally withdrew because of the expense, having spent $16 471 on the project. The coal had proved high enough in quality for the California market but too high in price (Golovin, 1862:109; ORAK 1859:117; USNA, roll 61, pt. 1, 13, 29v.–30, 106–106v., 182v.–183, 220–221).

The Kenai Coal Expedition failed to meet the American-Russian Commercial Company's expectations because, in the words of Russian officials, "local circumstances" created "difficulties and hardships" that rendered the operation "problematical". The coal itself was extracted with difficulty. Mining was done with picks by both the adit method (whereby a tunnel was dug horizontally from the shore into the coal bed) and by the shaft method (whereby a shaft was sunk vertically from the surface into the deposit). In both cases passages had to be dug through fine, wet sand—one of the most difficult of all mining tasks. Adit mining yielded coal of disappointing quality, so in 1857 a shaft (Mine No. 1) was sunk in the centre of the middle coal basin 180 metres from the shore. At the five-metre level water flooded the shaft; hand pumps proved inadequate, and mining ceased until a steam-driven pump was installed in 1858. Drainage tunnels also had to be dug. Governor Voyevodskiy visited English Bay in the summer of 1857 and reported that "coal mining was extremely difficult and slow because of the necessity of tunnelling". By the spring of 1859 the shaft was twenty-one metres deep (fourteen metres in sand and seven in clay) and the four adits were 514 metres long altogether (460 metres in coal and fifty-four in sand). It took at least twice as much work to dig the fourteen as it did the seven metres of the shaft because the sand damaged the water pump. The shaft was not expected to strike coal until it reached a depth of nearly forty-nine metres. Meanwhile, the adits (two of which were for drainage) had produced 4200 tons of coal. The correct mining of coal still had not begun by 1860, owing to malfunctioning of the water pump, and the shaft could not be completed. During the winter of 1860–61 a second shaft (Mine No. 2) was dug, and by the spring it had produced 200 tons of "good" coal. The upper coal seam was 2.7 to 3.7 metres thick and yielded 70 per cent coal at a depth of fifteen to eighteen metres very close to the shore. The coal was raised from the shaft "very slowly" by means of a horse-powered windlass. The first shaft, which had "cost so much labour and time and promised an abundant output of coal immediately", finally had to be abandoned, for the steam-driven water pump was damaged by fire in 1861 and the head miner had died. The second shaft was also subject to flooding. In 1862 a drainage basin and ditch had to be excavated. Because the ceilings of the mine were so thin pillars were essential. These required that about 30 per cent of the available coal be sacrificed to them. Eventually timbers were used; some 600 being cut between the spring of 1862 and the spring of 1863. (*Doklad*, 1863–64:II, 198; Golovin, 1862:108–110; ORAK 1858:51–53, 1859:118–119, 1860:40; Pierce, 1975:107; USNA, roll 61, pt. 1, 30, pt. 2, 91v., roll 62, pt. 2, 89, roll 63, pt. 1, 196v., pt. 2, 75v., roll 64, pt. 2, 47v.).

The mining site was problematical externally as well as internally. In Governor Voyevodskiy's words, the shore was "very high and nearly sheer". The anchorage was also beset by large tides and big swells, for Coal Cove was exposed to strong and prolonged westerly winds. Loading and trans-shipment were therefore quite difficult operations. The great distance to the California market meant that Kenai coal was not competitive, a disadvantage compounded by the fact that the American-Russian Commercial Company's ships came empty for coal. In Furuhjelm's opinion coal mining failed because of the mine's remoteness within the colony (costly supply) and of the colony's remoteness from world markets (costly delivery). Furuhjelm also castigated the Russian-American Company for taking too long to launch the coal trade. He pointed out that in 1850, when the first steamships appeared in San Francisco Bay, even the lowest grade of coal could have commanded high prices there, but by the time Coal Cove's output appeared on the California market, coal from England, Australia, Chile, Vancouver Island, Oregon, and California itself was available. In his words, "the company was again, as usual, too late". (*Doklad*, 1863–64:II, 200–201, 572; Golovin, 1862;109; Pierce, 1975:107; USNA, roll 61, pt. 2, 91v.-92, roll 62, pt. 1, 77).

Mining was further handicapped by insufficient and inexperienced workers. Governor Johan Furuhjelm (1859–63) reckoned that with a full complement of 131 men the mine could produce thirty to thirty-five tons of coal per day, but this complement was never reached. In 1857 it took three-and-a-half days to mine one ton of coal (USNA, roll 62, pt. 1, 52–52v.). The existing and insufficient workforce of forty men was further reduced in the spring of 1856, when eighteen of them became "seriously ill' with scurvy. One died. An attempt the previous year to exploit local fresh fish and wildfowl to help prevent scurvy had failed (Pierce, 1975:107; USNA, roll 61, pt. 1, 106v.). Enoch Furuhjelm complained that most of the workers were "hard-drinking good-for-nothings", and the soldiers (from the two officers and 100 men of the 14th Siberian Line Battalion that had been posted to New Archangel in 1854 after the outbreak of the Crimean War) "hardly knew how to use an axe". After a Tlingit attack in 1855 the battalion was doubled to four officers and 200 men in 1856–57 (ORAK 1854–55:36, 1856:11). Experience proved that the use of natives for heavy work in coal mining and ice cutting was "hopeless" because they soon became exhausted or unwell, and few Creoles were willing to be hired. By 1861 most of the mining was done by soldiers, who were thereby unable to attend to their proper duties. They no sooner became experienced miners, a process usually taking two or three years, than they finished their tour of duty. Furthermore, the native and Creole labourers were paid by the day, not by their amount of work or output of coal, so that they did not necessarily do what they were paid to do. Experienced workers would have received more pay but would also have required less supervision and produced more coal. Furuhjelm himself was irreplaceable. He was induced by rises and gratuities to stay until 1862, when finally he left (*Doklad*, 1863–64:II, 198–199, 201; Pierce, 1975:106; USNA, roll 61, pt. 1, 102–102v.).

The labour shortage affected all operations, construction included. The dock was still not finished by the summer of 1857, two years after mining began, and no storage shed had been built by the spring of 1859. Meanwhile, coal was simply stockpiled on the open ground, where it deteriorated under exposure to the elements. In 1862–63 some coal was even left in the mine for want of storage space on the dock. Furthermore, the coal was not sorted. According to the American engineer Fraser, it took ten tons of Kenai coal to equal seven tons of Newcastle coal, but that with sorting the ratio could have been reduced to ten to eight or even ten to nine. He added that Kenai coal was suitable for everything except coke (*Doklad*, 1863–64:II, 200; ORAK 1858:53; USNA roll 62, pt. 1, 77, roll 64, pt. 2, 47v.). In the colony coal was used for firing steamships and founding cast iron fittings (*Doklad*, 1863–64:II, 198).

Thanks to these "difficulties and hardships", little coal was mined at great cost. Furuhjelm's task was to mine 2000 tons per year, but from 1857 through 1859 only 2760 tons were extracted. The total value of the coal produced was 13 086 roubles. However, the cost of production in 1859 alone was 24 571 roubles. Between the summer of 1859 and the summer of 1861 mining expenses totalled 42 123 roubles and revenues only 10 877 roubles for a deficit of 31 246 roubles. In 1862 Governor Furuhjelm ordered the production of 1000 tons of coal annually, but that year only 850 tons were mined. By 1861 the expedition was in a position to recoup its losses, since no more expenditures were necessary for building or repairing. But by then the Russian-American Company was already flagging in the face of waning governmental support. In early 1864 the Head Office ordered the shutdown of the venture, and in the autumn the mine was already closed. The company was already importing coal from Vancouver Island. In the summer of 1865 Governor Maksutov visted English Bay and reported that the "locality . . . does not offer any advantages whatever for a settlement, except woods and hills, and there is no suitable site for either vegetable gardens or cattle pastures." Coal mining, he found, had been replaced by fish salting (*Doklad*, 1863–64:II, 201–202, 411; ORAK 1862:43; Pierce, 1975:107; USNA roll 63, pt. 2, 75–75v., roll 64, pt. 1, 29, 56v.-57, pt. 3, 42v., 64, roll 65, pt. 1, 115–115v.).

FISH AND TIMBER

The 1855 contract between the Russian-American and American-Russian Commercial Companies stipulated trade in fish and timber as well as ice and coal. Fish and timber were probably the most obvious and abundant resources of the Gulf of Alaska, and the Russians had long exploited both for colonial needs. Fish—fresh, dried, smoked, and salted—was the staple of the colonial diet for natives and Russians alike, although runs were seasonal and even cyclical. For example, at New Archangel the herring run occurrred in late March and early April and lasted three weeks, and the salmon run varied from "very, very small" to "extremely prolific". Principally salmon, herring, halibut, and cod were caught. Mainly salmon were salted for export: humpbacked (pink) were the most abundant and coho (silver) the most delicious. They were caught and salted at Lake Redoubt just south of New Archangel and at New Archangel itself, where barrels were also made (Table 9.4). A large stone shed for fish salting and storing was completed at the colonial capital in 1853 (*Doklad*, 1863–64:II, 188; Golovin, 1862:105; ORAK 1853:23).

Much timber was used for ships (fir, tamarack, cedar), buildings (spruce), firewood (fir and hawthorn), furniture, barrels, charcoal, sawdust, etc. At New Archangel in 1852, 12 000 barrel staves were made for one Russian-Finnish Whaling Company ship, and from 1854 through 1858 3500 barrels

Table 9.4. Amount of salmon salted for export at New Archangel and Lake Redoubt, 1846–1866.

Year	Barrels*	Year	Barrels*
1846	125	1857	0
1847	206	1858	1070
1848	211	1859	282
1849	636	1860	865
1850	0	1861	1050
1851	455	1862	?
1852	255	1863	1091
1853	600	1864	288
1854	715	1865	618
1855	488–545	1866	864
1856	700		

*Assuming 55 fish per barrel.

Sources: Golovin, 1862:106; USNA, roll 51, 458v., roll 52, 325v., roll 54, 209–209v., roll 55, 125v., roll 56, 124v., roll 57, 251, roll 58, 189, roll 59, 308v., roll 60, 25, roll 61, pt. 1, 85, pt. 2, 50, roll 62, pt. 1, 63v., pt. 2, 71v.–72, roll 63, pt. 1, 76v., pt. 2, 39v.–40, roll 64, pt. 1, 59v., pt. 2, 41v., pt. 3, 14v., roll 65, pt. 1, 57–57v., pt. 2, 33, pt. 3, 53v.

were coopered. Around 1860 the colonial capital required 788 900 cubic feet of firewood annually (Golovin, 1862:111). Timber had to be shipped to the Aleutian, Pribilof, and Commander Islands and the coasts of Bristol Bay and Norton Sound, which were treeless. Colonial demand was heavy. From 1852 through 1860 Russian America's annual timber requirement averaged 1855 trees of various sizes, including 940 for construction. At New Archangel during the 1820s up to 1000 trees were felled yearly; in 1826 fourteen to eighteen men were kept constantly busy sawing timber, and they were able to meet the demands of the colonial capital only, whose buildings did not last long in the strong winds and heavy rains. The dank climate and the fire hazard limited the life span of buildings to ten to twenty years (*Doklad*, 1863–64:II, 206–207; Khlebnikov, 1976:99; USNA, roll 30, 25v.).

It was the establishment of sawmills—at Lake Redoubt (at the outlet of

Deep Lake) in 1832, Serebrennikov [Silver] Bay (at the mouth of the Kirenga river [Sawmill Creek] just north of New Archangel in 1847, and at New Archangel itself in 1853—that enabled the company to produce enough timber for both internal needs and export markets. As an experiment, in 1847, 240 boards were shipped to California, where they brought the same price as on the Sandwich Islands. However, California imposed a tariff on foreign timber, and Californians preferred redwood lumber because of its softness. Subsequently timber and fish were exported, but in Governor Rudakov's words, "very seldomly and in a very negligible amount" (Tables 9.5 and 9.6). It was hoped that the 1855 contract would stimulate the export trade in timber and fish. However, the American-Russian Commercial Company, which had reluctantly agreed to take these commodities irregularly, refused after one year to accept timber, fish and, for good measure, coal as well. Occasionally thereafter, some timber and fish were shipped to San Francisco on the ice company's returning vessels

Table 9.5. Exports of timber by the Russian-American Company, 1849–1858.

Year	Amount	Value
1849	22 974 bd. ft. of lumber	1313 roubles
	3 logs	57
	4 prefabricated buildings	1060
1850	70 bd. ft. of firewood	33
	122 logs	339
	1 block	19
	3 prefabricated houses	1017
1851	12 987 bd. ft. of lumber	74
	245 bd. ft. of firewood	115
1852	28 bd. ft. of firewood	13
	other	277
1853	40 708 bd. ft. of lumber	233
1854	14 000 bd. ft. of lumber	234
	560 bd. ft. of firewood	263
	other	22
1855	46 525 bd. ft. of lumber	266
	1512 bd. ft. of firewood	710
	other	75
1856	26 891 bd. ft. of lumber	154
1857	1512 bd. ft. of firewood	1091
1858	31 250 bd. ft. of lumber	179

Sources: *Doklad*, 1863–1864:II, supp. xvi; Golovin, 1862:186–187.

Table 9.6. Exports of salted fish by the Russian-American Company,
1849–1859.

Year	Amount	Value
1849	255 barrels	1814 roubles
1850	100	429
1851	158	626
1852	0	0
1853	160	686
1854	610	2616
1855	399	1710
1856	610	2614
1857	700	5500
1858	1070	8407
1859	282	2216

Sources: *Doklad*, 1863–1864:II, supp. xvi; Golovin, 1862:1862, 186–187.

but primarily in order to provide full cargoes. In the spring of 1858 Governor Voyevodskiy reported that "the ice trade is now the sole branch of general trade at San Francisco under contract to the American-Russian Commercial Company and in any case the most profitable". (ORAK, 1859:119; USNA, roll 54, 282v.-283, roll 59, 380, roll 61, pt. 1, 231v., roll 62, pt. 1, 74v.).

Several obstacles impeded the export trade in timber and fish. In 1855 Governor Voyevodskiy admitted that "our fishing industry is as yet still weakly developed". He added that Russian American salmon was "much better" than Columbia River salmon but brought "much less" on account of the method of salting and the size of the barrels. It was found that Hawaiian salt was "not suitable" for salting fish. Baja Californian salt from San Quintin, although dearer, was better. Consequently, in 1855 100 tons of salt were brought to New Archangel from San Quintin, and detailed "Directions for Fish Salting" were issued by the governor. The American-Russian Commercial Company wanted the Russian-American Company to expand fishing but the Russians had neither the capital nor the manpower to do so. Both coopering and salting were expensive, and there was a shortage of barrels. In 1856 Governor Voyevodskiy told the American-Russian Commercial Company that fishing had to be restricted to New Archangel, rather than expanded, because of limited manpower, which was being concentrated on ice cutting and coal mining. And in 1858 Voyevodskiy reiterated that the Russian-American Company could not afford the resources (at least 100 workers, a schooner, buildings, salt, and iron) to develop fishing on a large scale unless the ice trade became unprofitable. Which did not happen. Besides, sometimes, as in 1857, the colony's fish runs failed. Governor Voyevodskiy reported in the spring of 1858 that "last summer the fish [salmon] run at New Archangel was very meagre, and it was not possible to spare any for sale". Similarly, the colonial capital's salmon run was "very unsatisfactory and short" in 1863, "very late and very short" in 1864, and "very meagre" in 1866. Moreover, the California market was not always bullish. In 1856 the demand in California for fish and timber was "very insignificant", and the American-Russian Commercial Company did not import any. Governor Voyevodskiy acknowledged that because of the "current low prices", fish would be stocked only "sporadically" and fish exports would be "negligible for the present." At the beginning of 1857 he again reported "low prices for fish and timber on Pacific Ocean markets" and added that "fish do not bring large profits, and timber is much more profitable."[6] (*Doklad*, 1863–64:I, 120, II, 189; Golovin, 1862:106; ORAK 1856:31; USNA, roll 60, pt. 2, 15v., 25, 97–97v., roll 61, pt. 1, 13v., 105v., 219v.-220, pt. 2, 13v., roll 62, pt. 1, 32v., 76v.-77, roll 64, pt. 3, 14v., roll 65, pt. 1, 57–57v., pt. 3, 53v.).

But the export trade in timber likewise did not flourish. It, too, suffered from a shortage of labour. There were other problems. In 1852 the sawmill operated for a "short time" only on account of insufficient water in the river (USNA, roll 59, 12v.-13). But when New Archangel's sawmill was converted to steam in 1855 in preparation for the expected demands of the 1855 contract, it worked so well that the supply of wood could not keep pace with the sawing of wood thanks to the shortage of hands for felling. Certainly there was not enough manpower to meet the timber needs of both the domestic and the export markets; colonial demand was too strong, especially at New Archangel, where logging was done mostly by soldiers. For example, during Governor Voyevodskiy's five-year term (spring, 1854–summer, 1859) 797 000 wooden shingles were required to roof thirty-three buildings in the colony. Its sawmills were able to make only 300 000 of this number, and the remainder had to be imported from San Francisco.[7] Also during Voyevodskiy's term, the ice houses and dock on Woody Island required 300 000 square feet of lumber and the fish trade 3500 barrels; little wonder that during the same period only 65 000 square feet of lumber, 1665 linear feet of round wood, and four spars were exported to California. Additional spars, which could be sold more profitably than any other form

---

[6] The Russian-American Company even exported some timber to China and Chile in 1860.

[7] Shingles provided the "best and cheapest" roofing. They did not require painting and were quite durable, lasting at least ten years without major repairs, which were not difficult to make. The roof of a building thirty metres long and twelve metres wide needed up to 50 000 shingles and 114 kilogrammes of nails [ORAK 1859:104]).

of timber, might have been exported if the Russian-American Company had had more ships. The California market for timber, however, sometimes sagged, as it did for fish. In 1856, for instance, timber exports were hampered by "low prices in California for sawn and round wood". And, in 1861, Governor Furuhjelm, who had been ordered by the Head Office in 1859 to increase timber exports, replied that to do so would be unprofitable because of "low prices for timber in S. Francisco". Besides, Russian American timber could not compete in California with Oregon timber (Douglas fir), which did not have to be shipped as far and was therefore cheaper. The Company's lack of a warehouse in San Francisco was another handicap (*Doklad*, 1863–64:II, 206; Golovin, 1862:110, 126; ORAK 1859:100, 103; USNA, roll 61, pt. 1, 105, roll 63, pt. 2, 44–44v.). Still another hindrance to trade according to Golovin was that Kostromitinov was not a suitable commercial agent for the company in San Francisco. He had been given the post as a reward for long service but did not know English, was too old, and was not sufficiently active or resourceful (Golovin, 1862:126–127).

CONCLUSION

If it had not been for ice, Russian America's trade with California would have been negligible. There were simply too many expenses for the upkeep of ships, the payment of harbour fees and customs duties, and the maintenance of agents for trade to profit. In order to reduce costs the company withdrew its San Francisco agent (Pëtr Kostromitinov) at the end of 1861 and replaced him with a private agent (Martin Klinkovstrem), whose commission amounted to five per cent of the cost of goods bought in California for the company and $100 for each ton of company products sold in California. This economy was too little and too late, however. Company operations were too remote and too inefficient to compete. Not only were some competitors closer to the main markets of the North Pacific, they were not hamstrung by monopolistic complacency and technological backwardness. The ice trade succeeded only because it faced little competition. The company's workers had no vested interest in the new activities because they stood to gain little from them. Moreover, they were neither numerous enough nor skilled enough (witness pelt curing and fish salting). Thanks to the immobility imposed on the bulk of the Russian population by serfdom, and the greater allure of Siberia, Russian America had always suffered from a shortage of competent personnel. The few that did come were soon reduced by overwork, insalubrity, accidents, disease, hunger, drunkenness, and even desertion. For instance, in 1860 at New Archangel, an average of thirty persons per day suffered from syphilis (USNA, roll 63, pt. 1 81v.). The abysmal living conditions occasionally drove company workers to desertion. In 1853 six crew members of the brig *Shelekhov* jumped ship at San Francisco (USNA, roll 60, pt. 1, 22v.). In 1846 Governor Teben'kov advised the Head Office that "there is much work but few men," adding that 150 of the 400 employees at New Archangel and Lake Redoubt were not able-bodied. And in 1851 Governor Rosenberg complained that the colony needed 300 additional employees (i.e., sixty per cent more man-power!). But they were not forthcoming. The company was either unwilling (for fear of reducing dividends) or unable (for want of funds) to endow its programme of diversification with sufficient capital and labour (machinery, vessels, technicians, agents). Much had to be expended on supplying Russian America with provisions and goods—another chronic problem—by means of company and chartered ships from St. Petersburg and Hamburg, company and American ships from San Francisco, and company ships from Ayan. The Russian-American Company never had much scope for manoeuvring and adjusting to circumstances beyond its control. What little they had was steadily eroded during the 1860s when the Tsarist government, perhaps because of the very failures of diversification but certainly because of the greater promise of Amuria, steadily withdrew its support. In 1867 Russia's only overseas colony was sold (*Doklad*, 1863–64:II, 211, 220; ORAK 1861:39–41; USNA, roll 51, 426, roll 57, 333).

REFERENCES

Davydov, G. I., (1977). "Two Voyages to Russian America, 1802–1807", trans. Colin Bearne, Kingston.

Doklad komiteta ob ustroistve russkikh amerikanskikh koloniy, 2 vols., St. Petersburg (1863–1864).

Doroshin, P., (1868). "Kamenyy ugol' v byvshikh amerikanskikh vladeniyakh Rossii," *Gornyy zhurnal* 10, 45–57.

Golovin, Captain-Lieutenant, (1862). Obzor russkikh koloniy v Severnoy Amerike, *Morskoy sbornik* 57, 19–193.

HBCA [Hudson's Bay Company Archives], A.11/62, 1843–49, 1849–52; A.11/63.

Hinkley, Ted C., (1967). Ice from "Seward's Icebox", *Pacific Historian* 11, 28–38.

Khlebnikov, K. T., (1973). "Baranov," trans. Colin Bearne, Kingston.

[Khlebnikov, K. T.], (1976). "Colonial Russian America," trans. Basil Dmytryshyn and E. A. P. Crownhart-Vaughan, Portland.

ORAK [Otchët Rossiisko-Amerikanskoy Kompanii Glavnago Pravleniya za odin god . . .], 21 issues, St. Petersburg (1843–1865).

Ostenstad, W. L., (1977). A lucrative contract: The HBC and the Pacific ice trade, *The Beaver* 308, 36–40.

Pierce, Richard A., (1975). The Russian coal mine on the Kenai, *Alaska Journal* 5, 104–108.

Portlock, Captain Nathaniel, (1789). "A Voyage Round the World . . .," London.
Rimskiy-Korsakov, V., (ed.) (1863). Iz putevykh pisem P. N. Golovina, *Morskoy sbornik* 6, 101–182, 275–340.
Saul, Norman E., (1972). Beverley C. Sanders and the expansion of American trade with Russia, 1853–1855, *Maryland Historical Magazine* 67, 156–170.
Tikhmenev, P. A., (1978). "A History of the Russian-American Company," trans. Richard A. Pierce and Alton S. Donnelly, Seattle.
TsGIAL [Tsentral'nyy gosudarstvennyy istoricheskiy arkhiv v Leningrade], f. 1, 263, op. 1, d. 2,095.
USNA [United States National Archives], File Microcopies of Records in the National Archives: No. 11, "Records of the Russian-American Company 1802–1867: Correspondence of Governors General," 77 rolls (1941).

The author is grateful to the Hudson's Bay Company for permission to consult and quote their archives.

Subject Index